GENDERED RELATIONSHIPS

edited by

Julia T. Wood

The University of North Carolina at Chapel Hill

MAYFIELD PUBLISHING COMPANY
Mountain View, California
London • Toronto

Library of Congress Cataloging-in-Publication Data
Gendered relationships / Julia T. Wood, editor.
     p.   cm.
    Includes bibliographical references.
    ISBN 1–55934–430–X (pbk.)
    1. Sex role. 2. Gender identity. 3. Interpersonal relations.
4. Man–woman relationships. 5. Race relations. 6. Social classes.
I. Wood, Julia T.
HQ1075.G467   1995   95–22985
305.3—dc20   CIP

Manufactured in the United States of America
10 9 8 7 6 5 4 3 2

Mayfield Publishing Company
1280 Villa Street
Mountain View, California 94041

Sponsoring editor, Holly J. Allen; production, Publishing Support Services; manuscript editor, Melissa Andrews; text and cover designer, Donna Davis; art director, Jeanne M. Schreiber; manufacturing manager, Randy Hurst. The text was set on 10.5/13 Sabon by Publishing Support Services and printed on 50# Thor Offset by Malloy Lithographing, Inc.

We dedicate this book to our students,
who have taught us as much about gender
as we have taught them.

CONTENTS

PREFACE

Typically, relationships and gender have been considered independent areas of academic study. Thus, they have been generally addressed in discrete courses with separate textbooks. Disconnecting gender and relationships, however, limits insight into the complex ways in which they shape one another. To appreciate the continuous cycle of influence between gender and relationships, this book concentrates on the ways that gender shapes and is expressed in relationships, while it is simultaneously shaped by and expressive of relationships.

Because research on gender is substantial and wide in scope, no single book can discuss comprehensively how gender is created and how it affects our lives. *Gendered Relationships* focuses specifically on reciprocal influence between gender and relationships. This means we don't emphasize the institutional bases for gender, except as they surface in particular relationships. Likewise, we don't focus on gender as an issue in politics or public policy.

Gendered Relationships pursues two primary lines of inquiry. One is how gender creates and is created in relationships between people. We trace ways that individuals become gendered through interacting with others, and we consider how our gendered identities influence the patterns and dynamics of our own relationships.

The second line of inquiry interrogates how individuals reflect, reinforce, and sometimes challenge social views of gender by the ways they communicate in particular relationships. We want to appreciate how individuals' actions perpetuate, modify, or alter prevailing views and expectations of women and men and relationships between them.

Gendered Relationships is divided into four parts. Part I, Foundations for Studying Gender and Relationships, includes three chapters. In the first chapter, I delineate the intricate relationships among gender, personal identity, communication, and relationships. After clarifying distinctions between gender and sex, I describe how communication weaves gender into individual identity and, in turn, how gender is sustained by the ways individuals structure their relationships and communicate with one another.

In Chapter 2, Cheris Kramarae calls attention to intersections among gender, race, and class, especially as those are shaped by language. Her analysis illuminates the subtle and complex ways in which views of gender, race, and class, and the connections among them are crafted by communication. Terms for defining and thinking about masculinity are different for African Americans and European Americans, gay and straight men, and middle- and working-class males. Femininity means different things and carries different obligations in South Africa, Korea, the United States, and Mexico. To understand gender, then, we must appreciate how it interacts with multiple dimensions of selfhood and how all of those are socially constructed.

In Chapter 3, Marsha Houston and I discuss the challenges and opportunities of relationships between people of different races and classes. Like gender, race and class are basic to identity, and they influence our expectations of relationships and the ways we interact with others. Our chapter highlights points of tension and occasions for growth that often accompany communication across the lines of race and class, and we offer suggestions for improving understanding.

Four chapters compose Part II of the book, Gendered Personal Relationships. In Chapter 4, Carol Bruess and Judy Pearson discuss relationships in families. Focusing primarily on parent–child relationships, Bruess and Pearson reveal both obvious and subtle ways in which parents' communication encourages girls to become feminine and boys to become masculine. Often called "the cradle of civilization," families are extraordinarily powerful in shaping our first senses of ourselves and of what it means to be male or female in this society.

The next three chapters consider ways in which gender sculpts friendships. In Chapter 5, Fern Johnson explains how women typically develop "closeness in dialogue" through friendships in which personal communication holds center stage. Her insightful account of women's friendships highlights uniquely feminine rhythms and priorities.

In Chapter 6, Chris Inman provides a rich analysis of closeness between male friends. He contends that men typically achieve closeness by doing things with and for one another, rather than relying primarily on communication to build closeness.

In Chapter 7, Lee West, Jennifer Anderson, and Steve Duck explore patterns and dynamics of friendships between women and men. Since women and men differ somewhat in their preferred ways of interacting, mixed-sex friendships require understanding and respecting different interaction styles and goals and developing abilities to "speak each other's language." This chapter traces friendships between women and men across the life span and highlights both the values and dilemmas of this type of relationship.

Part III focuses on gender in romantic and sexual relationships. Chapter 8, by Clyde Hendrick and Susan Hendrick, explores the fascinating relationship between gender and styles of loving. Drawing on research that identifies some general differences in women's and men's styles of loving, the Hendricks trace how gendered identities shape expectations and experiences of romantic love. Chapter 9 extends the foregoing discussion by tracing how gender affects heterosexual relationships over time. In this chapter, I describe gendered styles of communicating caring, conflict, and closeness, and I discuss difficulties that sometimes grow out of dissimilarities in women's and men's communication styles.

Paralleling the chapters on heterosexual intimacy is Chapter 10, in which Michelle Huston and Pepper Schwartz give attention to gay and lesbian romantic commitments. Contradicting popular opinion, they point out that straight and gay men are alike in many ways, just as lesbian and straight women have many likenesses. Of greater consequence than affectional preference is gender, which influences gay and lesbian relationships as profoundly as it does heterosexual ones.

Turning to the darker side of romantic relationships, the last two chapters in Part III focus on particularly dangerous and dismaying implications of gender as it is currently constructed in Western culture. In Chapter 11, Sheryl Perlmutter Bowen and Paula Michal-Johnson discuss gender-related issues in negotiations regarding safer sex in an era under the shadow of AIDS/HIV. The research they review reveals that gendered tendencies of women and men put many of us at risk in sexual encounters. Whereas feminine socialization to defer and accommodate encourages women not to insist on safeguards, the gendered identities of men may foster risk taking and unwillingness to accede to their partners' request for protection.

In Chapter 12, Jacquelyn White and Barrie Bondurant focus on the alarming prevalence of violence in intimate relationships. Their analysis reveals that both enacting and tolerating violence are fostered by socially constructed gender prescriptions. To the extent that masculinity is viewed in terms of power and domination and femininity is associated with deference and loyalty to relationships, violence between intimates is not only understandable, but sadly, predictable. All of the chapters in

Part III underscore the role of gender in shaping romantic relationships and the indentities and well-being of the people in them.

In Part IV, Gendered Professional Relationships, we turn our attention to the ways that gender affects and is reflected in women's and men's relationships in the workplace. Chapter 13, by Bren Ortega Murphy and Ted Zorn, discusses gendered interaction between men and women in professional roles. Based on extensive research, as well as years of experience in consulting with organizations, Murphy and Zorn identify differences in the orientations, expectations, and communication styles that women and men bring to the workplace. Also valuable is their discussion of ways women and men can learn to understand each other's language and work comfortably together as colleagues.

In Chapter 14, Shereen Bingham describes gendered dynamics that underlie and sustain sexual harassment, as well as toleration of it by victims and by organizations. Looking at sexual harassment both on campuses and in the workplace, she explains how women's and men's gendered identities and pervasive social views of the sexes cultivate abuses by administrators, teachers, bosses, and others in positions of power.

Moving beyond discussions of gendered forms of interaction between individuals, in Chapter 15 Elizabeth Natalle invites us to consider the gap between expectations and realities of the modern workplace. Her discussion sheds light on the ways in which professional environments continue to reflect largely masculine attitudes, norms, and assumptions. In addition, she dispels some persisting misconceptions about women's and men's communication in work settings.

Taken together, the chapters in this book offer broad and varied insights into ways that gender shapes relationships and is, in turn, shaped by them. From our earliest interactions in the nuclear family to adult romantic and professional relationships, gender affects who we are, how we act, how others perceive and treat us, and even our tendencies to inflict or suffer violence. In underlining the centrality of gender to personal identity and relationships with others, the chapters in this book enrich insight into the gender dynamics at work in relationships throughout our lives.

The original idea for *Gendered Relationships* has evolved and improved as a result of the contributions of many people. At the top of the list of individuals who have enhanced this book is Holly Allen, who has been as generous in providing editorial guidance and insight as she has been in giving personal support. Without her encouragement, direction, and talent, this book would not exist.

The authors and I are also indebted to a number of scholars who made time to review the manuscript for this book. For unusually perceptive and helpful suggestions, we thank Judith Bowker, Oregon State University; Patrice Buzzanell, Northern Illinois University; Valerian J. Derlaga, Old Dominion University; Kathryn Dindia, University of Wisconsin at Milwaukee; Sandra Metts, Illinois State University; Susan Sprecher, Illinois State University; and Barbara Winstead, Old Dominion University.

Julia T. Wood
The University of North Carolina
Chapel Hill, North Carolina

THE CONTRIBUTORS

Jennifer Anderson earned her B.A. from California State University–Bakersfield and her M.A. from Miami University of Ohio, both in Speech Communication. She is presently a Ph.D. candidate at the University of Iowa Department of Communication Studies, working in the area of gender and relationships.

Shereen G. Bingham is an associate professor of Communication at the University of Nebraska at Omaha, where she teaches in the areas of gender, interpersonal, and organizational communication. Her research focuses on how people use communication to enact, perpetuate, and respond to sexual harassment.

Barrie Bondurant is a doctoral candidate in social/personality Psychology at the University of North Carolina at Greensboro. Her research focuses on gender issues in aggression. She is currently investigating factors that influence how women label rape experiences.

Sheryl Perlmutter Bowen is an assistant professor of Communication Arts and associate director of Women's Studies at Villanova University. She studies sensitive health communication processes, including personal relationships and AIDS discourse and culturally sensitive HIV education. She is co-editor of *Transforming Visions: Feminist Critiques in Communication Studies* (1993).

Carol Bruess is a faculty member in Ohio University's School of Interpersonal Communication where she also received her Ph.D. in 1994 at the age of 25. She has presented her research on gender, marital, and family communication at over a dozen national, regional, and international conferences and has had her work published in national and international journals. She has been honored as Ohio University's Kanter Fellow and as recipient of the Speech Communication Association's Dissertation of the Year Award.

Steve Duck earned his B.A. and M.A. from Oxford University, UK, and his Ph.D. from the University of Sheffield, UK. He is now the Daniel and Amy Starch Distinguished Research Professor at the University of Iowa where he holds appointments in the Communication Studies Department and the Psychology Department. He founded the *Journal of Social and Personal Relationships,* which he currently edits, and the International Network on Personal Relationships, the professional multidisciplinary organization for the study of relationships. He has written or edited over 30 books on relationships.

Clyde Hendrick is a professor of Psychology and dean of the graduate school at Texas Tech University. During the past decade, he has conducted research in many areas of social psychology, focusing primarily on close relationships. He has co-authored or edited 11 books and published over 100 journal articles. He serves as co-editor, with Susan S. Hendrick, of the Sage Series on Close Relationships.

Susan S. Hendrick is a professor of Psychology and director of the Counseling Psychology Program at Texas Tech University. She has conducted research in the areas of close relationships and counseling processes. She has authored or co-authored 5 books and published over 60 journal articles, chapters, and reviews. She serves as co-editor, with Clyde Hendrick, of the Sage Series on Close Relationships.

Marsha Houston is an associate professor of Communication at Tulane University. She has chaired the Feminist and Women's Studies Division of the Speech Communication Association and is co-editor of the book *Our Own Voices: Essays in Culture, Ethnicity, and Communication.*

Michelle Huston is a graduate student in the Department of Sociology at the University of Washington. She holds a bachelor's degree in Sociology from the State University of New York at Plattsburgh (1992). While the focus of her interests seems to change periodically, she always seems to come back to the exploration of sexuality and gender.

Chris Inman is currently working on his doctorate; he completed his M.A. in Communication Studies at the University of North Carolina at Chapel Hill. He works in the area of gender and close relationships, specializing in the study of men's relationships. He is active in the International Network of Personal Relationships and has served on Network committees.

Fern L. Johnson is a professor of English at Clark University in Worcester, Massachusetts. She specializes in language and culture, with emphasis on gender, race, and ethnicity in the United States. She publishes widely in journals and edited books, and has presented numerous papers in the United States and abroad. She is the 1994 winner of the Speech Communication Association's Robert J. Kibler Memorial Award.

Cheris Kramarae is Jubilee Professor of Liberal Arts and Sciences, and professor of Speech Communication at the University of Illinois, where she coordinates the Women's Studies Program. She is author, editor, or co-editor of 11 books, including *Women and Men Speaking; Technology and Women's Voices; Amazons, Bluestockings, and Crones: A Feminist Dictionary;* and *Women, Information Technology, and Scholarship.* With Dale Spender, she is editing a Women's Studies international encyclopedia.

Paula Michal-Johnson is an associate professor of Communication Arts at Villanova University. Her research into sensitive health communication processes involves personal relationships and AIDS discourse, culturally sensitive HIV education, and disclosure of HIV in home health care.

Bren Ortega Murphy received her Ph.D. in Communication Studies from Northwestern University in 1984. She is currently an associate professor of Communication at Loyola University–Chicago, where she also serves as dean for College Programs in the School of Arts and Sciences. She publishes and consults primarily in the area of gender representation in popular culture as well as the impact of gender in professional settings. Other scholarly interests include service learning and the teaching of communication ethics.

Elizabeth J. Natalle (Ph.D., Florida State University) is an assistant professor and director of graduate studies in Communication Studies at the University of North Carolina at Greensboro. She is also on the Women's Studies faculty at UNCG and teaches a course on gender and communication theory. Dr. Natalle's research interests include feminist criticism, interpersonal process, and issues of metatheory regarding gender and communication.

Judy C. Pearson is director of the Northern Virginia Graduate Center and associate dean of the graduate school at Virginia Polytechnic Institute and State University. She is the author of numerous books including *Lasting Love: What Keeps Couples Together; Communication* *in the Family: Seeking Satisfaction in Changing Times;* and *Gender and Communication.* She has made her research available to the general public through articles in about 250 newspapers including *USA Today,* in over a dozen magazines including *Newsweek,* and on several television programs including "CBS This Morning."

Pepper Schwartz is a professor of Sociology at the University of Washington and associate chair of the department. Her most recent book is *Peer Marriage: How Love Between Equals Really Works.* She is also co-author (with Philip Blumstein) of *American Couples,* a study of heterosexual and homosexual couples.

Lee West earned her B.A. from San Francisco State University and her M.A. from the University of Wisconsin–Milwaukee. She is presently a Ph.D. candidate at the University of Iowa Department of Communication Studies, working in the area of social construction of identity.

Jacquelyn W. White, Ph.D., a social psychologist, is a professor of Psychology at the University of North Carolina at Greensboro, and a member of the Women's Studies Coordinating Council. She is currently conducting a longitudinal investigation of relationship violence, following students' experiences with dating violence and sexual assault from adolescence through the collegiate years.

Julia T. Wood is the Nelson R. Hairston Distinguished Professor of Communication Studies at the University of North Carolina at Chapel Hill. Her teaching and research focus on gender and personal relationships. During her career, she has written 10 books, edited 6 others, and published over 50 articles and chapters. In 1984, she co-founded the National Conference on Gender and Communication Research, which meets in the spring of each year.

Theodore E. Zorn received his Ph.D. in Communication from the University of Kentucky in 1987. He is currently an associate professor at the University of North Carolina at Chapel Hill. His teaching, research, and organizational consulting center on interpersonal communication in organizations, particularly the role of social cognitive and communicative processes in work relationships.

PART
ONE

FOUNDATIONS FOR
STUDYING GENDER
AND RELATIONSHIPS

GENDER, RELATIONSHIPS, AND COMMUNICATION

JULIA T. WOOD

Not long ago, I was playing a question game with my 4-year-old niece Michelle. When I asked her who she was, she immediately replied, "I'm a girl." Only after declaring her sex did she proceed to describe her likes and dislikes, family, and so forth. In focusing on being a girl, Michelle underlined the centrality of sex to personal identity.

If asked to describe yourself, like Michelle, you would probably note you are a woman or a man before describing your personality, background, hobbies, ambitions, and appearance. According to historian Elizabeth Fox-Genovese (1991, p. 20), "To be an 'I' at all means to be gendered."

In Western society, gender is fundamental to social life and to individuals' identities, roles, and options. The influence of gender is evident in everything from social policies and laws to intimate interaction. What gender means and how we embody it depend directly on communication that expresses, sustains, and changes views of women and men. As we communicate in families, schools, playgrounds, media, offices, and Congress, we continuously re-create our understandings of cultural life, our relations with others, and ourselves as women and men.

Of the many contexts in which gender is defined and enacted, a particularly important one is our relationships with others. Our earliest relationships in nuclear families weave gender into our basic self-concepts. Later in life, we form friendships and romantic relationships in which we express our gendered identities, and we participate in

3

professional associations in which gender may affect how we act and how others perceive and treat us. Relationships and gender influence each other, so that relationships define gender, and gender, in turn, sculpts the character of relationships. Thus, gender is both created by and creative of relationships.

This chapter traces connections among gender, our identities as women and men, communication, and relationships. We'll begin by defining gender and its impact on our lives. Next, we'll explore gender as a personal, social, and relational phenomenon. Finally, we'll highlight the formative role of communication in creating, sustaining, and revising social understandings and expectations of women and men.

UNDERSTANDING GENDER

Although *sex* and *gender* are often used as synonyms, actually they are distinct concepts (Epstein, 1988; Scott, 1986; West & Zimmerman, 1987; Wood, 1994b, 1994c, 1995a). Sex is innate, but gender is socially created and learned by individuals. Being born male or female does not necessarily lead to thinking, acting, and feeling in ways a culture prescribes for men or women. Instead, biological sex is transformed into culturally constructed gender as we interact with social structures and practices that express, uphold, and encourage individuals to embody prevailing views of women and men. As we communicate with others, we learn how society defines the sexes, and we craft our personal identities to reflect or resist social expectations. For example, society encourages women to be sensitive to relationships and to others' feelings, and many women reflect these feminine prescriptions in their concrete behaviors. Men are generally urged to be competitive and emotionally controlled, and these learnings surface in how many men communicate.

Sex

Sex is a biological quality that is determined by genetics and hormones. The terms *male* and *female, woman* and *man, girl* and *boy* refer to biological sex. Even before birth, sex is established, and, short of radical procedures, it remains stable throughout our lives. Of the 23 pairs of chromosomes that provide the blueprint for human identity, one pair controls sex. The usual chromosome patterns are XX for females and XY for males. (Less standard patterns are XO or XXX for females and XXY or XYY for males.) Both before and after birth, hormones govern secondary sexual characteristics such as facial hair, menstruation, and proportion of muscle and fat tissue (Jacklin, 1989).

Recent research also suggests that biological sex may influence tendencies toward specialization in the human brain. In general, females are more adept in using the right brain lobe, which controls creative abilities and intuitive, holistic thinking. Males are generally more skilled in left brain functions, which govern linear thinking and abstract, analytic thought (Hartlage, 1980). Females typically have more developed corpora callosa, which are the bundles of nerves connecting brain lobes. Thus, females may have an advantage in crossing from one side of the brain to the other and in using both brain hemispheres (Hines, 1992). Research linking sex and hemispheric brain specialization, however, doesn't prove that sex determines brain activity. It is equally possible that males and females are socialized in ways that lead to differential development of ability in the distinct lobes of the brain (Breedlove, 1994).

Currently there is no conclusive evidence of sex differences beyond those associated with physiology, hormonal activity, and brain specialization. Perhaps you're thinking that these limited differences don't explain extensive distinctions in how men and women act, perceive themselves, and are seen and treated by others. If so, you're perceptive. To make sense of pronounced and numerous dissimilarities in how the sexes act and are perceived, we need to understand gender.

Gender

Unlike sex, which is innate and stable, gender is learned, and it varies in response to experiences over a lifetime. We acquire gender as we interact with others and our social world. As we enter diverse situations and relationships during our lives, our understandings of gender continuously evolve. Gender terms such as *feminine* and *masculine* and *womanly* and *manly* reflect socially constructed views of women and men.

Gender consists of meanings and expectations of men and women that are created and upheld by social processes and structures. For example, women are expected to be sensitive to others, nurturing, and emotional, and men are expected to be independent, assertive, and emotionally reserved (Doyle, 1989; Tavris & Baumgartner, 1983). This gendered aspect of identity is particularly evident in patterns of caregiving. Although sex determines that women and not men carry fetuses, give birth, and lactate, gender accounts for the expectation that women will assume primary responsibility for caring for children and others.

Studies (Risman, 1987, 1989) have shown that men can be as loving, nurturing, and responsive to children as women, yet our society continues to expect women to be more involved than men in parenting (Okin, 1989). Likewise, women are expected to care for elderly individuals, so daughters generally assume greater responsibility than sons in caring for parents, and wives typically provide more care to in-laws than married sons do (Aronson, 1992; Wood, 1994e). Social expectations that women should care for others are reflected in and perpetuated by practices such as maternity leaves and schools' tendencies to call mothers before fathers about children. It is gender, not sex, that explains why caring is expected of and assigned to women more than men.

Because gender surpasses sex in explaining patterned differences in social life and the roles, status, rights, activities, and self-concepts of individual women and men, the remainder of this chapter focuses on gender.

SOCIAL CONSTRUCTION OF GENDER

We are sexed beings even before birth, but we acquire gender in the process of social interaction. As we communicate with others, we learn the meanings and values of our culture (G. H. Mead, 1934). In particular, we learn how our culture defines women and men and what it regards as appropriate roles, activities, and identities for each.

Gender Is Variable

What gender means is not universal across time and social groups. In fact, views of men and women vary from culture to culture and at different times within a single culture. The rugged, physically strong exemplar of manhood that held sway in the U.S. in the 1700s was replaced when the Industrial Revolution created a paid labor force in which a man's worth was measured by what he earned (Cancian, 1987; Wood, 1994b). The European American model of women as dainty decorations was displaced by a view of them as hardworking partners in the family livelihood during the agrarian era in the United States. When European American men were redefined as primary breadwinners in the public sphere, the Western ideal of womanhood was revised to that of homemaker (Cancian, 1987).

Gender also varies across cultures. For instance, in Nepal, both sexes are expected to be nurturing, and men are as likely as women to take care of children and elderly people. In other societies, men are more emotional and concerned with appearance than women, while women are more independent and emotionally restrained than men (M. Mead, 1934/1968). In still other cultures, more than two genders are recognized and celebrated, and individuals sometimes change their gender (Kessler & McKenna, 1978; Olien, 1978).

Even within the United States, gender varies among social groups. Because gender is socially created, it makes sense that different social circumstances would cultivate dissimilar views of the sexes (Haraway, 1988; Harding, 1991). For example, Gaines (1995) has shown that among blacks and Hispanics, both sexes have strongly communal orientations. As a group, African American women are also less deferential than white women and, thus, less inclined to smile and defer to men (Halberstadt & Saitta, 1987) and less likely to tolerate abuse passively (Uzzell & Peebles-Wilkins, 1989). Research indicates that lesbians tend to be somewhat more autonomous than their heterosexual sisters (Huston & Schwartz, 1995).

Gender also intersects with other social categories such as race, class, age, and affectional preference (Spelman, 1988). Thus, a heterosexual black attorney will understand and enact gender (as well as class, race, and sexuality) differently than a white working-class man or a gay accountant in Germany. Because gender varies across time and social groups and in relation to other socially constructed categories, it's a mistake to regard women and men as homogeneous groups. Among members of each sex there is substantial variation due to diverse social circumstances that contour the lives of individual women and men. Cheris Kramarae elaborates this idea in Chapter 2.

Normalizing Masculinity and Men

To create and sustain the meaning of gender, social processes and structures normalize arbitrary and often limiting views of the sexes. We thus come to take for granted the "reality" of social views that have been made to seem so natural that we seldom notice or critically evaluate them. Although *gender* is often misunderstood as a synonym for *women*, men are also gendered, since society imposes expectations on both sexes. Just as heterosexuals, as well as lesbians, gays, and bisexuals, have affectional preferences, and Caucasians, as well as people of color, have racial identity, men, as well as women, are gendered.

We tend to think of race as referring to non-Anglos, sexuality as indicating gays, lesbians, and bisexuals, and gender as describing women because whites, heterosexuality, and men have been normalized in Western culture (Wood, 1995a, 1995c). They are the standard against which all others are measured. Heterosexual patterns and activities are the assumed norms for romantic relationships, which invites us to perceive lesbian, gay, and bisexual relationships as abnormal. Similarly, in professional contexts, the behaviors and orientations of white men are the model against which the conduct of women and people of color is judged. By designating one group as *the* standard, we implicitly define everyone outside of that group as deviant, nonstandard, or other. In this manner, cultures construct a narrow vision of what or who is normal (Harding, 1991; Wood & Duck, 1995) and, also, of what or who is abnormal.

Like whiteness and heterosexuality, masculinity is not an absolute standard, but one that is socially constructed as normative. This implies that it is open to critique and change. More complete views of sexuality, professionalism, and other aspects of life would reflect all those who make up the human community and who participate in social life.

PERVASIVENESS OF GENDER

Because gender infuses the entire social order, it is difficult to notice, much less question, prevailing views of women and men. Becoming aware of how society creates and sustains gender enables social progress and personal change.

Gender Is a Pervasive Aspect of Cultural Life

Gender shapes and is evident in everything from personal relationships to public life. Families often divide labor along gendered lines so that boys are assigned independent, outdoor chores such as mowing the lawn, while girls are expected to participate in cooking and cleaning to provide comfort to others (Burns & Homel, 1989; McHale, Bartko, Crouter, & Perry-Jenkins, 1990). These different chores inscribe gender by encouraging boys to be independent and adventurous and girls to respond to others. Public policies, too, bespeak cultural views of women and men (Okin, 1989). Despite some changes, our laws still grant substantial presumption to women in child custody cases, which reflects gendered views of women as caregivers and men as detached from family ties (Coleman & Ganong, 1995).

Gender Is Difficult to Notice

Even though gender pervades our lives, its character and effects are difficult to perceive. Just as we seldom notice air and fish are unaware of water, for the most part we do not realize the myriad ways in which gender infuses our everyday lives as individuals and our collective life as a culture. This is because the meanings of gender that our society has constructed are normalized, making them a constant taken-for-granted background that can easily escape notice. It's difficult to grasp the ways in which gender is normalized when so many aspects of ordinary life make arbitrary views of women and men seem natural: From pink and blue blankets in hospital delivery rooms, to dolls advertised for girls and trains for boys, to guidance counselors who advise women to enter caring professions and men to pursue high-powered careers (Spender, 1989), social constructions of gender surround us at every turn, and they work together to naturalize arbitrary social meanings.

Developing a critical awareness of processes that naturalize views of women and men empowers us to make informed, deliberate choices about how we will embody gender and how we will support or resist prevailing views of women and men. Wise choices about personal identity and social impact begin with recognizing the scope of gender in life.

SCOPE OF GENDER

Gender is a facet of individual identity, a primary principle of social life, and a powerful dynamic in relationships.

Gender as Personal Identity

For most of us, gender is concretely experienced as part of personal identity. We think of ourselves and others as more or less masculine and feminine. Perceiving yourself as feminine or masculine affects the clothes you wear, what and how much you eat, whether you feel safe walking alone at night, and how closely your self-esteem is tied to success in a career and/or relationships. You may feel it is unfeminine to curse or be insensitive to others, or unmasculine to cry or show weakness. In these and other ways, we experience gender as part of personal identity, and it guides how we think, feel, and act.

Gender as a Principle of Social Life

Yet gender is more than personal. It is also a system of social meanings that is constructed and sustained by a variety of cultural structures and practices. Families, schools, laws, the military, professions, religious orders, and businesses are social structures that reflect and reproduce the gender ideology of a culture. Patterns of interacting and roles are social practices that sustain gender ideology. For example, research indicates that parents tend to encourage daughters to be cooperative and attentive to others' needs, and encourage sons to be competitive and assertive of their individual rights (Fagot, Hagan, Leinbach, & Kronsberg, 1985). Many workplaces allow maternity but not paternity leaves, an inequity that reflects and sustains views of women as caregivers. The still-prevalent tendency of women to assume the names of their husbands is a practice that reflects the belief that a woman's identity is based on her relationship to a man.

Another illustration of social practices that prescribe and sustain gender comes from West's (1995) in-depth study of battered women. He reports that many women who are brutalized by their intimate partners seek support from clergy only to be told that they should stay in their marriages, regardless of the danger to their well-being and perhaps their lives. Multiple social structures and practices establish and sustain society's gender ideology.

Gender and Relational Concepts

Social expectations of women and men are realized in particular relationships (Wood, 1994b). Elizabeth Fox-Genovese (1991, p. 120) notes that "in practice gender exists not as an abstraction, but as a system of relations...the specific roles that [societies] assign to women and to men." As we interact with others, we discover how they see us and what they expect of us (G. H. Mead, 1934). We assess our feelings, thoughts, actions, and appearances by comparing ourselves to others. Thus, gender is both taught and concretely embodied in relationships. Consider a few examples:

- For 20 years in a row, a national survey has found that the linchpin of manhood is being a good breadwinner (Faludi, 1991). The link between manhood and professional success (Doyle, 1989; Wood, 1994c) surfaces concretely in relationships. In a study of wives who outearned husbands, Hochschild (1989) found that both spouses were ashamed of her higher salary, and they worked together to sustain a private understanding of their relationship that portrayed the husband as the leader and the wife as dependent on him.

- In heterosexual couples, both women and men continue to assume women should and will do most of the child care and homemaking (Wood, 1994b, 1994e). Even when both partners work outside of the home, only 20% of men assume half of home responsibilities (Hochschild with Machung, 1989).

- In professional contexts, women and men are perceived and treated differently, regardless of their formal titles. For example, women flight attendants are subjected to more abuse from passengers than their male peers. Further, male attendants demand deference from females of equivalent rank and resist women's authority (Hochschild, 1983). Because women are expected to be sensitive to others, working women are assumed to be more open to and interested than men in peers' and subordinates' personal problems (Wood, 1994d).

- Even in the 1990s, men are expected to be sexually aggressive and women to be sexually available. Television shows, films, magazines, and music videos normalize men's sexual aggression, which sheds light on the prevalence of sexual harassment and the still widespread belief that it is normal and acceptable to treat women as sexual objects (Bingham, 1995; Strine, 1992; Wood, 1992, 1995b).

Masculinity and femininity are themselves relational concepts, because the meaning of each is tied to the other. The deference widely associated with femininity requires someone to whom to defer. Likewise, the assertiveness generally associated with masculinity is not an absolute quality, but depends on others who yield. Softness exists in relation to hardness; emotional restraint is meaningful in juxtaposition to emotional expressiveness; independence gains its character in contrast to dependence. It is virtually impossible to conceive of masculinity and femininity apart from one another. In the daily life of relationships, abstract social meanings of gender are transformed into the concrete realities of individual thoughts, feelings, and actions.

DISCURSIVE (RE)CONSTRUCTION OF GENDER

Communication is the most fundamental process that creates, upholds, and alters gender (Bingham, 1995; Weedon, 1987). From public discourse to mediated messages to private talk between intimates, communication reflects social understandings of gender and expresses how individual men and women embody it in their personal identities. For instance, research indicates that men interrupt women more often than women interrupt men (Beck, 1988; DeFrancisco, 1991; Mulac, Wiemann, Widenmann, & Gibson, 1988). When we observe a specific man interrupt a particular woman and see her allow it, we are witnessing a concrete performance of gender. He assumes he should assert and dominate, which is consistent with social prescriptions for masculinity. She displays deference in keeping with social views of women.

Communication Creates and Sustains Gender

The philosopher Michael Foucault realized that communication is a pivotal force in establishing and regulating social life and personal identity. According to Foucault (1978, p. 18), communication is the primary process through which social reality is created because in communication "something is formed." This implies that communication defines experience and establishes meaning. As Spender (1984) has pointed out, language shapes what we perceive. Words confer social existence on what a culture considers important. For instance, the term *date rape* was only recently coined. Before the term entered our language, many women whose dates forced them into sexual activity had no socially authorized way to describe what had happened or to label it as wrong and a violation (Wood, 1992). In like manner, all meanings of ourselves and our world are formed in and fortified by communication on playgrounds, over the breakfast table, in congressional debates, and in schools.

Social views of women and men are established and normalized through ongoing symbolic interaction in society. From family conversations to political discourse to intimate dialogues, communication constructs perspectives of men and women, and at the same time, individuals use communication to embody or resist social meanings. As children, we learned that boys are made of "snakes and snails and puppy dog tails," and girls are made of "sugar and spice and everything nice." Gendered expectations are further communicated through parents' distinctive treatment of daughters and sons. Despite convincing evidence of the detrimental effects of sex-stereotyped childrearing (Morrow, 1990), many parents still perceive and treat boys and girls differently. Parents tend to expect and encourage sons to be independent, active, and tough and daughters to be social and interpersonally sensitive (Jones & Dembo, 1989; Safilios-Rothschild, 1979; Stern & Karraker, 1989; Thompson & Walker, 1989; Thorbecke & Grotevant, 1982). From nursery rhymes to parental instruction, family communication teaches children society's expectations of women and men.

Peers' communication reinforces parental messages about gender. Boys learn early that being afraid will earn them epithets of *sissy, wimp,* and *mama's boy,* and girls discover peers will reject them if they aren't nice to others (Maccoby & Jacklin, 1987; Martin, 1989). Gender is also reinforced in childhood games. Football, for instance, teaches boys to compete, assert themselves, and focus on achieving clear-cut goals. Games that girls typically play (jump rope and house) encourage and reward cooperation and responsiveness to others (Maltz & Borker, 1982).

Communication in schools further fortifies social views of the sexes by rewarding girls for being cooperative and quiet and boys for competing and asserting themselves (Epperson, 1988; Sadker & Sadker, 1986; Wood & Lenze, 1991). A survey of over 1,300 studies revealed that teachers give males more attention and encouragement than females ("Sexism in the Schoolhouse," 1992). Thus, communication in schools echoes the meanings of gender expressed in other contexts.

As individuals enter into adult romantic relationships, social views of the sexes surface in communication between partners, especially heterosexuals. For instance, female and male college students share gender stereotypes about appropriate dating scripts. Both sexes think men should initiate relationships and plan activities other than sex (Rose & Frieze, 1989). Both sexes also expect women to be relationship experts (Tavris, 1992; Wood, 1994b) and men to be more powerful (Anderson & Leslie, 1991; Reissman, 1990). Further, an alarming number of college men and women perceive abuse, including physical violence, as a male prerogative in romantic relationships (Goldner, Penn, Sheinberg, & Walker, 1990).

Communication upholds cultural values by reinscribing and naturalizing socially constructed patterns of meaning, perception, and sense making. Also, most of us internalize prevailing social values in the process of communicating. Referring to this as "governance," Foucault (1982) asserts that we learn cultural values in the process of learning language, and this predisposes us to think and act in ways that affirm and reproduce the existing social order. Thus, as we interact with others throughout life, we learn society's meanings for gender, and we are encouraged to accept and embody them in our own lives (Wood, 1994a).

Communication Changes Gender

As we've seen, gender is not static, but consists of fluid social meanings that vary across time and social groups and in relation to other aspects of identity. Social views of men and women change as a result of communication by and between individuals. In other words, individuals can and often do use communication to re-form understandings of what it means to be feminine or masculine. The athletic woman of the 1990s would have been disparaged as unfeminine in 1950, and women's participation in professional life was not widely accepted even two decades ago. Hillary Rodham Clinton embodies a new vision of women, one that could not have been attempted in the 1970s. Likewise, Bill Clinton's sensitivity to others and his personal comfort with a strong wife would have been unacceptable in the era dominated by John Wayne as the male ideal.

We notice public figures who offer new models of men and women because they are in the limelight. Yet, less famous people also resist constraining definitions of the sexes and usher in alternative visions. For example, career women become more assertive, ambitious, and comfortable using power the longer they participate in professional life (Epstein, 1981; McGowen & Hart, 1990). As women inhabit professional roles, they alter how they conceive and enact their gender. In turn, this influences how others view men and women and relations between them.

In ordinary family life, too, communication instigates changes in how women and men define themselves and each other. For example, Kaye and Applegate (1990) reported that men who take care of elderly people become more aware of others' feelings and more generous in responding to others' needs than men who are less involved in caregiving. Many modern men, who are more actively involved with children than their own fathers were, communicate an alternative definition of manhood and fatherhood.

Children of today who see mothers who are assertive as well as nurturing and fathers who provide personal care as well as financial support develop broader understandings of gender than those learned by many members of previous generations. Thus, much of the communication that creates, sustains, and challenges socially prescribed meanings of gender occurs in the private sphere of relationships.

SUMMARY

In this chapter, we have seen that gender is a social construction. It consists of the meanings culture attributes to men and women and the personal and social effects of those meanings on individuals' concrete lives. Abstract social meanings of gender are learned through social interaction and realized in daily life as we communicate with others in our social and personal relationships. As we interact with family members, friends, intimates, and work associates, we participate in the ongoing cultural creation of gender. Both in accepting or rejecting prevailing views of women and men and in the ways we personally embody gender, each of us influences the continuous (re)construction of gender.

Although gender is normalized through numerous and intricately entwined social structures and practices, we can choose to become critically aware of how arbitrary views of the sexes are naturalized and to take an active role in shaping the impact of gender on our personal and collective lives. It takes courage to question prevailing values and to resist social expectations of how we should be. The easy course is to accept current prescriptions for gender without question or challenge.

Yet, in every generation, individuals take issue with prevailing views of men and women and change social understandings of who they are and should be. For example, from 1848 until 1920, a number of women and a few men challenged then-prevalent views that women were not entitled to own property, pursue higher education, or vote. Resistance to social views of women in that era led to substantial changes in women's rights and opportunities. Similarly, men's movements have contested the macho John Wayne view of manhood and have provided an alternative vision of masculinity as both sensitive and strong, both individualistic and committed to others. As agents of social change, each of us has the capacity to affect what gender will mean in our society. Cultivating and acting on critical consciousness of gender empowers us to influence our personal destinies and the life of our culture.

Perhaps communication as a fulcrum of changing gender is best illustrated in a conversation I overheard between my niece and her playmate Steven. He announced, "I am the father so I get to go to work each day and you have to stay home." Michelle's response was swift and sure: "I don't want to stay home. You do that. I'm going to work." Regardless of how these two 4-year-olds work out roles in their make-believe family, they are engaged in constructing the meaning of gender and what it implies for their personal identities and their relationship with each other. Like Michelle and Steven, each of us is engaged in the social construction of gender and, thus, the continuous creation of our relationships, our society, and ourselves.

QUESTIONS FOR REFLECTION AND DISCUSSION

1. Think about the ways in which masculinity and male patterns are normalized in contexts such as professions, athletics, and media. How are norms and standards of male athletes made to seem appropriate for all athletes? How are masculine modes of doing business represented as natural and right?

2. How do media reproduce cultural views of women and men? Watch children's programs on Saturday morning and notice the roles of characters of each sex. Which sex is more active, adventurous, and successful? Which is more dependent, quiet, and unsuccessful?

3. Examine science texts used in courses for any grade level. Notice the number of women and men scientists who are mentioned.

Notice pictures used to illustrate scientific work. What view of scientists is normalized by communication in textbooks?

4. Interview a local attorney, preferably the district attorney for your area. Ask her or him to describe trial strategies used by lawyers and assumptions held by jurors that affect verdicts in rape and sexual assault cases. With others in your class, discuss how the information you gain from the interview sheds light on gender ideology.

REFERENCES

Anderson, E. A., & Leslie, L. A. (1991). Coping with employment and family stress: Employment arrangement and gender differences. *Sex Roles, 24,* 223–237.

Aronson, J. (1992). Women's sense of responsibility for the care of old people: "But who else is going to do it?" *Gender and Society, 6,* 8–29.

Beck, A. (1988). *Love is never enough.* New York: Harper & Row.

Bingham, S. (Ed.). (1995). *Conceptualizing sexual harassment as discursive practice.* Westport, CT: Praeger.

Breedlove, S. M. (1994). Sexual differentiation of the human nervous system. *Annual Review of Psychology, 45,* 389–418.

Burns, A., & Homel, R. (1989). Gender division of tasks by parents and their children. *Psychology of Women Quarterly, 13,* 113–125.

Cancian, F. (1987). *Love in America.* Cambridge, MA: Cambridge University Press.

Coleman, M., & Ganong, L. D. (1995). Family reconfiguring following divorce. In S. Duck & J. T. Wood (Eds.), *Understanding relationship processes, 5: Confronting relationship challenges* (pp. 73–108). Thousand Oaks, CA: Sage.

DeFrancisco, V. (1991). The sounds of silence: How men silence women in marital relations. *Discourse & Society, 2,* 413–423.

Doyle, J. A. (1989). *The male experience* (2nd ed.). Dubuque, IA: William C. Brown.

Epperson, S. E. (1988, September 16). Studies link subtle sex bias in schools with women's behavior in the workplace. *Wall Street Journal,* p. 27A.

Epstein, C. (1981). *Women in law.* New York: Basic Books.

Epstein, C. F. (1988). *Deceptive distinctions: Sex, gender and the social order.* New Haven: Yale University Press.

Fagot, B. I., Hagan, R., Leinbach, M. D., & Kronsberg, S. (1985). Differential reactions to assertive and communicative acts of toddler boys and girls. *Child Development, 56,* 1499–1505.

Faludi, S. (1991). *Backlash: The undeclared war against American women.* New York: Crown.

Foucault, M. (1978). Politics and the study of discourse. *Ideology and Consciousness, 3,* 7–26.

Foucault, M. (1982). The subject and power. *Critical Inquiry, 8,* 777–789.

Fox-Genovese, E. (1991). *Feminism without illusions*. Chapel Hill, NC: University of North Carolina Press.

Gaines, S. (1995). Relationships between members of cultural minorities. In J. T. Wood & S. W. Duck (Eds.), *Understanding relationship processes, 6: Off the beaten track: Understudied relationships*. Thousand Oaks, CA: Sage.

Goldner, V., Penn, P., Sheinberg, M., & Walker, G. (1990). Love and violence: Gender paradoxes in volatile attachments. *Family Process, 19,* 343–364.

Halberstadt, A., & Saitta, M. (1987). Gender, nonverbal behavior, and perceived dominance: A test of the theory. *Journal of Personality and Social Psychology, 53,* 257–272.

Haraway, D. (1988). Situated knowledges: The science question in feminism and the privilege of partial perspective. *Signs, 14,* 575–599.

Harding, S. (1991). *Whose science? Whose knowledge? Thinking from women's lives*. Ithaca, NY: Cornell University Press.

Hartlage, L. (1980, March). *Identifying and programming for differences*. Paper at the Parent and Professional Conference on Young children with Special Needs, Cleveland, OH.

Hines, M. (1992, April 19). [Untitled report]. *Health Information Communication Network, 5,* 2.

Hochschild, A. (1983). *The managed heart: Commercialization of human feeling*. Berkeley: University of California Press.

Hochschild, A. (1989). The economy of gratitude. In D. Franks & E. D. McCarthy (Eds.), *The sociology of emotions: Original essays and research papers* (pp. 95–113). Greenwich, CT: JAI Press.

Hochschild, A., with Machung, A. (1989). *The second shift*. New York: Viking/Penguin.

Huston, M., & Schwartz, P. (1995). In J. T. Wood & S. W. Duck (Eds.), *Understanding relationship processes, 6: Off the beaten track: Understudied relationships*. Thousand Oaks, CA: Sage.

Jacklin, C. N. (1989). Female and male: Issues of gender. *American Psychologist, 44,* 127–133.

Jones, G. P., & Dembo, M. H. (1989). Age and sex role differences in intimate friendships during childhood and adolescence. *Merrill-Palmer Quarterly, 35,* 445–462.

Kaye, L. W., & Applegate, J. S. (1990). Men as elder caregivers: A response to changing families. *American Journal of Orthopsychiatry, 60,* 86–95.

Kessler, S., & McKenna, W. (1978). *Gender: An ethnomethodological approach*. New York: John Wiley.

Maccoby, E. E., & Jacklin, C. N. (1987). Gender segregation in childhood. *Advances in Child Development and Behavior, 20,* 239–287.

Maltz, D. N., and Borker, R. (1982). A cultural approach to male–female miscommunication. In J. J. Gumpertz (Ed.), *Language and social identity* (pp. 196–216). Cambridge, UK: Cambridge University Press.

Martin, C. L. (1989). Children's use of gender-related information in making social judgments. *Developmental Psychology, 25,* 80–88.

McGowen, K. R., & Hart, L. E. (1990). Still different after all these years: Gender differences in professional identity formation. *Professional Psychology: Research and Practice, 21,* 118–123.

McHale, S. M., Bartko, W. T., Crouter, A. C., & Perry-Jenkins, M. (1990). Children's housework and psycho-social functioning: The mediating effects of parents' sex-role behaviors and attitudes. *Child Development, 61,* 1413–1426.

Mead, G. H. (1934). *Mind, self, and society.* Chicago: University of Chicago Press.

Mead, M. (1935/1968). *Sex and temperament in three primitive societies.* New York: Dell.

Morrow, F. (1990). *Unleashing our unknown selves: An inquiry into the future of femininity and masculinity.* Westport, CT: Praeger.

Mulac, A., Wiemann, J. M., Widenmann, S. J., & Gibson, T. W. (1988). Male/female language differences and effects in same-sex and mixed-sex dyads: The gender-linked language effect. *Communication Monographs, 55,* 315–335.

Okin, S. M. (1989). *Gender, justice, and the family.* New York: Basic Books.

Olien, M. (1978). *The human myth.* New York: Harper & Row.

Reissman, C. (1990). *Divorce talk: Women and men make sense of personal relationships.* Brunswick, NJ: Rutgers University Press.

Risman, B. (1987). Intimate relationships from a microstructural perspective: Men who mother. *Gender and Society, 1,* 6–32.

Risman, B. (1989). Can men mother? Life as a single father. In B. Risman & P. Schwartz (Eds.), *Gender in intimate relationships.* Belmont, CA: Wadsworth.

Rose, S., & Frieze, I. H. (1989). Young singles' scripts for a first date. *Gender and Society, 3,* 258–268.

Sadker, M., & Sadker, D. (1986, March). Sexism in the classroom: From grade school to graduate school. *Phi Delta Kappan,* pp. 512–515.

Safilios-Rothschild, C. (1979). *Sex-role socialization and sex discrimination: A synthesis and critique of the literature.* Washington, DC: National Institute of Education.

Scott, J. (1986). Gender: A useful category for social analysis. *American Historical Review, 91,* 1053–1075.

Sexism in the schoolhouse. (1992, February 24). *Newsweek,* p. 48.

Spelman, E. V. (1988). *Inessential woman: Problems of exclusion in feminist thought.* Boston: Beacon Press.

Spender, D. (1984). Defining reality: A powerful tool. In C. Kramarae, M. Schultz, & W. O'Barr (Eds.), *Language and power* (pp. 9–22). Beverly Hills: Sage.

Spender, D. (1989). *Invisible women: The schooling scandal.* London: Women's Press.

Stern, M., & Karraker, K. H. (1989). Sex stereotyping of infants: A review of gender labeling studies. *Sex Roles, 20,* 501–522.

Strine, M. S. (1992). Understanding how things work: Sexual harassment and academic culture. *Journal of Applied Communication Research, 20,* 391–400.

Tavris, C. (1992). *The mismeasure of woman.* New York: Simon & Schuster.

Tavris, C., & Baumgartner, A. (1983, February). How would your life be different? *Redbook,* pp. 92–95.

Thompson, L., & Walker, A. (1989). Gender in families: Women and men in marriage, work, and parenthood. *Journal of Marriage and the Family, 51,* 845–871.

Thorbecke, W., and Grotevant, H. D. (1982). Gender differences in adolescent interpersonal identity formation. *Journal of Youth and Adolescence, 11,* 479–492.

Uzzell, O., & Peebles-Wilkins, W. (1989). Black spouse abuse: A focus on factors and intervention strategies. *Western Journal of Black Studies, 13,* 10–16.

Weedon, C. (1987). *Feminist practice and poststructuralist theory.* Oxford, UK: Basil Blackwell.

West, J. T. (1995). Understanding how the dynamics of ideology influence violence between intimates. In J. T. Wood & S. W. Duck (Eds.), *Understanding relationship processes, 5: Confronting relationship challenges* (pp. 129–150). Thousand Oaks, CA: Sage.

West, C., & Zimmerman, D. H. (1987). Doing gender. *Gender and Society, 1,* 125–151.

Wood, J. T. (1992). Telling our stories: Narratives as a basis for theorizing sexual harassment. *Journal of Applied Communication Research, 4,* 349–363.

Wood, J. T. (1994a). Engendered identities: Shaping voice and mind through gender. In D. Vocate (Ed.), *Intrapersonal communication: Different voices, different minds.* Hillsdale, NJ: Lawrence Erlbaum.

Wood, J. T. (1994b). Engendered relations: Interaction, caring, power, and responsibility in close relationships. In S. W. Duck (Ed.), *Understanding relationship processes 3: Social context and relationships* (pp. 26–54). Newbury Park, CA: Sage.

Wood, J. T. (1994c). *Gendered lives: Communication, gender, and culture.* Belmont, CA: Wadsworth.

Wood, J. T. (1994d). Issues facing nontraditional members of academe. In G. M. Phillips, D. S. Gouran, S. A. Kuehn, & J. T. Wood (Eds.), *Professionalism: A survival guide for beginning academics.* Cresskill, NJ: Hampton Press.

Wood, J. T. (1994e). *Who cares: Women, care, and culture.* Carbondale, IL: Southern Illinois University Press.

Wood, J. T. (1995a). Feminist scholarship and research on relationships. *Journal of Social and Personal Relationships, 12,* 103–120.

Wood, J. T. (1995b). Saying it makes it so: The discursive construction of sexual harassment. In S. Bingham (Ed.), *Conceptualizing sexual harassment as discursive practice* (pp. 17–32). Westport, CT: Praeger.

Wood, J. T. (1995c). *Relational communication: Change and continuity in personal relationships.* Belmont, CA: Wadsworth.

Wood, J. T., & Duck, S. W. (1995). In J. T. Wood & S. W. Duck (Eds.), *Understanding relationship processes, 6: Off the beaten track: Understudied relationships.* Thousand Oaks, CA: Sage.

Wood, J. T., & Lenze, L. F. (1991). Strategies to enhance gender sensitivity in communication education. *Communication Education, 40,* 16–21.

CLASSIFIED INFORMATION: RACE, CLASS, AND (ALWAYS) GENDER

CHERIS KRAMARAE

...within a system of interlocking race, gender, class, and sexual oppression, there are few pure oppressors or victims. --COLLINS, 1990, P. 194

Talking about race, class, and gender together is not easy, and not even always desirable. These systems have important historical and contemporary differences as well as connections. Each needs our concentrated, critical attention. They are not discrete systems, however and we too seldom consider the ways they interweave. For example, when we focus on the terms *homosexual* and *gay,* we may forget that there are many gays who are women *and* people of color *and* working class *and* poor *and* disabled *and* old *and* Jewish (see Barbara Smith's 1983 discussion, p. 415).

Have you heard the term *women and minorities*? Have you noticed that it makes minority women invisible? Have you ever heard (or used) the term *Asian American*? Do you hear how it blurs differences among people from Nepal, China, Japan, Malaysia, and other Asian countries? We often hear the phrase *women of color,* but seldom hear *men of color.* Are all men white? These examples of everyday talk reveal the power of language in shaping—and distorting—our perceptions of individuals.

This chapter is an invitation to focus on ways in which language creates and reproduces views of gender, race, class, and sexual orientation, as well as on ways language represents or fails to represent connections among these. My style is deliberately unconventional as I call attention to the language we use for ourselves and each other. My choices of labels in this chapter are also somewhat irregular; rather than forcing a false standardizing, I have tried to use "appropriate terminology" for the particular context, including the labels used by authors. For a discussion of the reasons for the changes in one set of labels, see Tom W. Smith's (1992) essay on the terms *Colored, Negro, Black,* and *African American.*

FINDING WAYS TO THINK ABOUT RACE, CLASS, AND GENDER

Race, class, and gender are all involved in our nation's critical debates and in the language and other aspects of our everyday interactions, even if not always explicitly. In interactions with, for example, people whom we have known for a long time, we may not be conscious of race, class, gender, and sexual orientation and the ways they sculpt our talks. We just talk to friends and acquaintances in different ways.

In interactions with strangers, however, we usually do an immediate "processing" of race, sex, and class. If you have ever had the experience of not knowing whether the person you were talking to was a woman or a man, you will likely have found that "normal conversation" was impossible because most of your focus would probably have been on trying to determine, through attention to the person's physical, behavioral, or language traits, who she or he "really was." Even in telephone conversations with strangers, you assess these primary characteristics and adapt your communication accordingly.

Although some people participating in the various new electronic forums argue that this medium allows us to correspond with others without knowing or caring about the race, class, gender, age, occupational status, sexual orientation, or physical characteristics of those with whom we "talk," gender at least is usually very much an issue. Our names often carry this information, and since an estimated 85 to 95% of those participating on the Internet are male, women often stand out, or are made to stand out. In many of the interactive forums, where people make up characters, often a great deal of interaction is directed toward determining the "real" gender of the players. Jeanie Taylor and her colleagues (1993) give examples of the sexual harassment on the nets and of the many other ways in which these new forums are gendered.

The labels we call each other are not "mere rhetoric" but critical behaviors. The labels are intimately involved in the ideas we have about ourselves and thus about our relationships. Power, subordination, love, hatred, anger, hostility, cooperation, solidarity, and resistance are expressed in part through selective addressing and labeling. Language is not a substitute for action, but is itself action. In this chapter, the focus is on the actions embedded in the labels we use.

Models for Talking About Race, Class, and Gender

There are several models or approaches for talking about the relationship among race, class, and gender. Some people have studied how women and men have talked about the power relationships in their everyday lives. For example, Philomena Essed (1991) listens to the way race, class, and gender—interrelated processes, as she demonstrates— are actively structured in the talk in shops, the street, schools, and workplaces. These processes take place through the formulation and application of rules, laws, and regulations, but also through such every-day interactions as sexual harassment, name calling, verbal threats, ridicule, and jokes.

Others bring together essays on these systems of oppression in practice and theory, in order to encourage our moving back and forth, using each to examine the others. For example, Paula Rothenberg (1992), in her edited book of essays about the ways that racism, sexism, and classism pervade American life, offers readers a variety of ideas about the causes and cures of economic, legal, and social inequalities, suggesting that developing a critical understanding of the nature and causes of race, class, and gender oppression is the first step toward moving beyond it. Margaret Andersen and Patricia Hill Collins (1995) and Elizabeth Spelman (1988) also offer a collection of essays that inspect the interrelationships of race, class, and gender.

Another approach encourages us to reflect on the ways that we have been taught to respond to various "differences" in similar ways—by ignoring, copying, or destroying the differences, depending on where we think they and we are in a hierarchy. For example, in the chapter "Age, Race, Class, and Sex: Women Redefining Difference," Audre Lorde (1984) encourages us to consider the ways differences are linked, by pointing to the similarity of the definitions:

> *Racism, the belief in the inherent superiority of one race over all others and thereby the right to dominance. Sexism, the belief in the inherent superiority of one sex over the other and thereby the right to dominance. Ageism. Heterosexism. Elitism. Classism.* (p. 115; her italics)

They operate from, in general, the same assumption of inferiority–superiority.

We gain additional information from looking at labels. Currently we have a lot of controversy in the United States about social identity—who gets to say who or what they are, and what terminology is being forced on what other groups. We hear most, of course, from people who have the best access to lecterns and other means of public voice. Some people who don't see any reason for a change in relationships among groups either reject the changes in terminology or wish for a quick, permanent change if there must be one. In a discussion about social categories, I heard a white woman say to a woman who called herself Latina, "Okay, I'll call you what you people want to be called—Latino, Latina, Chicano, Chicana, Hispanic, Mexican American, whatever. Just tell me what it is you want to be called!" She was speaking as if these are all one group of people, as if there were, or should be, one static terminology system that one could learn and then apply easily in all further interactions, and as if our current relationships were set for all time.

Others who want change call for a variety of strategies, including the use of new terminology or new definitions in their own interactions, and they argue from the ideas of equality expressed in our laws. Others use dictionary definitions as *the* authority for determining the meanings of the labels. For example, one person, on a "soc.culture.african" newsgroup electronic bulletin board, responding to a comment about Caucasians, wrote:

> I can see you take "Caucasian" to be white....The two are completely different....Here's the dictionary definition of Caucasian: a member of a racial group, or its descendants, originally inhabiting Europe **and parts of North Africa, western Asia and India**, complexion varies from **fair to very dark**, hair texture ranges from **kinky to straight**...So you see, Indians are in fact Caucasians. (March 8, 1993)

Here the assumption is that "the dictionary definition" (the particular dictionary unnamed, as if dictionaries are all—regardless of year of publication, size, and collection process—interchangeable) takes precedence over any other justifications of terminology.

Limitations of Dictionary Definitions

Many of us were taught, in grade school and high school, to treat dictionaries as *the* authority on language usage. However, the makers of dictionaries, as well as most contributors, are themselves members of particular social groups, usually the dominant groups. Like the rest of us, dictionary editors hear and read selectively and from their own social positions. They usually give us very little information about the labels, relying instead on "usage," which generally means what is printed in publications controlled by elites. Dictionaries are useful archives of some kinds of information, but they tell us very little about what labels are used with what reasons and with what effect in which situations.

Those who know the English language well understand that some English terms easily can be used as insults. Once a speaker learns what *trash* is, he or she knows that calling someone *white trash* or *Black trash* is an insult. Most of us who become familiar with a language and a culture learn that some words have historically been used as insults. However, there is no simple way of culling out acceptable terms from unacceptable (to the person named) without knowing about race, gender, class, and sexual conflicts. Some nonnative speakers of English are puzzled when, after they have learned that *Nigger* is a provocative, aggressive word, they hear it used by some African Americans for each other—in humor, or to chastise each other, or to point to a history of racism, or to move African Americans toward political activity, or to express love (Wilson, 1980, p. 16; see also the naming in Toni Morrison's *Beloved*, 1987).

Queer is a label that some heterosexuals use as an insult. However, it has been reappropriated by many lesbians and gays as a term of empowerment. Similarly, while many English speakers have learned that *girl* is a belittling term when used to address or describe an adult human female and *woman* is a respectful term, some of us have also learned that, from certain people at certain times, *girl* can be a desirable term for an adult woman. For example, bell hooks writes, "We use the word 'girl' in that way it is used in traditional African-American culture as a sign of intense womanist affection, not as a put down" (1990, p. 100). Labels thus can express various meanings, depending on the circumstance.

FOCUS ON RACE, CLASS, AND GENDER

Why a focus on race, class, and gender in particular? All cultures we know about place a lot of attention on gender. Many people in the United States are concerned with the subject of race. (In a relatively brief time period, Euro-Americans, mostly, killed Native Americans and took their land, captured Blacks to do the heavy labor on the confiscated land, and put Japanese in interment camps. Today, exploitation continues as Mexicans and other "nonnative" farm and domestic laborers work for poverty wages.) Class, although not as often explicitly discussed as gender and race, is a distinction that most North Americans and others frequently make. I write as a white, middle-aged, academic woman who has spent much of her adult life studying language and gender issues in the United States and in several other countries including South Africa. Both in the Untied States and in other countries, I have been identified and evaluated on the basis of race, gender, age, education, sexual orientation, weight, height, class, religion, and nationality, among other characteristics. However, my perceived race, class, and gender have been primary, and related, identifiers in many situations, so I am focusing on these. I am also particularly interested in the ways attitudes about gender have shaped the terms we've created to describe race and class.

Few of us can escape hearing and speaking about race, class, and gender, and thus few of us can avoid interpreting and having our terminology interpreted along these lines. As Doris Wilkinson (1990, p. 14) points out (in talking about the controversy over how Negroes/Coloreds/Blacks/African Americans have been and wish to be identified), these are not discussions of style, but substantive debates with philosophical, cognitive, and political implications.

The Language of Race

Language Constructs Race. Many social scientists point out that we do not perceive racial differences. We perceive differences of hair color and texture, height, bone structure, and skin color. We learn to associate those with racial classifications and with differing social values. This is to say that "races" do not exist apart from our creation. Examples are the Nazi creation of the Aryan race, and the U.S. creation of the labels *Asian* and *Asian American,* which suggest that people from Japan, Malaysia, China, Nepal, and Taiwan are somehow all the same.[1]

Most academics writing about race classification are quick to point out that there is nothing scientific about it. Yet many of our official

---

[1] While the focus in this essay is on gender, class, and race, I note that we can very usefully talk about other classifications in much the same way—as creations. Elana Dykewomon writes: "Being female is like being a Jew, or short—it's a fact—but what it 'means' is determined by culture, history, institutionalized power. No matter how clearly (or not) I perceive those things, I have few choices but to play my part or denounce it. Biology *becomes* destiny seems more like it" (1993, p. 7).

documents set forth a classification system that ignores the fluidity of social and economic features and treats them as immutable "facts." While one of the common category schemes of race has been division into Negroid, Mongoloid, and Caucasoid, some modern classifiers have listed as many as 30 races (Nelson, 1982). However, for much of the 20th century, physical anthropologists haven't been able to agree on where the genetic boundaries are between these groups.

Language Justifies Racism. The "science of race" based on biological and genetic discourses became popular around the turn of the century and was a compelling proposal for many Euro-Americans; many of them thought African Americans were inferior and welcomed the support of academic and scholarly authority for their beliefs and actions (Brooks & Cutbirth, 1990). Scientific racism did not crowd out other types of proof, however. For example, the Bible has been used by some to support declarations of the innate limitations of white women and of African Americans as compared to white men.

Recently, we have seen a resurgence of arguments that African Americans are inherently less intelligent than whites. However, specialists are not in agreement about what is inherited or what intelligence is. Some researchers have shown that in "enriched" environments in which children receive a great deal of nurturing, the heritability factor actually goes up, suggesting that we need to think of heritability, as well as intelligence, as being organic and in flux rather than set forever. Some researchers equate intelligence only with acquisition of knowledge needed for formal schooling, while others suggest that we consider the existence of various types of intelligence—including artistic, physical, and relational knowledge—and point out that we know too little about relationships among these (Coughlin, 1994).

While there is much we don't know, we can see that not only race but class assumptions are involved in how we think about intelligence. Likely, most of us are ready to assume, without thinking about where that assumption comes from, that the children of Fortune 500 executives are going to be smarter than the children of auto mechanics. We should also note the assumption that the "smart gene" (not yet discovered!) is transmitted primarily through the male lineage.

Language Establishes Gender and "Mixed Race." Many of the problems of race categories become clear when we try to determine who or what counts as mixed race. Popular ideas about this vary dramatically from country to country and from decade to decade. For example, people in Belgium who might describe themselves as "mixed" would be called African Americans in the United States (unless they "pass" as white). In most of Latin America, the same people would not be categorized as a group at all. In South Africa, they would be called Coloured (Banton, 1980).

There are not, of course, any pure races. In any "race mixing," women are involved. But women's involvement has been talked about in quite different ways from men's involvement. For example, in Euro-American colonies in the United States, white men might excuse other white men who had sexual intercourse with, or raped, Black women, but white men did not excuse white women, who, in order to retain their "good name," should remain white, "unsoiled" by any sexual mixing with Black or Native American men. African American women never were allowed a "good name" in the category systems imposed by whites (Brent, 1973).

Sometimes called "white children of slavery," the "mulatto" daughters received different labels and treatment at slave markets than did the "mulatto" sons (see Forbes, 1988, for a discussion of the use of the term *mulatto*). In the mid-19th century, there were slave markets of "fancy girls"—especially fair "mixed-race" girls and women who were sold at high prices to white men (Williamson, 1980, pp. 68–69).

In Southern literature, the Southern white lady is charm, beauty, and refinement while the "mulatto" woman is a marginal, tragic person. While the mulatto image has existed since the beginning of novel writing in the United States, Southern writers of literature focus more on the mammy than the mulatto, likely in order to play down the existence of miscegenation (Sims-Wood, 1988). The "mammy" label is used for a nonmulatto women who is very black, with large breasts and head covered with a kerchief; she is loyal, sexless, religious, and superstitious (Christian, 1980, p. 11). Many of us have learned about these race labels from authors, publishers, song writers, and film directors.

Language Defines Minority Status.   Usually, the term *minority* is applied to a group of people who have the following characteristics: They are in a subordinate position, They are numerically inferior to the rest of the population in a region, and they have some interest in preserving their ethnic, religious, or linguistic heritage. But there are difficulties with this kind of definition. Numerical superiority doesn't always mean dominance. Consider South Africa politics where a relatively small number of whites have ruled. And there's the problem of determining the boundaries between such "regions" as town, country, state, and nation. Do we have to look to the legislative structure of a country in order to figure out who the minorities are?

Another definition might read as follows: Minorities are people who because of physical or cultural characteristics are set aside in various ways and thus experience prejudice, discrimination, and marginality by dominant groups. Many people labeled minorities have physical or linguistic traits that make them relatively easily distinguishable, or they are encouraged or forced to have distinguishable traits or signs (for example, Jews in Nazi Germany were forced to wear patches and were branded with numbers).

Language Erases Identity. Women have a special tie to the term *minority* as in that strange and revealing phrase *women and minorities.* Women are not, of course, a small group, but they are often considered and treated by dominant groups as marginal. Further, minorities are not all men, although this phrase encourages that perception and "leads to the invisibility of minority women and the invisibility of the issues which affect them," argues Judy Scales-Trent (1990, p. 338). As she points out, while seemingly everyone has a named place in each of the categories of race, class, and gender, in actuality for some people some of the categories are not considered equally applicable:

> For example, for black men, the sex category is invisible. Black men are "powerful" through their masculinity, and therefore often do not focus on the gender attribute of their identity. For white women, the race category is invisible. Their race is an attribute of power, and therefore they often do not think of themselves as having a race. For white men, all categories are invisible. White men are just regular people! They are the paradigm of what is normal. All the rest of us wear some stigma of "otherness." (p. 338)

This discussion helps us understand why the editors of the *New York Times* could assume that we would understand the race and sex of the two people mentioned in the headline "Woman and a Black Are Proposed for U.S. Attorney Posts in New York" (March 31, 1993, p. A14).

Increasingly, women who are labeled *women of color* are talking about how that term is used primarily to describe African Americans or Black women in Canada, which helps to make invisible, for example, Native American (or First Nation), South Asian, Puerto Rican, and Muslim Caribbean women.

We need to ask who is served by the labels. As one woman, now living in Canada, writes, "Living in Trinidad, I was clear who I was and who the other people around me were." Now, she is constantly put in the position of explaining her identity, and her experiences as an Indo-Caribbean woman never fit into the traditional categories, since most North Americans think that the Caribbean heritage is only a Black heritage. She attributes colonialism and white supremacy for the identity crisis she and so many other women experience (Ahmad, 1994, p. 29).

Once the divisions have been established by those who control language, and once cultural practices and policies have been built on those arbitrary divisions, we all learn how to apply the labels to others—and ourselves. The dominant group (of race, class, and gender) has fewer labels (because they do much of the labeling, but often do not consider themselves a group—they just *are*). Other groups must deal with the category system in some way. As Margaret Andersen and Patricia Hill Collins (1995) write:

> Language becomes especially problematic when we want to talk about features of experience that different groups share. Using shortcut terms, like *Hispanic, Latino, Native American,* and even *women of color*, homogenizes distinct historical experiences. Even the term *White* falsely unifies experiences across such factors as ethnicity, region, class, and gender, to name a few.... We do not know how to resolve this problem, but we want readers to be aware of the limitations and significance of language as they try to think more inclusively about diverse group experiences. (p. xix)

The Language of Class
Some people say that you are likely white and middle class (and nervous about slipping) if you feel anxiety, or annoyance, when the subject of class is brought up, and if you think education, occupation, and perseverance have as much to do with class as money. Lower in the class hierarchy, people think that class relates to money. Higher in the hierarchy, people think that it involves taste, values, and style, as well as money. Other elements often involved in determining class include waste (the "excess" you have), cleanliness, and type of transport used.

Language Constructs Class. Texts dealing specifically with class will often use the categories upper class, upper middle class, middle class, working class, and underclass; the number of classes and their names differ somewhat at different times and in different places. Recent terms are *the rich* and *the poor*. (Time changes the meaning of these words. During the 1980s and early 1990s, the rich got richer and the poor lost out even more. Meanwhile, politicians were talking more about middle class and including themselves in that term, although their salaries seemed upper class to most of the rest of us.) Other terms are *those supervised* and *those supervising; the employed, the unemployed* and *the employer* at the top; *bourgeois* and *proletariat; highbrow, middle-brow,* and *lowbrow; gentlemen* and *cads.*

In popular usage, sometimes one word or phrase is used to say something about class and social status, which usually means one's social prestige in relation to those around you. This one word or a phrase might come from the following overlapping categories.

Hierarchical movement: Upward-bound, downward-and-falling, deserving.

Monetary: Affluent, independently wealthy, low income, welfare recipient (which, since 90% of the adults on welfare are female, is code for *poor woman*), welfare queen, newly rich, old wealth.

Education: Good social status, Mt. Holyoke degree, latchkey children, Ivy League, professional, laborer, cleaning person, well educated.

Values: Middle-class values, respectable poor, trash.

Living conditions: No indoor plumbing, one bathroom, three bathrooms, ghetto, homeowner, inner-city, renter, second home.

Occupations:[2] Unemployed, corporate lawyer, her husband is a doctor, new poor, white collar, blue collar, laborer.

Speech: Spanish-speaking, posh-speaking, illiterate. (This category gets little attention, although I think that speech is used by many as an indicator of class. In a show of her assumptions about race and class, a white manager once told me that she had hired a new secretary, "a Black woman but she speaks well.")

Intelligence: Dumb-ox, intelligent, ignorant, sharp.

Behavior: Well-bred, high class, trashy, feminine, masculine, wimp, nice, rough around the edges, pleasant. (I expand on this category below, because class as described and defined by behavior usually receives too little attention.)

Behavior Is Read as Class. Class is of particular interest to those who have something—such as inherited money, physical security, ways of making money from others, homes—that they want to protect. And they are likely to label the behaviors of others seen as threatening those belongings. In this respect, as in others, the dominant protect their privileges by imposing their stratification system and labels on the domi-

---

[2] We have an elaborate, if implicit, ranking system of occupations. The federal government recognizes more than 20,000 occupations, and most U.S. adults can sort many of these out along lines of income, education, and estimates of prestige. Many of these occupations are considered gender-related.

nated. Many of the terms involving class are actually based on behavior rather than on money, education, occupation, and so on. In an article (in a reputable academic journal) on "the underclass in the United States," Vijai P. Singh (1991), perhaps unconsciously, uses many middle-class value terms to describe the faults of the "underclass": They don't know "the value of education, of holding a job, of raising children in a two-parent family, or of being a law-abiding citizen" (p. 507). They have a "high propensity for crime, poverty, poor education and out-of-wedlock births" (p. 509). They are angry and aggressive.

The aggressive-behavior label works somewhat differently for women and men in various class, race, age, and gender categories. Many whites tend to link aggressiveness closely with young Black men. "An aggressive woman" might be a label attached to a Jewish woman, a feminist of any social category, or any woman who stands up for her rights! She is likely considered more an irritant than a threat. She simply (and not so simply) doesn't know "her place."

The rich no longer exhibit their wealth as conspicuously as when they owned big houses set back but visible from the street. Now their houses are out of sight, sometimes on islands, behind locked gates (or visible only by helicopter). The upper middle class often have big houses with high pillars, visible from the street.

Rich women who do show their wealth (for example, by wearing jewels and expensive clothing) seem to be particularly reviled if they are thought not to have made their money themselves. The fact that their fathers and/or husbands likely made their money off the "less fortunate" isn't usually considered much of an issue.

Definitions of the poor often assume deviant behavior and race distinctions. The poor supposedly are freeloaders who take money for no work. Poor men are supposedly the cause of rising crime rates, while poor women supposedly have children in order to increase their welfare checks. In white middle-class terms, "the underclass" members are often assumed to be men and women of color, who not only are poor but are likely to abuse drugs; so of course the children of "those people" are thought to suffer. But this white middle-class lumping together of "others" is based on a profound ignorance of the cultures of various groups, including ignorance of the range of white behavioral and class differences. For example, what about the research that indicates that Latina women smoke, drink, and abuse drugs less frequently than do Black or Anglo women—cautious behavior that aids the health of Latina babies? And what about the research that tells us that Latinos are less likely than Blacks and only slightly more than Anglos to participate in government-subsidy programs? And yet, as a group,

Latina/os are still poor. And what are we to make of the evidence that many people who come to the United States with strong cultural strengths do everything right and are still poor? We might well ask, What is it about the economic policies of this country that make it very difficult for increasing numbers of people of color and white women to have healthy living conditions? Whose behavior do we need to be critiquing?

Language (En)genders Class

In several ways, concepts of class are gendered. First, class, as discussed in most academic work, is male. Many theorists talk about class as if the divisions primarily involve men, who occasionally have wives. Second, we know from experience (including the fear of many so-called working-class or middle-class married women who worry that only a husband stands between them and poverty), as well as from the work of feminist sociologists, that class means quite different things and is defined in different ways by women.

Men writing about class often forget, at least momentarily, that there are any women in any class. For example, one writer (Fussell, 1983) writes about how clothing determines whether a person is middle class or upper class. The principle is that the wider the difference between one's working clothes and one's best clothes, the lower the class. He writes, "Think not just of laborers and blue-collar people in general, but of doormen and bellboys, farmers and railway conductors and trainmen, and firemen" (p. 45). In much academic literature, men inhabit all of the class clothing.

Feminists point out that the causes of poverty differ not only for women and men in general, but also for women of color and white women. For example, women of all colors are in the lowest paying occupations, with few opportunities for improvement. In 1940, 70% of Black women working outside their homes were working in other people's homes; only 6% were doing so in 1980. In 1940, 1% of employed Black women were in clerical jobs; by 1980, almost 30% were in clerical and service (but not household) jobs. However, the wages remain low, and there has been an erosion of assistance programs for women heading families. In addition, these days Black women are not participating in as much financial collaboration with Black men. There are fewer employment possibilities for Black men, and when Black men lose jobs, they have a more difficult time than do white men in finding new jobs (Claude, 1986). From white politicians we've heard about the pathology of the Black family, but not as much from those politicians about the pathology of the nation in which racism and sexism are governing policies, though they are not acknowledged.

One urban study found that the average man experienced a 42% increase in his standard of living within a year of divorce, while the average women experienced a 73% decline (Weitzman, 1985). These divorced women do not talk about their class in the ways that most men theorists would predict. They are more likely than men to discuss values. For example, many of them realize that they do not fit into the social class theories because although they may live in less-than-middle-class neighborhoods, they feel that they have middle-class values. One divorced woman who was unemployed, living with her mother and her daughter in a very small house, pointed out that the books in her bookshelf would mean that she wouldn't be listed as living in poverty (Grella, 1990). The values, beliefs, and economic criteria that go into class self-definitions are different for men and women. Class is gendered.

Language Links Control to Class.   Some people have suggested that the world can be divided into "command" and "obey" classes. Although this single-criterion, dichotomous view of class might seem too static a division (since for many people the amount of command or obey they are expected to display is highly situational), the introduction of "control" into a discussion of class is useful. Many people who have possessions and income talk about the poor as those who, basically, haven't taken control of their lives and moved up. Particularly if they are men, the recommendation is that they should just decide what they want to do and then do it. But, according to the middle-class view, even women should exercise control, especially control of emotions. As one feminist who identified herself as working class says:

> Most middle-class people are encouraged to operate from the head, and not to acknowledge or value their own and others' feelings. They may be encouraged to *talk* about feelings, but not necessarily to express or really feel them. At the same time, our expression of emotion is something we're criticized for or put down for. Middle-class women (among others) find it difficult when we're expressing those intense feelings—perhaps our anger and our frustration challenge them around places they have privilege. (Anna Willats in Ignagni et al., 1988, p. 81)

Is it possible that many middle-class people have accepted, without much question, the emphasis on control, and that this focus on control affects middle-class thinking about class and difference? On the one hand, feminists, in particular, have been critical of men's wish to "master" their environment—whether other people, other animals, or the land. On the other hand, as Irene Diamond (1994) points out, many feminists also talk about control of their bodies, control of reproduction, and control of their lives. Do middle-class feminists, in their wish to reform or do away with the race, gender, and class hierarchies, also put a lot of emphasis on control? How does a focus on control fit with feminists' stated goals of coalitions, harmony, and cooperative efforts? Will women continue to separate themselves (from each other and from the rest of the earth) if they continue to accept without question the necessity to "control" their lives?

The Language of Class Obscures Racism.   In the apartheid system of South Africa, white politicians seldom talked about race. They discussed "ethnic groups," but "race" divisions were seldom mentioned. Ethnic labels, such as Zulu and Bantu, have been used by whites as a way of avoiding discussion of racism. In the United States today, some sociologists suggest that we no longer discuss race but only ethnic groups, probably for the same reason. Yet, for many Euro-Americans, ethnicity often means aspects of cultural background that can be stressed or not depending on the context. I can state, when I wish, that I am half Dutch, although I have spent only a couple months in the Netherlands and know very little about the religion or the language of my grandparents. I have at certain times used this half-Dutch identification. However, most of my friends do not know that I ever define myself in this way. Note that I do not define myself as from the Dutch "race." Compare this choice of identification with the ways people in "racial groups" often identify themselves and are often identified by others.[3]

Others who write about governmental policy, including Supreme Court Justice Antonin Scalia, are suggesting that the emphasis of affirmative action programs be changed to a focus on class rather than on race and gender. Then the poor, of whatever color and history, could be helped, the argument goes. However, since affirmative action programs are designed to help remedy past and current discrimination, this proposed shift in focus seems a tactic to avoid dealing with the racism and sexism of centuries. The proposal does not recognize that, for example, an unemployed Black woman is likely to have quite different, more

---

[3] Many whites are likely to identify themselves more often as Italian, Dutch, German, and so on, than as whites. Because *white* does not work as a parallel term for *Black* or *Native American*, I have used a capital letter for one but not the other. See Bonnie Thornton Dill (1988) for a discussion of other labels for white North Americans of European descent.

restrictive options than an unemployed white man. (The proposal also doesn't seem to recognize that most government social programs, other than the affirmative action programs, *are* based on income.) What is particularly interesting for our discussion is that race, gender, and class are slippery categories and, in fact, are sometimes substituted for one another in political discussions. None of them is a "scientific term." All of them are used in the struggle over conflicting economic interests. All of them are involved in many kinds of resistance, unification, and coercion.

This chapter is in no way a primer for the use of social category terms regarding race, class, and gender. In the English language, there are more than 1,000 labels just for women and men sorted into various race and ethnic groups. Most of them have not been mentioned in this chapter—most of them are considered derogatory by the people to whom they are applied. Rather, my hope is that this chapter heightens our awareness of the importance of the labels, and their intersecting nature in our relationships and in our visions of the future. Labels that denote hierarchies of age, religion, sexual orientation, physical ability, and ethnicity also are interconnected in the systems of inequality. We wouldn't need the labels connected with all of these divisions if some of the people living before us and some of us today had not wanted to establish and maintain hierarchies of privileges. These hierarchies exist; we need to critique them, which is one way of starting to understand and topple them. Understanding these hierarchies is the purpose of this chapter and those that follow. As you read about gender in personal, social, and professional relationships, consider the language that is used and what identities it constructs, obscures, and erases.

QUESTIONS FOR REFLECTION AND DISCUSSION

1. How do you label yourself? What does that label include, exclude, erase, and imply? Are there labels that others apply to you that you resent? For what reasons?
2. Think of some of the terms that you, friends, and family have used to discuss the class of others. You may wish to revise the categories and add to the list of class terms suggested in this essay.
3. Peggy McIntosh (1988, 1995) argues that those of us who (because of white, middle-class, heterosexual privilege) don't use labels frequently to define our race, class, and sexual orientation have a special need to consider the issues discussed in this essay. Draw up a

list of the everyday type of privileges you have, or don't have, that you are dependent on. You might start with items such as:

I can (not) forget my race label most of the time in dealing with teachers and sales clerks.

I do (not) worry that the way I talk will be used in evaluations of my intelligence.

4. What are the assumptions implicit in the categories of "immigrant woman," "woman of color," and "visible minority"? For people so identified are there possibilities of assimilation into the "mainstream"? How do these labels affect the lives of people to whom they are applied? What are the economic implications of each? Is the term *immigrant* used as regularly for someone from Great Britain or Germany as it is for someone from "non-Western" countries?

5. Why do you think the author decided to capitalize the word *Black*? What does this suggest about the way language shapes our understanding?

REFERENCES

In the Reference section, I include the full names rather than only the first initials because I believe it is important in this essay to recognize the sex of each author.

Ahmad, Fawzia. (1994). "How do you identify?" *Canadian Woman Studies/ Les Cahiers de la femme, 14*(2), 29–30.

Andersen, Margaret L., & Collins, Patricia Hill. (1995). Preface: Toward inclusive thinking through the study of race, class, and gender. In Margaret Andersen & Patricia Hill Collins (Eds.), *Race, class, and gender: An anthology (*2nd ed., pp. xi–xx). Boston, MA: Wadsworth.

Banton, Michael. (1980). The idiom of race. *Research in Race and Ethnic Relations, 2,* 21–42.

Brent, L. (1973). *Incidents in the life of a slave girl.* San Diego: Harvest/HBJ.

Brooks, Dwight E., & Cutbirth, Craig. (1990, November). *The negro as "beast": Scientific definitions of African–Americans.* Paper presented at the annual meeting of the Speech Communication Association, Chicago, IL.

Christian, Barbara. (1980). *Black women novelists: The development of a tradition, 1892–1976.* Westport, CT: Greenwood Press.

Christian, Barbara. (1985). *Black feminist criticism: Perspectives on Black women writers.* New York: Pergamon Press.

Claude, Judy. (1986). Poverty patterns for Black men and women. *The Black Scholar, 17*(5), 20–23.

Collins, Patricia Hill. (1990). *Black feminist thought: Knowledge, consciousness, and the politics of empowerment.* Boston, MA: Unwin Hyman.

Coughlin, Ellen K. (1994, October 26). Class, IQ, and heredity. *Chronicle of Higher Education,* pp. A12, A20.

Diamond, Irene. (1994). *Fertile ground: Women, earth, and the limits of control.* Boston, MA: Beacon Press.

Dill, Bonnie Thornton. (1988). Our mothers' grief: Racial ethnic women and the maintenance of families. *Journal of Family History, 13,* 415–431.

Dykewomon, Elana. (1993). Our bodies are the flags. *Sinister Wisdom, 49,* 4–9.

Essed, Philomena. (1991). *Understanding everyday racism.* Newbury Park, CA: Sage.

Etter–Lewis, Gwendolyn. (1991). Standing up and speaking out: African American women's narrative legacy. *Discourse and Society, 2(4),* 425–438.

Forbes, Jack D. (1988). *Black Africans and Native Americans: Color, race and caste in the evolution of Red–Black peoples.* Oxford, UK: Basil Blackwell.

Fussell, Paul. (1983). *Class: A guide through the American status system.* New York: Summit Books.

Gimenez, Martha E. (1993). Latinos, Hispanics ... what next! *Heresies, 27,* 39–42.

Grella, Christine. (1990). Irreconcilable differences: Women defining class after divorce and downward mobility. *Gender and Society, 4(1),* 41–55.

hooks, bell. (1990). *Yearning: Race, gender, and cultural politics.* Boston, MA: South End Press.

Ignagni, Esther, Parent, Deb, Perreault, Yvette, & Willats, Anna. (1988). Around the kitchen table. Toronto Rape Crisis Centre—Working Class Caucus. *Fireweed, 26,* 80.

Lorde, Audre. (1984). *Sister Outsider.* Freedom, CA: Crossing Press.

McIntosh, Peggy. (1988, 1995). White privilege and male privilege: A personal account of coming to see correspondences through work in Women's Studies. In Margaret L. Andersen & Patricia Hill Collins (Eds.), *Race, class, and gender: An anthology,* (2nd ed., pp. 76–87). Boston, MA: Wadsworth.

Morrison, Toni. (1987). *Beloved: A novel.* New York: Knopf.

Nelson, William. (1982). *Racial definition handbook.* Edina, MN: Alpha Editions.

Penelope, Julia. (1990). *Speaking freely: Unlearning the lies of the father's tongues.* New York: Pergamon Press.

Rothenberg, Paula S. (Ed.). (1992). *Race, class, and gender in the United States: An integrated study.* New York: St. Martin's Press.

Scales-Trent, Judy. (1990). Women in the lawyering process: The implications of categories. *New York Law School Law Review, 35(2),* 337–342.

Sims-Wood, Janet. (1988). The Black female: Mammy, Jemima, Sapphire, and other images. In Jessie Carney Smith (Ed.), *Images of Blacks in American culture: A reference guide to information sources* (pp. 235–256). New York: Greenwood Press.

Singh, Vijai P. (1991). The underclass in the United States: Some correlates of economic change. *Sociological Inquiry, 61(4),* 505–521.

Smith, Barbara. (1983, 1995). HOMOPHOBIA: Why Bring It Up? In Margaret Andersen and Patricia Hill Collins (Eds.), *Race, class, and gender: An anthology* (2nd ed., pp. 413–417). Boston, MA: Wadsworth.

Smith, Tom W. (1992). Changing racial labels: From "Colored" to "Negro" to "Black" to "African American". *Public Opinion, 56,* 496–514.

Spelman, Elizabeth. (1988). *Inessential woman: Problems of exclusion in feminist thought.* Boston: Beacon Press.

Taylor, H. Jeanie, Kramarae, Cheris, & Ebben, Maureen. (1993). *Women, information technology, and scholarship.* Urbana, IL: Center for Advanced Study, University of Illinois at Urbana-Champaign.

Weitzman, Lenore. (1985). *The divorce revolution: The unexpected social and economic consequences for women and children in America.* New York: Free Press.

Wilkinson, Doris. (1990). Americans of African identity. *Society, 27,* 14–18.

Williamson, Joel. (1980). *New people: Miscegenation and mulattoes in the United States.* New York: Free Press.

Wilson, Geraldine. (1980). Sticks and stones and racial slurs do hurt. *Interracial Books for Children Bulletin, 11*(3/4), 16, 18.

3

DIFFICULT DIALOGUES, EXPANDED HORIZONS: COMMUNICATING ACROSS RACE AND CLASS

MARSHA HOUSTON
JULIA T. WOOD

I met Meredith in a class, and one day she asked me to go shopping. I never felt so out of place in my life. We went to shops I never go in. I nearly keeled over when she paid $100 for a sweater. For dinner she picked a place where I paid $10 for a salad—it was all I could afford. I'll bet she's never gone in a Kmart or Wendy's.

My white friends don't mean to offend me, but they do. How am I supposed to feel when they say "I think of you as just like me." They never say they think of themselves as just like me. What they mean is, I seem white enough.

On campus I feel equal to my colleagues, but I dread social occasions. I don't know which fork to use, and I can't identify half the food they serve. I don't fit in.

Most of the time I like Michael, but when he starts bragging about himself and saying how great he is, I get really uncomfortable. I don't know why black people do that.

Differences in where we shop, what foods we eat, and how we talk about ourselves symbolize larger variations among social groups. The differences may generate tensions that are confusing and often painful. Seldom, however, do we talk about differences based on race/ethnicity and class, perhaps because we find it so difficult to deal with these issues in a society that claims to be "equal for all."

You might wonder why a chapter on race and class is included in a book about gendered relationships. The reason is that race, socioeconomic class, and gender interact to shape identity. Other chapters in this book focus on differences between social prescriptions for femininity and masculinity and the impact of those prescriptions on individual women and men. Gender, however, isn't independent of other socially constructed categories that affect who we are and can be. Gender interacts with race, class, sexual preference, ability and disability, age, and other socially constructed categories of identity (Samovar & Porter, 1994). For example, Native Americans, African Americans, Hispanics, Asian Americans, gays, lesbians, bisexuals, Buddhists, Jews, and the working class are distinct cultures in the United States, where the dominant group is European Americans who are middle class, white, heterosexual, and Protestant.

Thinking about how race and socioeconomic class create differences among members of each gender will help us realize that gender isn't the only source of human diversity. In addition to gender, differences in race and class divide people and often are seen as insurmountable barriers to good relationships. When we encourage students to interact with people of different races and classes, they often object. One black student bluntly proclaimed, "I don't need white friends," and a white student asked, "Why should I work to be friends with people who are different when it's so much easier to hang with people who are like me?"

Although these responses are understandable, they don't cultivate an ideally wide range of individual choices and social relations. Just as there are rewards from interacting with people who are like us, so too is there value in engaging differences. Relationships with members of our own social groups deepen identification with those groups, whereas relationships with people from different social groups enlarge our horizons and diminish divisions in society. This chapter, then, is an invitation and an opportunity for personal growth.

Of course, we can't give you a magic formula for communicating with people whose social groups differ from your own. We can, however, explain some reasons for common tensions and misunderstandings that arise when socially diverse people interact. In tracing how ethnicity and class shape communication, we'll discover that ethnocentric standards often distort how people perceive one another.

RACE AND CLASS STANDPOINTS

Although each of us is an individual, we also belong to multiple social groups that share common attitudes, values, and ways of relating to others. Even though we aren't usually aware of the influence of ethnicity and class, like gender, they powerfully sculpt identities and relationships. Some of the social groups to which we belong, such as gender and racial/ethnic groups, will likely remain stable throughout our lives, although their influence will be stronger in some situations than in others. Our membership in and identification with other groups, such as sexual orientation and socioeconomic class, may change as we age, interact with new people, change professions and locations, and add to the fund of experiences that makes each of us who we are.

Collaborating on this chapter gave the two of us opportunities to reflect on the social groups that influence our identities and the ways some of those have changed during our lives. Marsha is a middle-aged, African American college professor who's the parent of an adult son. Among the social groups that define her identity at this point in her life are African Americans, middle-aged women, single mothers, the United States middle class, and college professors. Some of the social groups that Julia uses to define herself overlap with those Marsha uses: Julia is also middle-aged and a college professor. Yet, Julia identifies with other social groups such as European Americans that aren't part of Marsha's identity. Also, Julia doesn't belong to the social group of mothers, which is primary in Marsha's identity. Like the two of us, you belong to many social groups that influence who you are, what you think and feel, and how you communicate and form relationships. Also like the two of us, your social roots parallel those of other people in certain respects and deviate from those of others in some respects.

In this chapter, we're interested in how two social groups that have particular salience in Western culture influence personal identities and relationships. Although we discuss racial/ethnic groups and socioeconomic classes separately so that we can clarify how each influences communication, keep in mind that, in reality, these and other social groups interlock in our identities. None of us is just a member of a particular ethnic group or a specific class. Instead, each of us experiences these and other social group identities in concert, and we often can't isolate the influence of any single group. Also, each of us relates to others as a complex individual who is defined and guided by multiple and fluid bases of identity.

Genesis of Diversity: Social Standpoints

Standpoint theory, which informs other chapters in this book, contends that the social groups to which we belong guide how we experience the world, ourselves, and relationships with others (Harding, 1991). Standpoints are shaped by historical and current circumstances.

Differences among social groups are produced and reproduced by cultural structures and practices that use criteria such as sex, class, sexual orientation, and race to assign individuals to groups that are accorded unequal status and opportunities. Modern Western culture confers privilege and value on Caucasians, heterosexuals, and the middle and upper socioeconomic classes, and it values other social groups less.

Members of each social group communicate in some ways that aren't shared by people outside that group. Although individual variations exist, most of us tend to adopt much of our groups' perspectives. Standpoint theory doesn't deny individuality, but it does contend that social groups influence how we view ourselves and others and how we act in the world. This implies that how any individual acts and thinks is not purely personal, since each of us is situated within and shaped by broader horizons of cultural life that make disparate experiences available to different groups.

Standpoint theory sheds light on the reasons members of diverse ethnic and class groups have different, sometimes conflicting, views of how to interact, show affection, and so forth. By extension, standpoint theory implies that all understandings are socially constructed, which reminds us there is no single right perspective, but a range of standpoints crafted by particular social locations.

ETHNIC AND CLASS CULTURES

Just as gender cultures influence how we think, act, feel, and communicate, so do ethnic and class cultures shape identity and behavior. Continuing this analogy, just as understanding different gender cultures enables us to communicate more clearly with one another, insight into different ethnic and class cultures enhances our ability to interact with people who belong to diverse social groups.

Race/Ethnicity as a Co-Culture

Race is a system of classifying individuals into arbitrary groups and assigning disparate meaning and value to the created groups. Racial or ethnic classifications affect the personal, social, educational, political, and material circumstances of individuals' lives. Consequently, these classifications shape how we view ourselves, others, and relationships.

Race as a Social Construction. Like gender, race is socially constructed. Obviously, people differ in skin color, but that physical difference isn't the basis of racial classifications. The term *white* wasn't used to describe race until Europeans colonized the United States. They invented the label *white* as a way to increase solidarity among European settlers who actually had distinct ethnic backgrounds. By calling themselves *white*, these diverse groups glossed over differences among themselves and used their similar, but not identical, skin hues to distinguish them from people whose skin was not whitish (Bates, 1994). *White*, in other words, is a term and a classification that legitimized the worst aspects of European expansion into the Western hemisphere, such as enslaving Africans and appropriating the lands and rights of Native Americans.

Prior to the Civil War, southern plantation owners invented a system of racial classification known as the "one-drop rule." According to this system, a person presumed to have even one drop of African blood was classified as black (Bates, 1994). Of course, the reference to "blood" was metaphorical, since there are no biological differences between African and European blood. This system classified a person as black if she or he had one African American and one European American parent, even if she or he was physically indistinguishable from European Americans. Invented racial classifications were codified into laws that remained in force well into the 20th century in many states. The same "one-drop rule" prevailed in South Africa for many years and was used to justify privileged status for the whitish minority in that country.

To appreciate how arbitrary racial classifications are, consider the term *Asian*, which is (mis)used to describe a range of people with vastly different physical features and cultural heritages. Malaysians, Taiwanese, Chinese, Tibetans, Japanese, and others are indiscriminately lumped together as Asians. The singular term *Asian* blurs distinctions among Asians that are at least as significant as differences between Asians and Caucasians. (*Caucasian* is another singular term to describe a range of people and heritages.)

Race and Standpoints. Although mythical and arbitrary, racial categories have real consequences in people's lives. One important consequence is that members of arbitrarily created racial groups develop common standpoints that reflect shared cultural history and traditions and the material conditions of their present lives. For example, although the United States became a biracial nation when the first European colonists arrived in the 16th century, and is now a multiracial nation, throughout most of this country's history whites have taken and maintained a position as the socially and economically privileged race. Disparate opportunities and status available to diverse racial/ethnic groups explain many differences in views of money, politics, social life, education, the meaning of race, and the interaction among members of different races.

The Hill–Thomas hearings in 1991 produced stormy arguments among people of different races. When Clarence Thomas was nominated to the Supreme Court in 1991, Anita Hill came forward to assert that he had sexually harassed her years before when she worked for him. Among many white women there was a shared belief that Anita Hill told the truer story.

When one of us (Julia) talked about the hearings with her good friend Melika, however, a heated debate erupted. Melika agreed that Thomas had harassed Hill, and she was concerned about that. Yet, she was deeply angry and embarrassed that Hill had dragged down a black man in front of an assembly of whites. Melika agreed with Thomas that the hearings were a "high-tech lynching." That charge didn't resonate with Julia, since none of her (known) ancestors had ever been lynched. As a white woman who had experienced sexual harassment, Julia saw sexism displayed by Thomas and the Senate committee. As an African American woman, Melika saw one more in a long list of racist stereotypes and attacks in a white system of (in)justice. These two women's different heritages led to dramatically dissimilar perceptions of what happened in the hearings.

Although Melika's perspective on the hearings was shared by a number of people of color, it was not the only response of people of color. Melika's perspective reflects black people's desire to mitigate negative stereotypes by refusing to discuss antisocial behavior by blacks in the presence of whites. Her attitude also reflects black women's traditional stance of solidarity with and protection of black men, sometimes against their interests as women. In contrast to Melika's view, a number of African American women and some African American men saw Thomas's invocation of "lynching" as blatant opportunism, and they viewed Hill as the true victim of both Thomas and the Senate committee. For example, 1,603 African American women signed a full-page ad published in a 1991 issue of the *New York Times* that began, "We are outraged by the racist and sexist treatment of Professor Anita Hill... who was maligned and castigated for daring to speak publicly of her own experience of sexual abuse."

More than conflicting judgments of Hill and Thomas, the disagreements outlined above reflect and are informed by distinct standpoints both within and across ethnic groups. Divergent perspectives are not uncommon in communication between people from different ethnic groups. By exploring the reasons behind some of these differences, we can better understand how ethnicity/race influences perception and communication and sometimes causes misunderstandings. Yet, our focus on commonalities created by racial/ethnic heritage and material life conditions doesn't imply that racial groups are homogeneous. They are diverse and include people whose various interlocking identities inform different angles of vision on their common heritage and standpoint.

Differing Values. Different standpoints generate diverse values (Wood 1993, 1995, in press). One of the most pronounced middle-class and European American values is individualism. Yet, emphasis on self is not so prominent in other ethnic groups. African Americans and Hispanics, for example, place great importance on family and community (Gaines, 1995). Koreans and members of many other Asian cultures also accent kinship and group ties more than individual identity (Park, 1979). The Korean emphasis on the group over any individual is reflected in language. Whereas European Americans say "my" to express ownership of things they don't exclusively own such as *my* town, *my* country, and *my* school, Koreans express shared ownership by saying *our* town, *our* country, and *our* school (Ferrante, 1992). The Korean word for individual, *kaein,* connotes undesirable selfishness (Underwood, 1977).

The difference between European Americans' regard for individualism and other ethnic groups' emphasis on family and community may promote misunderstandings. For example, Byron, an African American student in one of my classes, told me that his white friend Scott had been offended when Byron canceled a weekend get-together to go home and help take care of a sick aunt. Because Scott's culture didn't regard aunts as close family, he thought Byron didn't want to get together and used the aunt as an excuse. In Byron's culture, however, family includes cousins, aunts, uncles, grandparents, and others who take care of each other.

Assertiveness is another value that varies among ethnic groups. White middle-class groups in the United States admire people who assert their individual rights over those of others. Yet many other groups don't admire, and may actively disapprove of, self-advancement. Tamongs in Nepal value group harmony, so they routinely defer to one another. Harmony is also valued in many Asian societies, and disagreement is disparaged. Qualities such as assertion and deference have no absolute meanings. Instead, what they mean varies, sometimes dramatically, among ethnic groups.

Valaya, a student from China, was repeatedly scolded by peers and instructors for being passive. Since her arrival in the United States, others had encouraged her to assert herself and be strong in classes and personal relationships. What they didn't understand, Valaya told me, is that being strong doesn't require putting yourself first. In her culture, personal strength is displayed by honoring others, and assertion is a sign of selfishness and arrogance.

Differing Communication Styles.   "You play cards worse than my 2-year-old sister!" said Jamal as Emily laid down her card in a game of whist. Would you be insulted or hurt by Jamal's comment? Chances are you would be insulted if you are a European American like Emily, but you wouldn't be if you are African American. Like many African Americans, Jamal uses communication forms that aren't practiced by most European Americans. In this instance, he was relying on *indirection*—that is, criticism is made only indirectly (a more direct criticism would be, "You're a rotten card player"). What Jamal did/said was to "signify" to Emily that she didn't play cards very well (Gates, 1987; Houston, 1985; Mitchell-Kernan, 1972; Smitherman, 1977). He would have considered it appropriate (and fun) had Emily replied, "Yeah, maybe you should take lessons from her to help your own game."

Would you consider a person arrogant if she said, "I'm such a hot prospect on the job market that I set the chair on fire when I interview. I mean, I am so damn good that nobody else need apply"? Again, your race is likely to influence how you interpret this comment. Geneva Smitherman (1977) labels this "braggadocio" (it is also colloquially called "woofin'"). Braggadocio is intended as humor, not as sincere bragging. It is verbal artistry used to demonstrate wit and to dramatize interaction. Unless you understand braggadocio as stylized communication, not conventional bragging, you'll misunderstand what it means and reflects.

African Americans, as a group, also tend to be more confrontational and forceful in conversations among themselves than most European Americans (Ribeau, Baldwin, & Hecht, 1994). Thus, whites sometimes perceive African Americans as rude or impudent, and African Americans may regard whites as cold or unfeeling. One of us (Houston, 1994) has found that African American women often feel Caucasian women are dishonest or uninvolved in dialogue because Caucasians are reserved and subdued in both what they say and how they say it. The direct style of communication that is typical of many African Americans is illustrated in a story bell hooks often tells about getting off a plane when she went home and having her mother and sisters greet her with the unequivocal criticism "I can't believe you got on the plane looking like that!" (hooks, 1981).

Several scholars (Smitherman, 1977; Turner, 1949) claim that African American speech forms such as signifying and braggadocio are connected to the African oral tradition in which verbal artistry is highly valued. Other scholars (for example, Gates, 1987) argue that African Americans, like other people who have endured prolonged social stress, learned verbal artistry and ironic humor as coping skills. However we explain the differences, it's clear that ethnic groups shape standpoints on social life generally and communication in particular. Ethnically shaped styles of communicating are often misinterpreted by those outside a group.

Class as a Culture

The socioeconomic class into which we are socialized also influences our standpoint. Working-class, middle-class, and upper-class groups learn diverse communication styles. Like differences cultivated by ethnic and gender groups, differences fostered by class affect how we interact with others and how we interpret their communication.

Last year one of my students proudly announced to me that he had landed a job with a big insurance company. Knowing that Jordan was committed to social causes, I was surprised he had taken a job with a traditional bureaucratic company. When I asked why he took the job, Jordan replied, "Because they offered me a car and $30 thousand a year, that's why." As we talked about his decision, I came to appreciate what having a car and a good salary meant to a young man who had grown up on the fringes of poverty in a single-parent home. He had never owned a car, not even a used one, and he had gone through college never far ahead of the bills for tuition and fees. People who are economically secure may not understand or respect choices made by individuals raised in poverty.

Class is not simply a matter of income. Beyond current income, class also entails the *assumption* of economic security or insecurity and all of the material and social benefits associated with security and insecurity. In other words, class is a major aspect of who we are and how we live. Donna Langston (1992) explained the wide scope of class when she wrote that it is

> your understanding of the world and where you fit in; it's composed of
> ideas, behavior, attitudes, values, and language; class is how you think, feel,

act, look, dress, talk, move walk; class is what stores you shop at, restaurants you eat in; class is the schools you attend, the education you attain; class is the very jobs you will work at....Class is who our friends are [and] where we live and work. (p. 112)

Differing Values.   Like ethnicity and gender, class affects our values. Among members of the poorer classes, kinship and community ties are generally stronger than among members of the middle class (Cancian, 1987). Individuals are more likely to live near their families of origin and near the place they were raised. Members of the working and poor classes are also more likely to socialize with their kin than middle-class members. Working-class and poor communities tend to be tightly constructed, and members help each other out and pull together.

When people with different class backgrounds interact, misunderstandings may occur. Middle- and upper-class Western individuals, particularly European Americans, typically have fairly loose ties with families and socialize more with people outside of their kinship circles than those within them. Thus, they may regard working-class friends' close family ties as a form of overdependence. Conversely, poor or working-class people may disparage middle-class individuals' detachment from families.

Traditionalism is another value that is shaped by class. Members of the working and poor classes tend to adhere to relatively traditional sex roles: The man is the breadwinner and head of the house (even if the woman earns a higher salary than he does), and the woman is the homemaker and primary caregiver (even if she works outside of the home). These traditional values encourage rather sex-stereotypical differences in women's and men's power and status (Hochschild with Machung, 1989). Yet it is interesting to note that working-class husbands often do more homemaking chores than their middle-class brothers (Thompson & Walker, 1989).

Leisure-time activities are also shaped by class membership. Because middle-class people have good incomes and economic security, they have more leisure time than members of less economically comfortable classes (Langston, 1992). Not only do middle- and upper-class people have more leisure time, but they have the economic freedom to think about issues beyond basic survival. Thus, many middle-class people think and talk about matters such as dieting (not salient to someone who can barely feed a family), improving self-esteem (not a focus when every waking hour is devoted to one or more jobs), and finding coordinating accessories for a wardrobe (irrelevant if your clothes come from Goodwill and the Salvation Army). Members of the upper classes may also exploit working-class people, as exemplified in the practice of paying domestic workers minimum wages or less (Childers & hooks, 1990; Rollins, 1985).

Recreational activities also vary among classes. The higher your socioeconomic class, the more time you have for recreation. Going beyond disparities in leisure time, recreational choices are constrained by expense. It costs less to go bowling or to a Little League game than to attend a concert or a play. It costs less to eat at McDonald's than at a posh restaurant. It is cheaper to visit family for a vacation than to fly to Paris. More than we often realize, money controls a great deal of our lives and the experiences open to us.

Recreational choices also reflect class-related values. Among members of the upper and middle classes, education is revered. Private schools and elite colleges are privileges that can be enjoyed only by individuals who are economically well off. In addition, members of economically comfortable groups often choose to go to "important" movies, read "significant" books, and take classes for personal enrichment. Among members of the working and poor classes, however, excellent education is often not affordable. Perhaps disparities in educational quality explain why working-class individuals tend to regard education and intellectual pursuits with suspicion: In their view, book learning is no substitute for practical knowledge (Erkel, 1994). In addition, the "enrichment" alleged to come from reading fine books and attending important plays may be less alluring than pure fun to someone who works 40 hours a week in a job that offers little challenge or stimulation. In short, "an evening out" and "having a good time" may mean vastly different things to people with diverse class backgrounds.

What we've discussed so far illustrates some of the profound ways in which ethnicity and class shape our identities, values, activities, and communication styles. In the final pages of this chapter, we extend what we've learned to consider how we might communicate effectively with people of diverse ethnicities and classes.

COMMUNICATION AMONG MEMBERS OF DIVERSE SOCIAL GROUPS

Existing publications and conferences suggest four general guidelines for rewarding communication among people who have diverse ethnic and class heritages.

Understand That You May Not Understand

This is a foundation of effective communication with anyone, not just people who differ from us in ethnicity or class. However, acknowledging the limits of our insight into others is especially important when relating to people from different ethnic and class cultures. Instead of assuming you understand others, why not start with the notion that you may not? This allows you to avoid the mistake of imposing your meanings on others' behaviors and to open yourself to learning about meanings and communication styles that differ from your own.

In this chapter, we've noted incidents in which people didn't realize they had different meanings for the "same" behaviors. Scott didn't understand that family meant different things to him and his friend Byron. Emily didn't appreciate it when Jamal "signified on" her, and he didn't realize his comment would hurt Emily. The key insight we can derive from these examples is we may not understand others. The hurt that Scott and Emily felt didn't result from what Byron and Jamal did. Instead, it arose because friends didn't understand that they had different ways of communicating. We can't learn what others mean unless we begin with the realization that we may not understand them—at least not on their terms. The realization that standpoints shape how we communicate and interpret others' communication encourages us to acknowledge that we may not initially understand people outside of our social groups.

Don't Impose Your Standards on Other Social Groups

Have you ever noticed that many African American and Asian American models in Western magazines look more Caucasian than most people of African and Asian heritage? This reflects the fact that Western media (and perhaps the culture as a whole) impose a white standard of beauty and admire only individuals who approximate Anglo appearance.

The tendency to impose the standard of the dominant cultural group on people who are outside of that group also surfaces in relationships. As one woman from Mexico remarked to me, "I get along okay with people as long as I act white. If I act real white, they accept me. That means that they really don't accept me—the real me. To be accepted, I have to look and act like them."

It's natural to see others and how they act from the standpoint of our own social groups. Yet, doing so may make it impossible to have healthy relationships with people who differ from us. If we judge braggadocio by European standards, we'll assume those who do it are obnoxious egotists. If we judge European Americans by Korean standards, we'll regard them as selfish and pushy. If we judge a working-class man's order for a shot and a beer as uncouth, it's because we're applying middle-class standards. Becoming aware of the perspectives encouraged by our own social groups clears the way for us to recognize and consider the value of viewpoints of other social groups.

Nourishing curiosity toward some differences shifts us from thinking "That's wrong" to "That's interesting—what might I learn here?" As we learn about varied communication styles, we broaden our understanding of human relationships and the range of ways we can build connections with others.

Respect How Others Interpret Experience

In friendships between people of different social groups, tension may arise when one person does something that hurts or is offensive to the other. The tendency is to defend ourselves and/or to deny that any offense was meant. When Marsha's son Zuri was in elementary school, a white friend whose son Alan was in the same grade complained to Marsha about a group of black boys who persistently started fights with Alan. Feeling her ethnic group was under attack, Marsha quickly pointed out that Zuri had also been attacked by boys at his school. In retrospect, Marsha believes that her friend intended no accusation against blacks as a group, but only wanted to talk with another mother about her fears for her son's welfare. Marsha now realizes that her defensive response discouraged her friend from sharing her fears and feelings.

Another example of this tension occurred when Tami, an African American college student, was dismissed from an internship because her supervisor said, "You're just not working out." Tami was shocked, since her supervisor had frequently complimented her work, and she felt she was earning the respect of her peers. In discussing her feelings with several white friends, Tami suggested that the supervisor had dismissed her for racist reasons. Her white friends quickly asserted that racism had nothing to do with the situation, which led Tami to feel they thought she did something to cause the dismissal. Tami felt not only misunderstood, but also betrayed by her friends who both denied her interpretation of her experience and seemed to blame her for her misfortune.

Marsha's and Tami's stories are not unusual. The fear that our friend may associate us with offensive attitudes and behaviors of other members of our social groups may motivate us to cut short discussions about uncomfortable topics. But if we are to have friends of different races and classes, we cannot silence or deny how they experience the world. The least we can offer is a respectful hearing of our friends' interpretations, even though they may differ from our own. The most we can offer is empathy and support. Essential to listening respectfully to others and to supporting them is becoming aware of our own defenses—our reluctance to acknowledge, much less talk about, problems in our own social groups and our hesitance to admit any unfavorable attitudes we have about other social groups.

Acknowledge but Don't Totalize Differences

When we have a relationship with another person, it's natural to focus on our similarities. Yet this can inhibit relationships between people with different ethnic and class backgrounds. Repeatedly, African American and Asian American students tell us how frustrating it is when whites pretend to be unaware of race. "Of course they notice," insists one woman. "They're so busy pretending not to see I'm Asian that that's all they do see and all they deal with." Just as insightful is this comment from an African American friend of ours: "It's not just that people can't avoid seeing race. It's also that I'm insulted when someone treats me as not-black. I don't want my heritage erased any more than anyone else does."

Instead of glossing over differences, we should acknowledge them honestly and respect them as opportunities for personal growth. We expand our worlds when we are open to diverse values, behaviors, and communication styles.

Martin Buber (1972) illuminated the distinction between being open to others and surrendering our own views. It is possible, he argued, simultaneously to affirm the value of your ways and to acknowledge those that differ from yours. Buber referred to this as the "unity of contraries," which calls on us to appreciate the worth of our own patterns and beliefs and, at the same time, to respect others and their ways of seeing and acting. In other words, you don't have to abandon your own ways to honor different ways others employ.

Although acknowledging differences can be productive, we shouldn't overemphasize them. A Latina woman is of a different race than an African American woman, but each of them is more than just her race. A working-class person has a different heritage than a middle-class individual, but neither of them is defined only by socioeconomic class. When we treat others as if they are defined entirely by one facet of identity, we totalize them. For example, asking "What's the black perspective on this?" or "How do Asians see the issue?" pigeonholes people in terms of ethnic group.

To avoid ignoring or totalizing differences, we can recognize and learn from ethnic and class diversity that is part—but only part—of who we are. Recognizing both differences and commonalities provides an honest foundation for personal relationships. When people who have dissimilar social standpoints interact, they discover they have much in common and much they can learn from their differences (Gaertner, Mann, Murrel, & Dovidio, 1989).

Insensitive Talk

The phrases below can be "red flags" when used by members of privileged classes and ethnic groups in conversation with members of nonprivileged classes and ethnic groups.

"What's the black perspective on this?"

"I've suffered discrimination too."

"I know how you feel about racism/classism."

"I think of you as just like me."

"You're really exceptional."

"Your people..."

"It's remarkable how far you've come."

"Personally, I've never discriminated against Hispanics, Asian Americans, working-class people" (and so on).

"I've experienced sexism, so I understand racism."

SUMMARY

This chapter initiates a difficult dialogue about how ethnicity and class affect relationships. It would be comforting to believe that America is a classless society and that race is no longer salient in our lives. Yet, these are myths. We are socialized into cultures arranged along lines of race and class, as well as gender. Individually and together, our social groups shape how we see ourselves, others, and our experiences. Accepting that is a first step in learning to communicate across differences.

A second step is to realize that no way of relating is right or wrong in an absolute sense. Instead, we learn styles of interaction by participating in particular social groups. When we respect the validity of diverse communication styles, we grow beyond the perspectives of the groups in which we were originally socialized.

Because differences are so often disparaged or avoided, Caucasians don't want people of color in their neighborhoods, Protestants exclude Jews from their clubs, men are hostile to women in the workplace, heterosexuals disdain gays and lesbians, and African Americans form separate communities on predominantly white campuses. As long as we avoid or condemn communication that differs from our own, we can't prosper from diversity and we can't create a society hospitable to all who compose it. If instead we explore the opportunities for relationships with people of different races and classes, we heighten insight into ourselves and the range of human experience.

QUESTIONS FOR REFLECTION AND DISCUSSION

1. Reflect on how your ethnicity and class shape your values, perspectives, and ways of communicating. Where do you shop, eat, and live? What do you do for "a good time"?

2. Think about the messages about class you heard as a child. If you were middle or upper class, did you learn that televisions don't belong in living rooms? If you come from a working-class family, was it natural to have a television in the living room? How were meals served in your home? Were there communal dishes, a nicely set table?

3. How do you define family? Does your family include people other than parents, stepparents, and siblings? What is gained and lost by having an extended family and close ties with many relatives? How do extended or nuclear definitions of family shape perspectives on relationships?

4. As a class, discuss misunderstandings among members of different ethnic groups. It would be desirable to agree to guidelines for the discussion: Being open and honest are two important ones. Have members of each ethnic group describe how they perceive other ethnicities. Discuss discrepancies among perceptions.

5. Should we always be respectful of standpoints that differ from our own? Would doing so imply accepting sexual harassment, sexism, and racism?

REFERENCES

Bates, E. (1994, fall). Beyond black and white. *Southern Exposure*, pp. 11–15.

Buber, M. (1972). *Between man and man*. New York: Macmillan.

Cancian, F. (1987). *Love in America*. Cambridge: Cambridge University Press.

Childers, M., & hooks, b. (1990). A conversation about race and class. In M. Hirsch & E. F. Keller (Eds.), *Conflicts in feminism* (pp. 60–81). New York: Routledge & Kegan Paul.

Erkel, R. T. (1994, November/December). The mighty wedge of class. *Utne Reader*, pp. 100–103.

Ferrante, J. (1992). *Sociology: A global perspective*. Belmont, CA: Wadsworth.

Gaertner, S. L., Mann, J., Murrel, A., & Dovidio, J. F. (1989). Reducing intergroup bias: The benefits of recategorization. *Journal of Personality and Social Psychology, 57*, 239–249.

Gaines, S., Jr. (1995). Relationships between members of cultural minorities. In J. T. Wood & S. Duck (Eds.), *Understanding relationship processes, 6: Off the beaten track: Understudied relationships*. Thousand Oaks, CA: Sage.

Gates, H. L., Jr. (1987). The blackness of blackness: A critique of the sign and the signifying monkey. In H. L. Gates, Jr. (Ed.), *Figures in black* (pp. 235–276). New York: Oxford University Press.

Harding, S. (1991). *Whose science? Whose knowledge? Thinking from women's lives*. Ithaca, NY: Cornell University Press.

Hochschild, A., with Machung, A. (1989). *The second shift: Working parents and the revolution at home*. New York: Viking/Penguin.

hooks, b. (1981). *Ain't I a woman? Black women and feminism*. Boston: South End Press.

Houston, M. (1985). Language and black woman's place: Evidence from the black middle class. In P. Treichler, C. Kramarae, & B. Stafford (Eds.), *For alma mater: Theory and practice in feminist scholarship*. Urbana, IL: University of Illinois Press.

Houston, M. (1994). When black women talk with white women: Why dialogues are difficult. In A. Gonzalez, M. Houston, & V. Chen (Eds.), *Our voices: Essays in culture, ethnicity, and communication* (pp. 133–139). Los Angeles: Roxbury.

Langston, D. (1992). Tired of playing monopoly? In M. Andersen & P. Collins (Eds.), *Race, class, and gender* (pp. 110–119). Belmont, CA: Wadsworth.

Mitchell-Kernan, C. (1972). Signifying, loud-talking, and marking. In T. Kochman (Ed.), *Rappin' and stylin' out* (pp. 315–335). Urbana, IL: University of Illinois Press.

Park, M. (1979). *Communication styles in two different cultures: Korean and American*. Seoul: Han Shin Press.

Piper, A. (1994). Black pride for white people. *Utne Reader*, pp. 87–88.

Ribeau, S. A., Baldwin, J. R., & Hecht, M. L. (1994). An African-American communication perspective. In L. Samovar & R. Porter (Eds.), *Intercultural communication: A reader* (7th ed., pp. 140–147). Belmont, CA: Wadsworth.

Rollins, J. (1985). *Between women: Domestics and their employers*. Philadelphia: Temple University Press.

Samovar, L., & Porter, R. (1994). *Communication between cultures* (2nd ed.). Belmont, CA: Wadsworth.

Smitherman, G. (1977). *Talkin' and testifyin': The language of black America*. Boston: Houghton Mifflin.

Thompson, L., & Walker, A. J. (1989). Gender in families: Women and men in marriage, work, and parenthood. *Journal of Marriage and the Family, 51*, 845–871.

Turner, L. D. (1949). *Africanisms in the Gullah dialect.* Chicago: University of Chicago Press.

Underwood, H. G. (1977). Foundations in thought and values: How we differ. *Korea Journal, 17,* 6–9.

Wood, J. T. (1993). From "woman's nature" to standpoint epistemology: Gilligan and the debate over essentializing in feminist scholarship. *Women's Studies in Communication, 15,* 1–24.

Wood, J. T. (1995). *Relational communication.* Belmont, CA: Wadsworth.

Wood, J. T. (in press). The part is not the whole: Studying diverse relationships. *Journal of Social and Personal Relationships.*

PART
TWO

GENDERED
PERSONAL
RELATIONSHIPS

4

GENDERED PATTERNS IN FAMILY COMMUNICATION

CAROL J. S. BRUESS
JUDY C. PEARSON

What kinds of games did you play when you were a 5-year-old? When we were preschoolers, we played "school." The most envied role was "teacher," which we sought so that we could instruct, and perhaps discipline, our siblings. One of us played "church" (wherein a brother was *always* the priest who distributed vanilla wafers as communion, and the two female siblings were either nuns or ushers for imaginary parishioners). For both of us, our favorite activity was the game of "house," with the primary players being Mom, Dad, and baby. "House" involved a mother who cleaned the house, made the meals, and cooed at the baby, and a father who worked all day at the office and read the paper after work.

One of us has helped to raise four children and two stepchildren, and these siblings and stepsiblings also played house. The roles were not as stable, however, as when we were younger. One of the sons asked for a toy oven when he was 6 years old; another son requested a baby doll for Christmas whom he christened "Sophia" after his maternal grandmother. The oldest daughter refused to play games with boys unless she had a chance to win. By contrast, the youngest daughter loved makeup and "dress-up" from the time she knew how to role play. The two stepbrothers, too, enacted more traditional roles.

As our experiences—both past and present—imply, a discussion of family is incomplete without a discussion of gender. From the earliest age, we experience gender in the family in divisions of labor, roles, tasks, play, rules, and communication. In daily interactions, family members impart expectations of us as sons and daughters, mothers and fathers, and husbands and wives, and these expectations influence girls' and boys' identities. These gendered identities, in turn, inspire gendered career choices, communication styles, task expectations, styles of relating, and modes of engaging in the families we form as adults.

This chapter explores the links between gender and understandings of cultural life, ourselves, our communication, and our relationships. We hope you will be challenged to draw connections between images of yourself, the relationships and communication within your family, and your personal role in (re)creating or altering gender relationally, personally, and socially. The purpose of this chapter is to examine three (necessarily interrelated) gendered patterns of family communication; each reveals ways in which families embody—and continuously (re) create—gender. First, *gendered patterns of marital communication* are explored. Second, *gendered patterns of family roles* are examined. Finally, we discuss *gendered patterns of parenting*.

GENDERED PATTERNS OF MARITAL COMMUNICATION

Gendered understandings of relationship dynamics are manifest in the communication between spouses. Husbands and wives, especially in Western societies, come from two different cultures with different learned behavior and communication styles (Tannen, 1990). They are "intimate strangers" (Rubin, 1983) with the potential for many gendered misunderstandings.

Women's speech, in general, is based on notions of equality, supportiveness, expression of feelings, inclusivity, responsiveness, and personal disclosures (Pearson, West, & Turner, 1995; Wood, 1994a). Tentativeness is also characteristic of Caucasian women's communication, although less pronounced in the speech of African American women. With regard to women's speech, Wood (1994a, p. 142) explains: "Rather than a rigid you-tell-your-ideas-then-I'll-tell-mine sequence, women's speech more characteristically follows an interactive pattern in which different voices weave together to create conversations." Some men learn a very different style of speech, and thus define the goals of talk differently. Men often aim to establish status, maintain the floor (via talkativeness and humor), exhibit knowledge, solve problems, and assert themselves. Emotional and conversational responsiveness, tentativeness, and personal disclosures are typically underplayed in some men's speech (Pearson et al., 1995; Wood, 1994a). African

American men, however, tend to be more emotionally expressive and responsive than Caucasian men (Gaines, 1995). Men and women often operate out of distinctive speech communities, with styles that are different, "but equally valid" (Tannen, 1990, p. 15). These general communication patterns are discussed in depth by Julia Wood in Chapter 9 of this book.

Gendered communication styles might surface in actual, or perceived, self-disclosure, although findings are mixed. Early research suggested that women appear to self-disclose more than men (DeForest & Stone, 1980; Greenblatt, Gasenauer, & Freimuth, 1980; LeVine & Franco, 1981), disclose more negative information than men (Wheeless & Grotz, 1976), and disclose more intimate information than men (Gitter & Black, 1976). However, Dindia and Allen (1992) recently conducted a meta-analysis of 205 studies involving almost 24,000 subjects published between 1958 and 1989 in which sex differences in self-disclosure were studied. They conclude that actual sex differences in self-disclosure are not as large as researchers and theorists have suggested in the past, noting: "It is time to stop perpetuating the myth that there are large sex differences in men's and women's self-disclosure" (p. 118).

Dindia and Allen (1992) found extremely small differences in self-disclosure based on the sex of the discloser and the sex of the target. According to their meta-analysis, women, in general, disclose slightly more than men, although the statistical differences were extremely small. They also found that females disclose more with other females than males tend to disclose with females, but that females together are not more disclosive than males are with other males. Dindia and Allen argue that early research that reports sex differences in self-disclosure might be based on biased interpretations and/or research methods: "We may expect women to disclose more than men because we believe it is more appropriate for women to disclose than men" (p. 114).

Some researchers suggest that gender differences in self-disclosure are simply matters of gendered perception. Although Shimanoff (1985) found that wives *report* disclosing more, and valuing disclosure more, than husbands, observations revealed little actual difference in men's and women's patterns of self-disclosure. Why might this be so? According to Rubin (1983), some women might not recognize their husbands' comments as self-disclosures. A prototypical complaint of men is, "I tell her, but she's never satisfied....No matter how much I say, it's never enough" (Rubin, 1983, p. 71). Gendered styles of communication, as well as gendered expectations of that communication, contribute to this misunderstanding by socializing women and men into different views of what counts as self-disclosure.

The importance of self-disclosure may be overrated, particularly in the enduring relationship (Wood, 1995; Wood & Duck, 1995). Although self-disclosure plays an important role in the early stages of relational evolution, self-disclosive communication becomes less important than other types of communication in the enduring marriage. Also, couples' *perceptions* of disclosure may be more important than the amount of disclosure in which they actually engage; couples in happy marriages are more likely to positively distort their perceptions of disclosures received (Beach & Arias, 1983; Davidson, Balswick, & Halverson, 1983; Pearson, 1992).

Gendered styles of interacting (including actual or perceived self-disclosure patterns) might better be understood by examining the disparate ways that feminine and masculine individuals often express themselves (Wood, 1994a). Researchers have observed that men often do not express themselves and their feelings in feminine ways, just as many women do not use masculine means of expression (Wood, 1994a; Wood & Inman, 1993). Masculine modes of expressing closeness are different from feminine methods, which often involve "closeness in dialogue" (Wood, 1994a). Self-disclosure might represent an undesirable means of expression for many men who prefer instrumental demonstrations (such as doing a favor for a partner), or "closeness in the doing" (Swain, 1989). Gendered ways of expressing closeness represent how gendered socialization manifests itself in the communication of intimate partners.

Because men and women often talk at cross-purposes and often have different perceptions of their own and their partner's communication behavior, marital communication is particularly challenging. Do these differences affect marital satisfaction? It appears that gender at least affects one's *assessment* of marital satisfaction. Researchers have found that "her" marriage is not viewed as positively as "his" marriage; that is, when husbands and wives evaluate their marital happiness, husbands are more likely than wives to give it high marks (Bernard, 1972; Riessman, 1990). Women are more likely than men to perceive problems in communication and other relational dynamics because women, more than men, are socialized to be attentive to relational issues and problems (Tavris, 1992; Wood, 1993).

Marital satisfaction might be related to many husbands' ability to be expressive, to be clear, and to decode his wife's messages accurately (Balswick, 1988; Blumstein & Schwartz, 1983; Rubin, 1983). Because the masculine speech community does not encourage or value expressiveness, many wives complain that their husbands are deficiently expressive and nurturing (Davidson & Moore, 1992; Fitzpatrick & Indvik, 1982; Rubin, 1983). Men often express their feelings in instrumental (that is, "helping") behaviors like washing and waxing their wives' cars (Wood & Inman, 1993). Since women, in general, rely on verbal, emotional displays of feelings, they may fail to perceive instrumental actions as expressing emotion.

While gendered communication between spouses may result in misunderstandings, these differences may be improved over time. Sex-role differences are marked among younger people, but they become less salient as people age (Pearson, 1995; Sillars & Wilmot, 1989). "Sex-role crossover" might begin to occur as early as midlife (Cooper & Gutmann, 1987; McGee & Wells, 1982). Women often become freer to display more masculine traits, and many men are more likely to incorporate feminine behaviors into their communication repertoires. These relocations provide the opportunity for increased understanding between women and men.

GENDERED PATTERNS OF FAMILY ROLES

Each person in any system—whether it is a multinational corporation or a family—plays a role. The fulfillment of specific roles is essential to family functioning. Family roles are often linked to necessary family functions such as decision making and nurturance (Pearson, 1993) and to gendered expectations. The influence of gender particularly affects and reflects the roles of breadwinning, housework, and child care.

Breadwinning

Historically, men have been primarily responsible for providing for the financial needs of the family, particularly among Caucasians. Just as the wearing of white wedding dresses, fathers "giving away" their daughters, and wives adopting their husbands' names in marriage, traditions die hard. Although women are increasingly assuming equal breadwinning roles in families, most men and women still *prefer* husbands to be the primary breadwinners and wives to be homemakers, particularly after children are added to the family (Canter & Ageton, 1984; Herzog, Bachman, & Johnston, 1983; Reissman, 1990).

The role of "provider" remains intimately tied to perceptions of power in the family, reflecting continuing gender patterns. Young couples reveal that men and women still believe men should have more power in the arena of personal relationships (Riessman, 1990). An example is the fact that despite many of the nontraditional behaviors of dual-career couples, the marital satisfaction of these couples is still related to perceptions that both spouses fit sex-role stereotypes. Both husbands and wives in dual-career couples report more satisfaction if the husband is seen as more intelligent, competent, and of higher professional status than his wife (Yogev, 1987). Gender prescriptions require that men earn more and have higher job status than women; essentially, the partner who earns more tends to be the more powerful, particularly in heterosexual and gay relationships (Blumstein & Schwartz, 1983). Lesbians often do not embrace or enact a money-equals-power equation (Blumstein & Schwartz, 1983; see Huston and Schwartz, Chapter 10 of this book). Hence, viewing money and bread-winning as a source of relational power seems to reflect masculine perspectives more than feminine ones.

Straying from dominant prescriptions has relational consequences. As a wife's salary becomes greater than her husband's, marital satisfaction often decreases (Dersch & Pearson, 1986; Philliber & Hiller, 1979), and the probability of divorce increases (Trent & South, 1989). Some researchers estimate that for every $1,000 increase in a wife's salary, the possibility that she will divorce increases by 2% (Philliber & Vannoy-Hiller, 1990).

Still, women's participation in the paid work force has risen greatly in the last few decades. One of the most dramatic increases has been among women with children under the age of 6. In 1950, only 12% of women with children under age 6 worked outside the home. In 1988, 57.4% of these women with young children were employed outside the home (U.S. Department of Commerce, 1990). The most recent statistics reveal that over 65% of married women with children under 18 are in the labor force (U.S. Department of Commerce, 1990).

Reasons for, and the consequences of, women's increased participation in the family breadwinning role clarify the social meanings and consequences of gender ideologies. The most frequently cited reason for wives working outside the home is economic need (Israelson, 1989). However, many factors, including a woman's sex role, affect her decision to work (Krogh, 1985; Smith, 1985). Women who score high on traditionally masculine characteristics such as ambition, task orientation, and aggressiveness tend to be more satisfied if they have jobs outside the home than if they are full-time homemakers.

Husbands' attitudes also affect wives' decisions to work outside the home. The husbands of working women tend to be more profeminist than are the husbands of nonworking women (Smith, 1985). Age may be a mediating factor, since younger men report greater sensitivity to their spouses' needs and to the marriage in general, including a greater willingness to negotiate roles (McLeod, 1992).

Tied directly to these gendered patterns is another reality: Many employed wives are playing dual roles that require they work an extra shift—the first shift at work or at the office and a "second shift" at home (Hochschild with Machung, 1989). The reality, and consequences, of women's second shift, as we will see, are intimately connected to gender ideologies, and to the gendered politics of this particular family role.

Housework

Marriage has been criticized for perpetuating sex inequity. In discussing marriage, Johnson, Huston, Gaines, and Levinger (1992) recognized that "[m]arriage *is* about gender...and to a large extent about the gendered organization of labor" (p. 361). According to Riessman (1990), "Traditional marriage is a gendered institution—not just because women and men participate in it, but because the gender-based division of labor in it, in turn, creates inequality between women and men" (p. 15). The division of household tasks benefits the husband, often at the wife's expense.

Marriages, and families, do not exist outside of a gendered division of labor (Delphy, 1984). The gendered division of household work is central to the study of gender and family relationships, particularly as women increasingly share the breadwinning role.

As indicated earlier, dual-worker/dual-career marriages constitute approximately two-thirds of married families with children under 18 (Silberstein, 1992; Wilkie, 1991). Despite women's increased participation in the work force, men are not reciprocating by increasing their participation in household tasks. Wives' employment has minimal impact on husbands' involvement in domestic chores (Berk & Berk, 1979; Hochschild with Machung, 1989). Although some researchers suggest that for every one-dollar increase in the wife's income, the husband increases his household tasks by 20 minutes (Nickols & Metzen, 1978), others dispute claims that wives' earnings directly affect housework (Spitze, 1986). The bottom line is that only 20% of men in dual-worker families share equally in homemaking and child care (Hochschild with Machung, 1989).

The gendered imbalance of work in the home is staggering. Wives employed outside of the home perform three times more household duties than do their husbands (Berk, 1985; Kamo, 1988; Warner, 1986). These tasks amount to women doing approximately 15 additional hours per week of housework (Burley, 1991) and approximately 79% of the total housework (Burley, 1991). In sum, wives perform a month more of housework each year than their husbands (Hochschild with Machung, 1989). Not only are many women doing more work at home, but the nature of the tasks expected of women is qualitatively different from the chores assigned to men (Bruess, Dellinger, & Sahlman, 1993). Men are typically allocated tasklike "projects" (caring for patio furniture or water-sealing the deck), creative jobs (fixing the toaster), and/or responsibilities that are conducted seasonally or monthly (grilling hamburgers or seeding the lawn). Women's jobs include those that are required several times a day (washing dishes), mundane (folding the laundry), time consuming (running errands and making grocery lists), timely (planning and preparing meals), and simultaneous (fixing dinner while helping children with homework) (Beckwith, 1992; Hochschild with Machung, 1989).

Some couples report equal "sharing" of tasks, buying into the "upstairs/downstairs" or "inside/outside" myth (Hochschild with Machung, 1989). For these couples, outside (and/or downstairs) refers to a garage, basement, and/or yard; these are "his" responsibilities. Her responsibilities include the "upstairs" (and/or "inside"), which means the rest of the house (living room, bedrooms, family rooms, bathrooms, kitchen, and all the work associated with these rooms, such as laundry, dishes, and meal preparation). As a way to justify the second shift, many men *and* women in Hochschild and Machung's (1989) research jointly devised and embraced the outside/inside or upstairs/downstairs arrangement. However, such "half and half" arrangements are simply gendered myths that mask what remains a clearly lopsided division of tasks in most families.

The jobs most women assume in the home are many. The burden of their tasks is not only physical, but psychological as well. In fact, "psychological responsibility" is actually another job for many women (Hochschild with Machung, 1989). It involves the often necessary duty of "managing" the many other household jobs—remembering, planning, and coordinating tasks and reminding others of their responsibilities. Not only are women expected to do more tasks, but also they tend to adopt responsibility for making sure others' tasks get done.

Equally gendered are kinship responsibilities in families (Johnson et al., 1992). "Kinkeeping" is the function of maintaining contact with one's extended family and keeping other family members in touch with one another (Rosenthal, 1985). Families with kinkeepers report greater extended family interaction and greater emphasis on family rituals within the extended family and within the historical development of the family. Kinkeepers are more often women than men; grandmothers and mothers are more frequently placed in these roles than other family members (Bahr, 1976; Rosenthal, 1985). Men sometimes participate in the kinship role function by providing economic aid, but women are more likely to be involved in communication and relational activities (Bahr, 1976). Women also often assume responsibility for caring for elderly parents and parents-in-law. Again, men often provide instrumental support (money) while women most often assume responsibility for their parents' daily, personal care (Wood, 1994b). Family members define such activities as "women's work." The job is frequently passed from mother to daughter, and the position persists over time (Rosenthal, 1985).

What are the implications of the imbalance in shared housework and the additional burdens on women? The effects are detrimental for both marriages and families. The overburdening of women is related to dissatisfaction and depression among dual-career wives (Benin & Agostinelli, 1988; Ross, Mirowsky, & Huber, 1983). Women also suffer from more physical illness and emotional stress as a result of their extra duties (Hochschild with Machung, 1989).

Marital satisfaction is also related to task sharing; the happiest wives are in marriages where husbands share equally in household tasks (Yogev & Brett, 1985), and in marriages where they are satisfied with the amount of sharing or support they receive from their husbands (Pina & Bengston, 1993). Couples in one study reported that sharing tasks has a number of positive outcomes, such as increased communication, heightened intimacy, and improved decision-making abilities (Haas, 1980). However, wives who maintain traditional ideologies about marriage seem the least concerned about husbands who share household work. For wives with egalitarian beliefs about marital roles, marital satisfaction is closely linked to their husbands' involvement in housework (Pina & Bengston, 1993).

More equal sharing of household labor has positive effects on other familial relationships as well. Fathers who share tasks equally in their marriages report experiencing greater satisfaction in the fathering role, being more aware of their children's needs, and developing a maternal sense as they increased their domestic activities (Coltrane, 1989). Moreover, egalitarian families provide nonstereotypical role models for children.

How do you achieve an egalitarian marriage, or at least increase your chances for more equal task sharing? According to one study in which husbands and wives shared equally in housework, Coltrane (1989) found that the key factor influencing the equal division of household work was the attitude by both spouses that household work is not "women's work." Also important is how husbands and wives experience the division of labor and the roles in their primary families (Haas, 1980; Koopman-Boyden & Abbott, 1985). Husbands who had working mothers, and who were required to do chores as a child, were more likely to share household work.

Although women are encouraged in our society to "do it all" and be "superwomen" who handle careers, children, husbands, and in-laws with ease and grace, they seldom are warned about (or expect) the extra month of work each year that most men do not experience. Hochschild and Machung (1989) explain the "ironic heroism" of working mothers: "The common portrayal of the supermom working mother suggests that she is 'energetic' and 'competent' because these are her *personal* characteristics, not because she has been forced to adapt to an overly demanding schedule" (p. 24).

The politics of housework are not confined to bed sheets and dust-mops; the politics of housework are deeply saturated with images of gender. These conceptions are culturally constructed and reinforced, and then are further supported and enacted on various levels within the family. Next we explore another gendered family role: child care.

Child Care

Add a child to a family and what is the result? In books and movies (and sometimes in our dreams), adding a child is an idyllic time in which a couple experiences the beauty, poetry, and romance of the occasion. In reality, we know that the addition of children to the family increases stress and decreases marital satisfaction (Cox, 1985). Bill Cosby (1986) noted: "Having a child is surely the most beautifully irrational act that two people in love can commit" (p. 18).

Child rearing is important, yet, like other family roles, it often follows highly gendered patterns of cultural expectations and behaviors. Although men have increased their participation in the actual births of children, care for infant children is still assigned primarily to mothers. Even in egalitarian marriages, responsibilities regarding child care tend to become more traditional after children are born (Cox, 1985).

Many fathers report feeling unskilled in infant care. As compensation, they tend to emphasize their capacities as protectors and providers (Entwisle & Doering, 1988). According to researchers Harris and Morgan (1991), a father's breadwinning role mandates a less active, less compassionate role in parenting: "The traditional paternal role is the instrumental role as breadwinner. This role identifies some paternal responsibilities for training and discipline, but father–child relationships need not be close or compassionate" (p. 532), nor need the role involve the constant availability typically expected of mothers.

We might guess that in dual-career marriages, fathers would participate more equally in child care, since well-educated, middle-class men tend to be less sex-role stereotypical than their less-educated, lower class counterparts (Lamb, 1982). In fact, fathers in dual-career marriages do "assist" more than other fathers, and fathers' participation in child care has increased over the last few decades (Seward, Yeats, Seward, & Stanley-Stevens, 1993). However, "participating" is altogether different from "sharing equally." Fathers—even those in dual-career marriages—do not represent an egalitarian model of parenting (Bird, 1979; Hochschild with Machung, 1989; Seward et al., 1993).

Fathers' participation in child care is often in the form of recreational activities such as reading to children, playing with them, or teaching them (Thompson & Walker, 1989). Women often spend the majority of time taking care of mundane, repetitive child care activities (Bird, 1979), such as feeding, bathing, and other activities of primary caregiving (Katsh, 1981). The time many fathers spend with children is more occasional and enjoyable (as in a trip to the zoo on Saturday); the time mothers spend with children is more constant and boring (Burns & Hommel, 1989).

Some researchers optimistically suggest that fathers in contemporary dual-career families are "in a state of transition—moving from the traditional perspective of fatherhood toward a more egalitarian model" (Jump & Haas, 1987, p. 111). Until such a model is widely adopted—and embraced by a culture resistant to family-oriented men (Cohen, 1987)—gendered patterns of family structure, roles, and communication will remain concrete and distinct, reinforced by social expectations and continuously (re)created within and by families. Next, we explore parenting and parental communication as primary agents of children's gender socialization.

GENDERED PATTERNS OF PARENTING: CHILDREN'S SOCIALIZATION

From birth, male and female babies are treated differently both in American culture and around the world (Williams & Best, 1982). The process of socialization occurs in a variety of contexts and throughout our lifetime (Stanton, 1990), but it is most salient within the family.

Gender creates expectations of family members, as we discussed. The behaviors expected of "mommies and daddies," "sons and daughters," and "sisters and brothers" reflect social meanings of gender being (re)created and reinforced in our family relationships. The expectations parents have for children reflect parents' views of gender.

For instance, America's "boy preference" (Basow, 1992; Coombs, 1977) may be manifested in fathers' greater interaction with sons than daughters (Rossi, 1984). Too, differential descriptors are applied to babies within hours of their birth: Parents describe boys as "strong," "solid," and "independent," and depict girls as "cute," "sweet," and "delicate" (Handel, 1988; Stern & Karraker, 1989). In general, both mothers and fathers encourage, teach, question, and talk explicitly to their sons more than their daughters (Bronstein, 1988; Weitzman, Birns, & Friend, 1985). Males are valued more than females in almost every country in the world (Basow, 1992), a value that parents communicate, often unconsciously, to their children. In these ways, families foster, and children learn, social understandings of gender.

To understand the family is to understand the deeply embedded meanings of gender continuously communicated by parents. Parents' differential expectations for their daughters and sons are communicated both directly and indirectly. For example, parents often decorate children's rooms and bodies distinctively; gendered identities are fostered by the Power Ranger wallpaper and replicas of large machinery used to decorate a 2-year-old boy's room, and in the leggings and the black patent leather shoes strapped on the feet of a 3-year-old girl (Pomerleau, Bolduc, Malcuit, & Cossette, 1990; Richardson, 1988; Shakin, Shakin, & Sternglanz, 1985). After examining over 170 articles on sex-role stereotyping, Lytton and Romney (1991) concluded that sex- and gender-typing are the only areas in which mothers, fathers, and parents combined actually have an impact on children.

Because gendered prescriptions are pervasive and begin so early, it is surprising that children do not develop specific sex-role orientations earlier than they do. For instance, Doyle (1991) found that mothers begin to withdraw touch behaviors from sons around the age of 6 months. However, before the age of 3, children are rather flexible in their orientation: Boys are not yet doing only "little boy" things; girls have not yet learned to do only "little girl" things (Fine, 1987; Handel, 1988; Seegmiller, 1980). Around the age of about 3, the tendency to see oneself as consistently male or female (gender constancy) appears to develop in most children (Wood, 1994a).

Gendered identities are learned as families enact gendered patterns of behavior and communication in their everyday, mundane interactions.

For instance, parents encourage traditional sex roles for their female children when assigning chores. Daughters are routinely asked to perform more household jobs than are sons (Cloch, 1987; Mietus-Sanik & Stafford, 1985). Children also learn about gender by watching the roles and the relationship of their parents, such as who assumes the majority of child care and housework responsibilities (Hochschild with Machung, 1989), and who acts as the "relationship expert" (Wood, 1993).

Parents also shape understandings of gender in their communication, and their playful interaction, with children. Routinely, fathers emphasize independence and autonomy in their sons, while mothers encourage politeness, nurturance, and mutual activities in their daughters (Power & Shanks, 1989; Thompson & Walker, 1989). Fathers and their boys participate in more "dangerous and exciting" leisure activities (Lundgren & Cassedy, 1993); mothers are more likely to engage in social play (Belsky, 1980), tending toward more verbal and didactic interaction.

Parenting and gender-role research has been focused on heterosexual relationships. Families with gay or lesbian parents, too, are confronted with complexities of gender socialization. Lesbians, however, often hold less stereotypical perceptions of feminine behavior, believing their sons and daughters to be more similar in qualities than do heterosexual mothers (Hill, 1988). Lesbian mothers also tend to promote more traditionally masculine characteristics in their daughters. Gay men and lesbian women may be more sensitive to the constraints related to role restrictions and thus maximize nontraditional role modeling (Martin, 1993). However, both gay and lesbian parents note that the strength of cultural stereotypes often overwhelms their earnest attempts to minimize children's gendered attitudes and behaviors (Martin, 1993).

CONCLUSION

In this chapter, we explored gendered patterns of marital communication, family roles, and parenting. We learned that gender seeps into almost every aspect of our families, filtering our perceptions of the world, our views of family roles and relationships, and our expectations. We also learned that family communication is not immune to social meanings of gender, just as we, as individuals, are not immune to our families' prescriptions of, and influences on, who we are as women and men, girls and boys, mothers and fathers, and daughters and sons. Our jointly constructed gender ideologies—often those we learn and enact within the family—influence how we relate to and communicate with others. Indeed, you might recognize how your family has shaped your gendered participation in intimate, extended family, friendship, and even professional relationships. The chapters of this book invite you to explore these and other topics. We conclude this chapter by emphasizing that families cannot be understood without a consideration of gender. In multiple ways, each and every day, families normalize, reify, and ultimately embody social understandings of gender.

QUESTIONS FOR REFLECTION AND DISCUSSION

1. Construct a list of differences between how men and women often communicate in relationships. Observe or think about communication between your parents and other men and women. Do you see gendered patterns of communication in relationships? Are the communication patterns you observe and describe similar to those discussed in this chapter? Do you think that men and women generally have different conversational styles?

2. Observe the specific family roles, tasks, and communication patterns among gay or lesbian families and heterosexual families. Consider the families of African Americans, European Americans, Hispanic Americans, and other co-cultural groups. Also, think about your observations of, or experiences within, families from various countries or with various nationalities. Do you think gender ideologies (especially as they are enacted within the family) are culturally specific or vary in these family types? What did you observe that taught you about how men and women in the family are viewed in these cultures? What kinds of family roles did the men and women play in these families? How are they similar or different from the family roles in your own culture?

3. Make a list of *all* of the tasks that each person in your family typically performed (or is currently performing). Who assumed the large majority of chores in your family? Did the women or the men do a greater number of tasks, or did everyone share equally in tasks? Were there differences in the "types" of jobs that different people performed? Did it seem like someone in your family took responsibility for "managing" the work of the other family members? Who was this person? What other assignments did this person typically have?

4. Imagine you have your own ideal family and you are in charge of dividing tasks among family members. How will you organize the

division of labor in your family? How will you divide the house-work? Who will be responsible for child care? Will you hire outside help? Will this ideal scenario affect who you choose as a mate? How so?

5. Talk to men you know in various types of families. Ask them what types of pressure they (and they think other men) feel concerning their roles as fathers, husbands, partners, uncles, or brothers, in contemporary families. Are men often constrained by traditional gender roles such as "breadwinner" or "provider"?

6. Do you think men and women define relationship satisfaction differently? If you asked a large group of men to define a satisfying relationship, what kinds of characteristics or definitions do you think they would provide? What would a group of women tell you? Would their criteria for satisfying relationships be the same? If not, what types of problems seem to emerge from these discrepant definitions? Does our society inspire differences in men's and women's criteria for achieving satisfaction in relationships? Find specific examples in our culture—such as movies, songs, books, advertisements, or other cultural artifacts—that support your ideas.

REFERENCES

Bahr, H. (1976). The kinship role. In F. Ivan Nye (Ed.), *Role structure and analysis of the family* (pp. 360–367). Beverly Hills, CA: Sage.

Balswick, J. (1988). *The inexpressive male.* Lexington, MA: Lexington Books.

Basow, S. (1992). *Gender: Stereotypes and roles* (3rd ed.). Pacific Grove, CA: Brooks/Cole.

Beach, S., & Arias, I. (1983). Assessment of perceptual discrepancy: Utility of the primary communication inventory. *Family Process, 22,* 309–316.

Beckwith, J. (1992). Stereotypes and reality in the division of household labor. *Social Behavior and Personality, 20,* 283–288.

Belsky, J. (1980). A family analysis of parental influence on infant exploratory competence. In F. A. Pedersen (Ed.), *The father–infant relationship: Observational studies in a family setting* (pp. 87–110). New York: Praeger.

Benin, M. H., & Agostinelli, J. (1988). Husbands' and wives' satisfaction with the division of labor. *Journal of Marriage and the Family, 50,* 349–361.

Berk, R., & Berk, S. (1979). *Labor and leisure at home: Content and organization of the household day.* Beverly Hills, CA: Sage.

Berk, S. F. (1985). *The gender factory: The apportionment of work in American households.* New York: World.

Bernard, J. (1972). *The future of marriage.* New York: Bantam.

Bird, C. (1979). *The two paycheck marriage.* New York: Rosen & Wade.

Blumstein, P., & Schwartz, P. (1983). *American couples.* New York: William Morrow.

Bronstein, P. (1988). Father–child interaction. In P. Bronstein & C. Cowan (Eds.), *Fatherhood today: Men's changing role in the family* (pp. 107–124). New York: John Wiley.

Bruess, C., Dellinger, C., & Sahlman, J. (1993, May). *I'll mow the grass, you fix dinner: Engaged couples' expectations of task-sharing in marriage.* Paper presented at the meeting of the International Network on Personal Relationships, Milwaukee, WI.

Burley, K. A. (1991). Family-work spillover in dual-career couples: A comparison of two time perspectives. *Psychological Reports, 68,* 471–480.

Burns, A., & Hommel, R. (1989). Gender division of tasks by parents and their children. *Psychology of Women Quarterly, 13,* 113–125.

Canter, R., & Ageton, S. (1984). The epidemiology of adolescent sex-role attitudes. *Sex Roles, 11,* 657–676.

Cloch, M. (1987). The development of sex differences in young children's activities at home: The effect of the social context. *Sex Roles, 16,* 279–302.

Cohen, T. (1987). Remaking men. *Journal of Family Issues, 8,* 57–77.

Coltrane, S. (1989). Household labor and the routine production of gender. *Social Problems, 36,* 473–490.

Coombs, L. (1977). Preferences for sex of children among U.S. couples. *Family Planning Perspectives, 9,* 259–265.

Cooper, K., & Gutmann, D. (1987). Gender identity and ego mastery style in middle-aged, pre- and post-empty nest women. *The Gerontologist, 27,* 347–352.

Cosby, B. (1986). *Fatherhood.* New York: Berkley.

Cox, M. (1985). Progress and continued challenges in understanding the transition to parenthood. *Journal of Family Issues, 6,* 395–408.

Davidson, B., Balswick, J., & Halverson, C. (1983). Affective self-disclosure and marital adjustment: A test of equity theory. *Journal of Marriage and the Family, 45,* 93–102.

Davidson, K., & Moore, N. (1992). *Marriage and family.* Dubuque, IA: William C. Brown.

DeForest, C., & Stone, G. (1980). Effects of sex and intimacy level on self-disclosure. *Journal of Counseling Psychology, 27,* 93–96.

Delphy, C. (1984). *Close to home: A materialist analysis of women's oppression.* Amherst, MA: University of Massachusetts Press.

Dersch, C., & Pearson, J. C. (1986, April). *Interpersonal communication competence and marital adjustment among dual career and dual worker women.* Paper presented at the annual meeting of the Central States Speech Communication Association, Cincinnati, OH.

Dindia, K., & Allen, M. (1992). Sex differences in self-disclosure: A meta-analysis. *Psychological Bulletin, 112,* 106–124.

Doyle, J. (1991). *The male experience.* Dubuque, IA: William C. Brown.

Entwisle, D., & Doering, S. (1988). The emergent father role. *Sex Roles, 18,* 119–142.

Fine, G. (1987). *With the boys: Little league baseball and preadolescent culture.* Chicago, IL: University of Chicago Press.

Fitzpatrick, M. A., & Indvik, J. (1982). The instrumental and expressive domains of marital communication. *Human Communication Research, 8,* 195–213.

Gaines, S. (1995). Relationships between members of cultural minorities. In J. T. Wood & S. W. Duck (Eds.), *Understanding relationship processes, 6: Off the beaten track: Understudied relationships* (pp. 51–88). Thousand Oaks, CA: Sage.

Gitter, G., & Black, H. (1976). Is self-disclosing revealing? *Journal of Counseling Psychology, 23,* 327–332.

Greenblatt, J., Gasenauer, J., & Freimuth, V. (1980). Psychological sex type and androgyny in the study of communication variables: Self-disclosure and communication apprehension. *Human Communication Research, 6,* 117–129.

Haas, L. (1980). Role-sharing couples: A study of egalitarian marriages. *Family Relations, 29,* 289–296.

Handel, G. (1988). *Childhood socialization.* Hawthorne, NY: Aldine de Gruyter.

Harris, J., & Morgan, S. (1991). Fathers, sons, and daughters: Differential paternal involvement in parenting. *Journal of Marriage and the Family, 53,* 531–544.

Herzog, A., Bachman, J., & Johnston, L. (1983). Paid work, child care, and housework: A national survey of high school seniors' preferences for sharing responsibilities between husband and wife. *Sex Roles, 9,* 109–135.

Hill, M. (1988). Child-rearing attitudes of black lesbian mothers. In *Lesbian psychologies: Explorations and challenges,* edited by Boston Lesbian Psychologies Collective. Urbana, IL: University of Illinois Press.

Hochschild, A., with Machung, A. (1989). *The second shift: Working parents and revolution at home.* New York: Viking.

Israelson, C. (1989). Family resource management. *Family Perspectives, 23,* 311–331.

Johnson, M., Huston, T., Gaines, S., & Levinger, G. (1992). Patterns of married life among young couples. *Journal of Social and Personal Relationships, 9,* 343–364.

Jump, T., & Haas, L. (1987). Fathers in transition: Dual-career fathers participating in child care. In M. Kimmel (Ed.), *Changing men: New directions in research on men and masculinity* (pp. 98–114). Newbury Park, CA: Sage.

Kamo, Y. (1988). Determinants of the household division of labor: Resources, power, and ideology. *Journal of Family Issues, 9,* 177–200.

Katsh, B. (1981). Fathers and infants. *Journal of Family Issues, 2,* 275–296.

Koopman-Boyden, P., & Abbott, M. (1985). Expectations for household task allocation and actual task allocation: A New Zealand study. *Journal of Marriage and the Family, 47,* 211–219.

Krogh, K. (1985). Women's motives to achieve and to nurture in different life stages. *Sex Roles, 12,* 75–90.

Lamb, M. (1982). *Nontraditional families: Parenting and child development.* Hillsdale, NJ: Lawrence Erlbaum.

LeVine, E., & Franco, J. (1981). A reassessment of self-disclosure patterns among Anglo–Americans and Hispanics. *Journal of Counseling Psychology, 28,* 522–524.

Lundgren, D., & Cassedy, A. (1993). Girls' and boys' activity patterns in family leisure settings. In C. Berryman-Fink, D. Ballard-Reisch, & L. Newman (Eds.), *Communication and sex-role socialization.* New York: Garland.

Lytton, H., & Romney, D. (1991). Parents' differential socialization of boys and girls: A meta-analysis. *Psychological Bulletin, 109,* 267–296.

Martin, A. (1993). *The lesbian and gay parenting handbook.* New York: Harper Collins.

McGee, J., & Wells, K. (1982). Gender typing and androgyny in later life. *Human Development, 25,* 116–139.

McLeod, R. (1992, March 14). Poll on male attitudes finds 90's men sensitive, caring. *Austin American–Statesman,* pp. A1, A15.

Mietus-Sanik, M., & Stafford, K. (1985). Adolescents' contributions to household production: Male and female differences. *Adolescence, 20,* 207–215.

Nickols, S., & Metzen, E. (1978). Household time for husband and wife. *Home Economics Research Journal, 7,* 85–97.

Pearson, J. C. (1992). *Lasting love: What keeps couples together.* Dubuque, IA: William C. Brown.

Pearson, J. C. (1993). *Communication in the family: Seeking satisfaction in changing times.* New York: Harper Collins.

Pearson, J. C. (1995). Forty-forever years? Primary relationships and senior citizens. In N. Vanzetti & S. Duck (Eds.), *A lifetime of relationships.* Pacific Grove, CA: Brooks/Cole.

Pearson, J. C., West, R. L., & Turner, L. (1995). *Gender and communication.* Dubuque, IA: Brown & Benchmark.

Philliber, W., & Hiller, D. (1979). A research note: Occupational attainments and perceptions of status among working wives. *Journal of Marriage and the Family, 41,* 59–62.

Philliber, W., & Vannoy-Hiller, D. (1990). The effect of husband's occupational attainment on wife's achievement. *Journal of Marriage and the Family, 52,* 323–329.

Pina, D., & Bengston, V. (1993). The division of household labor and wives' happiness: Ideology, employment, and perceptions of support. *Journal of Marriage and the Family, 55,* 901–912.

Pomerleau, A., Bolduc, D., Malcuit, G., & Cossette, L. (1990). Pink or blue: Environmental stereotypes in the first two years of life. *Sex Roles, 22,* 359–367.

Power, T., & Shanks, J. (1989). Parents as socializers: Maternal and paternal views. *Journal of Youth and Adolescence, 18,* 203–217.

Richardson, L. (1988). *The dynamics of sex and gender: A sociological perspective.* New York: Harper & Row.

Riessman, C. (1990). *Divorce talk: Women and men make sense of personal relationships.* New Brunswick, NJ: Rutgers University Press.

Rosenfeld, L. (1979). Self-disclosure avoidance: Why I am afraid to tell you who I am. *Communication Monographs, 46,* 63–74.

Rosenthal, C. (1985). Kinkeeping in the familial division of labor. *Journal of Marriage and the Family, 47,* 965–974.

Ross, C. E., Mirowsky, J., & Huber, J. (1983). Dividing work, sharing work, and in-between: Marriage patterns and depression. *American Sociological Review, 48,* 809–823.

Rossi, A. (1984). Gender and parenthood. *American Sociological Review, 49,* 1–19.

Rubin, L. (1983). *Intimate strangers: Men and women together.* New York: Harper & Row.

Seegmiller, B. (1980). Sex typed behavior in pre-schoolers: Sex, age, and social class effects. *Journal of Psychology, 104,* 31–33.

Seward, R., Yeats, D., Seward, J., & Stanley-Stevens, L. (1993). Fathers' time spent with their children: A longitudinal assessment. *Family Perspectives, 27,* 275–283.

Shakin, M., Shakin, D., & Sternglanz, S. (1985). Infant clothing: Sex labeling for strangers. *Sex Roles, 12,* 955–964.

Shimanoff, S. (1985). Rules governing the verbal expression of emotions between married couples. *Western Journal of Speech Communication, 49,* 147–165.

Silberstein, L. (1992). *Dual-career marriage: A system in transition.* Hillsdale, NJ: Lawrence Erlbaum.

Sillars, A., & Wilmot, W. (1989). Marital communication across the life span. In J. F. Nussbaum (Ed.), *Life-span communication: Normative processes* (pp. 225–253). Hillsdale, NJ: Lawrence Erlbaum.

Smith, D. (1985). Wife employment and marital adjustment: A cumulation of results. *Family Relations, 34,* 483–490.

Spitze, G. (1986). The division of task responsibility in U.S. households: Longitudinal adjustments to change. *Social Forces, 64,* 689–701.

Stanton, A. (1990). *Communication and student socialization.* Norwood, NJ: Ablex.

Stern, M., & Karraker, K. (1989). Sex stereotyping of infants: A review of gender labeling studies. *Sex Roles, 20,* 501–522.

Swain, S. (1989). Covert intimacy: Closeness in men's friendships. In B. J. Risman & P. Schwartz (Eds.), *Gendered intimate relationships* (pp. 71–86). Belmont, CA: Wadsworth.

Tannen, D. (1990). *You just don't understand: Women and men in conversation.* New York: William Morrow.

Tavris, C. (1992). *The mismeasure of woman.* New York: Simon & Schuster.

Thompson, K., & Walker, A. (1989). Women and men in marriage, work and parenthood. *Journal of Marriage and the Family, 51,* 845–872.

Trent, K., & South, S. (1989). Structural determinants of the divorce rate: A cross-societal analysis. *Journal of Marriage and the Family, 51,* 391–404.

U.S. Department of Commerce, Bureau of the Census. (1990). *Statistical abstract of the United States, 1990.* Washington, DC: U.S. Government Printing Office.

Warner, R. L. (1986). Alternative strategies for measuring household division of labor: A comparison. *Journal of Family Issues, 7,* 179–195.

Weitzman, N., Birns, B., & Friend, R. (1985). Traditional and nontraditional mothers' communication with their daughters and sons. *Child Development, 56,* 894–896.

Wheeless, L., & Grotz, J. (1976). Conceptualization and measurement of reported self-disclosure. *Human Communication Research, 2,* 338–346.

Wilkie, J. (1991). The decline in men's labor force participation and income and the changing structure of family economic support. *Journal of Marriage and the Family, 53,* 111–122.

Williams, J., & Best, D. (1982). *Measuring sex stereotypes: A thirty nation study.* Beverly Hills, CA: Sage.

Wood, J. T. (1993). Engendered relationships: Interaction, caring, power, and responsibility in close relationships. In S. Duck (Ed.), *Processes in close relationships: Contexts of close relationships* (Vol. 3). Beverly Hills, CA: Sage.

Wood, J. T. (1994a). *Gendered lives: Communication, gender, and culture.* Belmont, CA: Wadsworth.

Wood, J. T. (1994b). *Who cares? Women, care and culture.* Carbondale, IL: Southern Illinois University Press.

Wood, J. T. (1995). *Relational communication: Change and continuity in personal relationships.* Belmont, CA: Wadsworth.

Wood, J. T., & Duck, S. W. (1995). Off the beaten track: New frontiers in relational research. In J. T. Wood & S. W. Duck (Eds.), *Understanding relationship processes, 6: Off the beaten track: Understudied relationships* (pp. 1–21). Thousand Oaks, CA: Sage.

Wood, J. T., & Inman, C. (1993). In a different mode: Masculine styles of communicating closeness. *Journal of Applied Communication Research, 21,* 279–295.

Yogev, S. (1987). Marital satisfaction and sex role perceptions among dual-earner couples. *Journal of Social and Personal Relationships, 4,* 35–46.

Yogev, S., & Brett, J. (1985). Perceptions of division of housework and child care and marital satisfaction. *Journal of Marriage and the Family, 47,* 609–619.

5

FRIENDSHIPS AMONG WOMEN: CLOSENESS IN DIALOGUE

FERN L. JOHNSON

Friendship is a very personal experience for women. I bring to the writing of this chapter not only my experience as a scholar of women's friendship but also my own friendships with women and my impressions of the dynamics of female friendship. Because real-life friendships form the substance that researchers seek to explain, I begin with four vignettes from my experience. Each reveals something of the character of female friendship.

> *My memories from grade school include vivid recollections of overhearing my mother's telephone conversations with her best friend who was having marital difficulty. In these early morning conversations, my mother's words and tone expressed love and comfort. I sensed that horrible things were happening to my mother's friend, even though she always appeared self-confident, energetic, and in control when I saw her.*

> *A college-age woman in my neighborhood recently transferred from a school in New England to one in the South. When I asked why she was transferring, she replied that she wanted to be with her best girlfriend, whom she missed terribly. She expressed confidence in her ability to get higher grades if she was in the same place as her friend. Although this young woman seemed to have little difficulty changing boyfriends, the relationship with her best girlfriend provided stability and continuity.*

> *On a visit to a local nursery to buy shrubs for the yard, I overheard a short conversation between my saleswoman and another saleswoman that was critical of the nursery's treatment of its employees. After I told her that I had heard the conversation, she disclosed that she and this other woman had become close friends at work simply through sticking together in a difficult situation. She went on to tell me that this woman had become her best friend and that they went out to dinner together on*

evenings when their husbands were busy with other things. They would "just talk and have a good time."

A woman who I know well was describing a close, nonromantic friendship that had developed with a male colleague at work. She remarked that what made the relationship so terrific and unusual was that "it feels like being friends with a woman." When asked what that meant, she replied, "We talk about everything, and he really knows what's going on with me."

HISTORY OF RESEARCH ON WOMEN'S FRIENDSHIPS

Each of the preceding stories reveals the vitality of female friendship. They reflect connection, intimacy, and sharing. Yet, until as recently as 20 years ago, friendship bonds among women rarely commanded serious scholarly attention. When Elizabeth Aries and I (Aries & Johnson, 1983; Johnson & Aries, 1983a, 1983b) set out in the late 1970s to study gender differences in friendships, we quickly discovered a dearth of information about friendships among women in contemporary society. Folk wisdom of questionable accuracy abounded about women's jealousies of one another, especially related to their competition for men; their "yackedy-yack" with each other; and their idling away of time. Homophobia too limited serious consideration of women's friendships by fostering fears about "latent lesbianism" (O'Connor, 1992; Raymond, 1986). Male folk wisdom further purported that women's intimacy with each other threatened the primacy of their relationships with men.

Several additional factors account for the long-standing inattention to close friendships among women. First, friendship has held relatively lesser status than relationships that are either obligatory or institutionalized, such as kinship or marriage. Second, women's friendships, like other aspects of women's lives, commanded little attention because they were considered less significant than men's friendships. As in so many domains of life, the experiences of women were rarely part of the published historical record, nor were they included on the roster of critical issues for interpersonal research and teaching. Third, the locus of women's friendships in more intimate and private contexts compared to the public spheres of the male world led to a dismissal of the importance of female friendship; in this context, women's friendships had been viewed as simply passing time in idle chatter/prattle or detracting from the more important matters of marriage, family, and paid labor. Summing up this state of affairs, Robert Bell (1981) noted that "an examination of American history shows that when friendship has been recognized it has almost always been as male friendship" (p. 55). Lillian Rubin (1985) is even more emphatic:

> From the Greek philosophers to modern writers...women's friendships didn't count, indeed were not even noticed. For just as women have been invisible in public life throughout the ages, so their private relations with each other have been unseen as well. (p. 59)

In contrast to this history, recent research on women's friendships has been substantial. Historians of women's lives have been especially important in ushering in the contemporary focus on women's friendship. Publication of Carol Smith-Rosenberg's work (1975, 1985) on the intimate connections among 19th-century women in America, Nancy Cott's (1977) account of women's relationships in early New England, and Lillian Faderman's (1981) history of women's romantic friendship and love all led the way for new scholarship in a broad range of fields. This chapter focuses on several themes emerging from this recent scholarship. The themes emerge from a summary of research on women's friendships, my own analysis and interpretation of that research, and studies that Elizabeth Aries and I have conducted on adult friendship.

The thematic approach that I take balances generalizations about women's friendships with distinctive patterns corresponding to particular circumstances that shape women's lives. Both feminism and postmodernism have taught us to respect the multiplicity of culture, gender, race, ethnicity, and nationality, and to exercise caution when generalizing about any group of people. Totally rejecting generalizations, however, makes it difficult to say anything at all about groups such as women. Because femininity and womanhood—including women's spheres and women's work—continue to carry particular (often negative or limiting) social meaning, it is important to risk some degree of generalization so that we can focus on the experiences of women in domains of importance to them, such as friendship. Same-sex friendships—both women's and men's—continue to be situated in a gendered society. Graham Allan (1989) comments that "same-gender friendships will continue to dominate until gender itself becomes an insignificant dimension of social experience" (p. 84). The likelihood of that happening is remote.

The characterizations of women's friendships that you read about here are not intended to be universal statements about all women's friendships or to exclude all men's and cross-gender friendships. If you are a woman reading this chapter, you will likely recognize these themes in your own friendships; if you are a man reading this chapter, these themes may clarify what you have observed about women's connections to one another. But you may also think of exceptions or have experiences quite different from what is described. Humans act in patterned ways, but we are slaves neither to biology nor to societal norms.

THEMES IN WOMEN'S FRIENDSHIPS

The nature of women's friendships has been studied using a variety of research methods. Some studies are historical and analytical, while others explore the dimensions of friendship between women through questionnaires or in-depth interviews, which can be an especially rich source of information about the qualitative dimensions of women's friendships. Five themes emerge from this scholarship.

Significant across all five themes is the centrality of communication as a valued activity. Whereas close friendships between men center on connection through activities (Aries & Johnson, 1983; Wood & Inman, 1993) such as playing poker, attending sports events, or belonging to clubs focused on common interests such as fishing and hunting, women friends tend to connect through communication. The first theme addresses this directly, and it runs through others as well.

Theme 1: Women's Friendships Are Typically Centered in Converstion. When Elizabeth Aries and I (Johnson & Aries, 1983b) interviewed a broad range of women about their close friendships, we were struck by the consistency with which they reported that extended conversation is vital to friendship. Talking often occurs as the explicit agenda for women friends, as in conversing over coffee or a meal or just sitting down to talk, but it also can be central in the context of other activities such as going for a walk, shopping, bowling, or picking berries. In Karen Walker's (1994) study of the friendships of working-class and middle-class women and men, she found that two-thirds of the women interviewed defined shared activities such as sports or aerobics as occasions to be together and talk. Often when women and men engage in the same activities, men's talk will focus on the activity itself (for example, analysis of the game), while women's dialogue is much more broad ranging.

The female preference for talk shows up early. In the preschool that my children attended, I often observed girls playing quietly together and using talk to direct their attention to one thing or another, while the boys were more physically engaged and active, using talk as a vehicle to get attention or to assert themselves. In an analysis of videotapes of same-sex friends, Deborah Tannen (1990) observed that second-grade girls easily talked together and shared personal stories, in contrast to boys of the same age who "exhibited discomfort in the situation of sitting in a room with nothing to do but talk" (p. 75). Marjorie Harness Goodwin (1990) documented that African American girls from preschool to high school spent much more time talking than in play activity. As girls mature, the mode of talk looks more and more like adult conversation.

The centrality of conversation for establishing intimacy and cementing relationships appears in many of the studies on women's friendship. The working-class and middle-class women who were interviewed by Walker (1994) said that they bonded with women friends through talk, support, and sharing of feelings. These women were of varied ethnic backgrounds and represented ages ranging from the 20s through the 40s. A sample of middle- and upper-middle-class women who were interviewed by Helen Gouldner and Mary Symons Strong (1987) reported that talking was central to friendship, which led these researchers to characterize women friends as "talking companions" (p. 60). Studies of college students demonstrate as well that women see their close friendships with one another as centered in talk and conversation (Caldwell & Peplau, 1982; Johnson & Aries, 1983a).

In sum, talking together, what some have called "really talking" to distinguish it from both superficial talk and monologue (Belenky, Clinchy, Goldberger, & Tarule, 1986), has value in and of itself in the close friendships of women. Talk is action, not a replacement for action. Talk is primary, not secondary. Talk is sought after, not incidental.

Theme 2: Women Friends Cultivate Interpersonal Intimacy Through Dialogue. Through "really talking" and sharing in dialogue, women friends create interpersonal intimacy. Many research studies point to this aspect of women's friendships, although in different ways. Research related to self-disclosure shows that women confide more about their private feelings, thoughts, and problems to their same-sex friends than do men (Aries & Johnson, 1983; Buhrke & Faqua, 1987; Dindia & Allen, 1992; Fox & Auerbach, 1985; Jourard, 1971). Women typically bond with one another by sharing emotions and feelings, which distinguishes close from casual or social friendships (Caldwell & Peplau, 1982; Johnson & Aries, 1983b; Walker, 1994). Indeed, women usually find their deepest emotional relationships with other women rather than with men—a finding contained in the popular "Hite Report" on women's love and sexuality (Hite, 1987) as well as in academic research.

Much of the intimacy developed in women's friendships occurs in the dyadic context. This dyadic foundation can be traced to the preference of adolescent girls for intense one-to-one friendships rather than extensive friendship networks (Savin-Williams, 1980). Even in teen cliques, dyads of intimacy often develop between particular best friends.

There is some evidence that intimacy is less a distinctive aspect of women's friendships under certain conditions. Intimacy may be less important after middle age (Goldman, Cooper, Ahern, & Corsini, 1981), and among the elderly, who are more likely to value what same-sex friends can do to enhance their morale and feelings of psychological well-being (Rook, 1989). One researcher suggests that in long-term friendships, men's intimacy levels resemble women's (Wright, 1988). The overwhelming pattern, however, locates women's closeness in dialogue, which fosters intimacy and reciprocal knowledge of personal identities.

Theme 3: Women's Friendships Serve Therapeutic Functions. In a society where therapists and counselors are part of the lives of many individuals at some time or another (even universities have resident counselors), it is difficult to uncouple "therapy" from the idea of psychological or mental instability or illness. Therapists and counselors, viewed as professionals rather than friends, often assist their clients to modify their behaviors, to feel differently about their circumstances, or to act differently in the face of their circumstances.

The dominant position of feelings in women's lives makes them, compared to men, more vulnerable to the "therapism" movement in the United States, which defined the problems of private life and personal identity as best dealt with by professionals who are uninvolved in one's daily life. Therapism also implies that mental health can be enhanced through interventions, most often provided by those in the mental health industry. Raymond (1986) cautions that therapism—in both professional and friendship contexts—can tyrannize women through the "overvaluation of feelings where women have come to believe that what really counts in their life is their 'psychology'" (p. 155).

Because the therapism movement has created a social need for therapy and broad-scale practices for "going into therapy" and "getting therapy," it is often difficult to unravel what is meant in the scholarly literature about the therapy function in women's close friendships. While therapy from a professional perspective entails some degree of client passivity, asymmetry in the therapist–client relationship, and structured interpersonal boundaries, the therapy function in women's friendship is much less rule-governed because it grows organically from the relationship. When women talk about their best friends, the image of positive, and often reciprocal, therapy often comes through vividly. Elizabeth Aries and I heard women recount how their friends had helped give them self-confidence and fresh perspectives on themselves, or had facilitated the courage to make important life decisions. More recently, Stacey Oliker's (1989) interviews with a diverse group of women confirmed that close women friends provide emotional support and help with problem solving and self-development. Oliker's research and other studies (Goldman et al., 1981; Gouldner & Strong, 1987; Rubin, 1985) verify that the therapeutic function in friendship offers deep emotional and personal assistance and facilitates self-development and self-knowledge. Therapy is a function within friendship, but is not necessarily the focus of the relationship; it is deep because it goes beyond the surface and requires intimate sharing, risk, vulnerability, and mutual caring. Although excessive or one-way therapy can strain a friendship, healthy therapeutic processes in friendship exist when each person gains support over time from the other, with the balance of needs shifting from person to person.

Marriage is one of the most frequently cited subjects of therapeutic dialogue between women friends. Oliker (1989) found that heterosexual, married women viewed their discussions with close friends about marital problems as helping to improve and invigorate their marriage relationships. She called this "collective marriage work" (p. 151). There is, however, conflicting evidence, suggesting that a woman may withdraw from her close friends if her marriage is in jeopardy (Cobb & Jones-Cobb, 1984). Going through a divorce sometimes weakens and changes friendships (Rands, 1988), especially in situations in which those friendships are embedded in couples' relationships. Even when close friends have been helpful during major life transitions such as separation or divorce, the interests and needs of the friendship partners can change dramatically, leading to estrangement.

For women who experience violent abuse by their partner or husband, friendship becomes especially precarious. Because of the stigma of abuse, many women feel ashamed and withdraw or hide from friends—who may want to offer help. Even so, the research available (Allan, 1989) suggests that many abused women do call on friends for support and comfort.

Whether continuous or intermittent, short term or long term, women's friendships provide support, assistance, and the basis for self-discovery and knowledge. In the positive sense of therapy, these relationships often provide a more active and creative approach to problem solving simply because, unlike the therapist–client relationship, they are reciprocal.

Theme 4: Women's Friendships Are Situated in Culture, Class, Life Position, and Affectional Circumstances.   In one sense, this theme points to variability rather than uniformity in women's friendships. In another sense, it localizes broader themes and shows how they evolve differently depending on life circumstances. Complexity within gender gives rise to differences in how women friends connect with one another at different ages, at various life stages, and within a multiplicity of cultural circumstances.

As with so many areas of knowledge, we know the most about white, married, heterosexual, middle-class women because they are more easily accessible to researchers. Thus, caution must be exercised in generalizing from this knowledge to the experiences of a broader diversity of women. As noted in Chapter 6, marriage itself tends to curtail close friendships to some extent because of both the greater demands of living in a marriage relationship and the greater domestic demands on women relative to men in marriage relationships (Johnson & Aries, 1983b). Time, especially leisure time, becomes an increasingly scarce resource in the context of marriage. Parenting young children · also places pressure on the formation and maintenance of close friendships (Oliker, 1989). From infant to toddler to teen, children absorb enormous amounts of time; moreover, responsibility for children continues to fall disproportionately on mothers; many men still participate minimally in child rearing, and many women are single parents. Yet intimate friendships between women are sustained in the contexts of marriage and parenthood, albeit in different ways at different points in the life cycle.

Separation and divorce are especially disruptive of friendship, with divorced women often experiencing a reduction in close friendships (Acock & Hurlbert, 1990; Gerstel, 1988). Divorce is a major transition that often involves a change in life direction, added economic and personal burdens, and—if children are present—reduced discretionary time and flexibility.

Intimate lesbian friendships (as distinguished from lesbian partners) differ from friendships of heterosexual women in two important respects. First, because deep friendship bonds tend to occur between lesbian partners, these bonds will often be maintained with former partners (Hite, 1987; Wood, 1994). Second, lesbians who do not closet their romantic relationships usually develop close friendship groups because of the desire to situate lifestyle issues in a larger network of social relationships.

The relatedness of social class to friendship patterns has also received attention, with several patterns emerging from the research. First, working-class women and those with limited economic resources are more likely to embed friendship in kinship relationships (Johnson & Aries, 1983a, 1983b; Komarovsky, 1967; O'Connor, 1992; Oliker, 1989). Sisters, cousins, aunts, nieces, mothers, and daughters in such circumstances are likely to identify female kin as close friends. Here, friendship is fused with the mutual assistance and entailment necessary for daily living. The close friendships of working-class women and those with limited income also are more geographically local than those of middle-class women (O'Connor, 1992), who have greater latitude to develop and sustain friendships across neighborhoods or expansive geographical distances. The critical localizing forces are relative scarcity of time (for example, separate leisure time for scheduling activities and time together) and money (to spend on transportation, long-distance phone calls, and so on). These research studies demonstrate concretely why caution is called for in generalizing from middle-class women's friendship patterns to those of women in other circumstances.

We have already seen that age has an impact on the nature of friendship ties among women. Adolescence, the teen years, and early adulthood tend to be times of considerable intimacy between best friends. This arises in large part from the orientation in mainstream U.S. culture toward personal identity formation and self-knowledge, and the accompanying struggle for self-definition. In contrast, middle age shows a leveling off of intimate exchange (Goldman et al., 1981), while elderly women often experience extreme isolation (O'Connor, 1992).

Finally, some preliminary conclusions can be drawn about the ways in which substantial professional or career responsibility affects women's close friendships. Gouldner and Strong (1987) conducted one of the few studies available that addresses friendship in the lives of working women. In their interviews with middle- and upper-middle-class women, they found that women in executive positions tend to be lonely. These women hesitate to form friendships in the workplace and have little time to develop and sustain friendships off the job. The researchers also described "the new breed" of professionals and middle managers in their 30s and 40s who place their friendships with women "at the core of their lives" (p. 156). This new breed develops networks of women friends with whom they remain connected as they move through their careers.

Unfortunately, research studies on women's friendships have seldom emphasized race and ethnicity. Yet anecdotal evidence suggests that ethnicity and race influence the content and functions of friendships in specific ways. For example, African American women call on their friendships with one another to deal with the constancy of racism in their lives and the lives of their families. In multicultural societies such as the United States, cultural groups who speak languages other than English also enact friendship in distinctive ways. My own community has a high concentration of Brazilian immigrants, many of whom work in low-paying, labor-intensive jobs. The friendships of the Brazilian women in this community cluster among kin and other Brazilians. They are contextualized by Brazilian cultural patterns as enmeshed with the local dynamics of a close-knit Brazilian-immigrant community, using Portuguese as the primary language for communication with one another, living in extended family situations, and negotiating the necessities of daily living.

Although most close relationships follow the adages that "likes attract" and "birds of a feather flock together," friendships across substantial differences do occur. Unfortunately, little is known about how friendships bridge the divides of cultural differences, especially race. One notable exception is the recent work of Mary McCullough (1992) who interviewed nine pairs of black and white women friends ranging in age from 16 to 80. She found these cross-race friends to be outside of both the black and white mainstream (for example, some came to the friendships because of strong religious commitments, some because they embrace feminism and lesbianism). The dynamics of these friendships featured dealing with both white guilt and black shame as well as negotiating their different communication styles. Another study (Lamphere, 1985) explores the ways in which women try to bridge their ethnic and racial gaps at work, including friendships. The particular difficulties in achieving closeness across race are also explored by Marsha Houston (1994), who writes from the perspective of an African American woman about the ways in which white women's communication often precludes authentic talk with black women (see Chapter 3).

Theme 5: Women's Friendships Are the Site for Both Conservation and Resistance of Gendered Social Structures and Processes.   Because friendships are historically, socially, and culturally contextualized, their functions and meanings bear an ideology. Getting to the core of ideology in female friendship has been particularly problematic because of the privatized nature of women's connections. With the rise in attention to female friendship came a sense of celebration that did not invite ideological analysis. Yet, there is a clear ideological character to women's friendships. Women's friendships carry political content, and they shape political consciousness in ways that both support and contest gendered social structures.

There is ample evidence that women's close friendships sometimes support prevailing gender ideologies by managing and privatizing the problems of women. The therapeutic function of friendship itself often focuses on living within conventional romantic or marriage relationships that are heavily gendered, as pointed out in Chapter 9. The feelings of rejection among teenage women when their best friends' romantic involvements relegate the friendship to second place likewise reflect a prevailing gender ideology favoring romantic, heterosexual pairing that subordinates and displaces women's closeness with one another. Oliker's (1989) discussion of how women's friendships establish "collective marriage work," in which the discussion of marital problems helps to improve and reinvigorate marriage, fits this conventional ideology as well.

Conservative social arrangements that separate people by race and class reflect another ideological facet underlying friendship. Strong forces toward friendships among people who are alike (McCullough, 1992) perpetuate prevailing ideologies of racial separation (if asked to name your best friends, few of you will identify people of another race). Social class identity likewise draws women together, which maintains class position (Jerrome, 1984; McCullough, 1992).

Women's friendship as supportive of prevailing gender ideologies can be a site for working through problems that arise in a relatively conventional gendered world. The private locales of conversation coupled with a dyadic focus keep the expression of gender-personal problems from public view. If we look at the constellation of gender–race–class, we see that power and privilege are replicated in friendship: Classes and races stay together, and women defuse their problems in living as women through private talk and dialogue with close women friends. This keeps much gender tension away from men and out of the public domain; rather, it is coped with privately by women friends. O'Connor (1992), in assessing a broad range of literature, concludes that women's friendships often "consolidate middle class life style, values, and privilege" (p. 187).

Women's close friendships, however, do offer sites for resistance to gendered social structures and processes that confine and constrain both women and men. Through friendship, women can find empowering self-definitions and strength of identity in the face of debilitating or problematic social definitions. Louise Bernikow (1980) incisively describes the role of women's friendship across cultures in balancing female role subordination: "Women friends help each other to remain perpendicular in the face of cultures that attempt to knock them over with the hurricane forces of ideology about what a woman should be or...denying the validity of their experience, denigrating their frame of reference, reinforcing female masochism, self-doubt, passivity, and suicide" (p. 144). In other words, female friendship often resists gender oppression and narrow definitions of womanhood.

Raymond's (1986) view of "thoughtfully passionate friendship" carries this idea further by suggesting that such friendships "help women become their own person" (p. 225), but do not lead them to sentimental or romantic subordination of the self to the friend. She views female friendship as having the power to facilitate authentic selves engaged in a life of worldly integrity. Raymond's vision for friends fits with the notion of resistance because it rejects the idea that friendship is little more than a safe place for coping with gender subordination. Her vision also rejects personal subordination of one friend to another through adoration. In her view, women friends—either as lovers or as nonlovers—can envision new worlds through the integrity of selves and the exchange of caring concern.

While Raymond's is a philosophical analysis of women's friendship, her vision finds evidence in several empirical studies. The "new breed" of connections among women friends found by Gouldner and Strong (1987) suggests "thoughtfully passionate" attachments. A similar image is evoked from Oliker's (1989) description of her interviewees as speaking of an "ethic of personal liberty" through which women friends respect one another's integrity. Consistent in all of these is the power of female friendship to create, affirm, or sustain moral orders that are held to be authentically important by women and not simply imposed on them through gendered social structures and processes. There is a fine line between that which conserves gender structures and that which resists, but friendships between women can do either or both.

TOWARD THE FUTURE

The last two decades have been important in elevating female friendship from the realm of triviality to the status of significance. This occurred largely because of the greater attention being paid to the lives of women in general, but also as a result of more holistic ideas about what constitutes a human life. Much of the work (my own included) on women's friendship bonds has affirmed their positive functions and validated their importance. This process of claiming the significance of women's bonds has at times been overly romantic and embedded in a particular cultural context.

To prevent an overly romantic view, thoughts about the future of female friendship must be seasoned with its harsher realities and challenges. Because of cultural, economic, and life-stage circumstances, many of the joys of friendship are not equally available to all women. As scholarship broadened, we learned that privilege favors friendship just as it favors the other finer things in life. Intimate friendship and "thoughtfully passionate" friendship evolve through genuine dialogue. All friendships have costs as well as benefits (Hayes, 1985; Rubin, 1985), but dialogue demands a special commitment of time as well as emotional and mental energy. The cultural complexity of society, women's increasing presence in leadership, managerial, and executive positions, plus the greater participation of women in public life all constrain the ways in which women relate to one another. The ideals of intimate dialogue and "thoughtfully passionate" friendship may in some ways be tied to the precise conditions that have kept women subordinate: domestic and emotional orientations, and privatized and personalized relationships.

The needs, demands, complications, challenges, and complexities of modern life present many opportunities, but they also threaten human connections. Cultural multiplicity, rapid change, economic hardship and uncertainty, the staccato tempo of technological advances, rampant consumerism, and familial disruption all tend to separate people from one another, creating the potential for alienation and isolation. Friendship—not as an optional, voluntary liaison but as a fundamental human relationship—offers a humane alternative to alienation. The nature and functions of women's friendship in particular offer a site for reciprocal caregiving, self-development, and assertion—a site for the kind of thoughtful engagement necessary to center ourselves in relation to other people and other worlds.

QUESTIONS FOR REFLECTION AND DISCUSSION

1. How do you distinguish *close* from *casual* friends?
2. Reflect on the idea that "likes attract." Are your closest friends similar to you in age, race, and social class? If so, why and how did this happen? If not, have there been any obstacles to the friendship?

3. How do you spend time with your closest same-sex friends?

    a. If you are a woman, do you think these closest friendships are centered in talk and conversation? Do you share intimate personal experiences and information?

    b. If you are a man, do you and your closest friends spend most of your time in joint activities or in conversation? If you do not get together to "just talk," why do you think this is so?

4. Reflect on the friendships of your mother, aunts, or grandmothers and ask yourself how they are similar to or differ from the themes described in this chapter.

5. Do you have any close friends of the opposite sex? If you do not, what precludes these friendships? If you do, what is the foundation for the friendship(s)?

6. Ask two men and two women in your age group the following questions, and compare the answers:

    a. Who is your closest friend?

    b. How do you spend time when with this friend?

    c. What about this friendship is most important to you?

REFERENCES

Acock, A. C., & Hurlbert, J. S. (1990). Social network analysis: A structural perspective for family studies. *Journal of Social and Personal Relationships, 7,* 245–264.

Allan, G. A. (1989). *Friendship: Developing a sociological perspective.* Boulder, CO: Westview Press.

Aries, E. J., & Johnson, F. L. (1983). Close friendship in adulthood: Conversational content between same-sex close friends. *Sex Roles, 9,* 1183–1196.

Belenky, M. F., Clinchy, B. M., Goldberger, N. R., & Tarule, J. M. (1986). *Women's ways of knowing: The development of self, voice, and mind.* New York: Basic Books.

Bell, R. R. (1981). *Worlds of friendship.* Beverly Hills: Sage.

Bernikow, L. (1980). *Among women.* New York: Crown.

Buhrke, R. A., & Faqua, D. R. (1987). Sex differences in same- and cross-sex supportive relationships. *Sex Roles, 17,* 339–352.

Caldwell, M. A., & Peplau, L. A. (1982). Sex differences in same-sex friendship. *Sex Roles, 8,* 721–732.

Cobb, S., & Jones-Cobb, J. M. (1984). Social support, support groups and marital relationships. In S. Duck (Ed.), Personal relationships: Vol. 5. Repairing personal relationships (pp. 47–66). London: Academic Press.

Cott, N. (1977). *The bonds of womanhood: "Woman's sphere" in New England, 1780–1835.* New Haven: Yale University Press.

Dindia K., & Allen, M. (1992). Sex differences in self-disclosure: A meta-analysis. *Psychological Bulletin, 112,* 106–124.

Faderman, L. (1981). *Surpassing the love of men: Romantic friendship between women from the Renaissance to the present.* New York: William Morrow.

Fox, M., & Auerbach, D. (1985). Age and gender dimensions of friendship. *Psychology of Women Quarterly, 9,* 489–501.

Gerstel, N. (1988). Divorce and kin ties: The importance of gender. *Journal of Marriage and the Family, 50,* 209–219.

Goldman, J. A., Cooper, P. E., Ahern, K., & Corsini, D. (1981). Continuities and discontinuities in the friendship descriptions of women at six stages in the life cycle. *Genetic Psychology Monographs, 103,* 153–167.

Goodwin, M. H. (1990). *He-said-she-said: Talk as social organization among black children.* Bloomington: Indiana University Press.

Gouldner, H., & Strong, M. S. (1987). *Speaking of friendship: Middle class women and their friends.* New York: Greenwood.

Hayes, R. B. (1985). A longitudinal study of friendship development. *Journal of Personality and Social Psychology, 48,* 909–924.

Hite, S. (1987). *Women and love: A cultural revolution in progress.* New York: Knopf.

Houston, M. (1994). When black women talk with white women: Why dialogues are difficult. In A. Gonzales, M. Houston, & V. Chen (Eds.), *Our voices: Essays in culture, ethnicity, and communication.* Los Angeles: Roxbury.

Jerrome, D. (1984). Good company: The sociological implications of friendship. *Sociological Review, 32,* 606–715.

Johnson, F. L., & Aries, E. J. (1983a). Conversational patterns among same-sex pairs of late-adolescent close friends. *Journal of Genetic Psychology, 142,* 225–238.

Johnson, F. L., & Aries, E. J. (1983b). The talk of women friends. *Women's Studies International Forum, 6,* 353–361.

Jourard, S. (1971). *Disclosure: An experimental analysis of the transparent self.* New York: John Wiley.

Komarovsky, M. (1967). *Blue collar marriage.* New York: Random House.

Lamphere, L. (1985). Bringing the family to work: Women's culture on the shop floor. *Feminist Studies, 11,* 518–540.

McCullough, M. (1992). *Black and white women's friendships: Claiming the margins.* Unpublished doctoral dissertation, Temple University, Philadelphia, PA.

O'Connor, P. (1992). *Friendships between women: A critical review.* New York: Guilford Press.

Oliker, S. J. (1989). *Best friends and marriage: Exchange among women.* Berkeley: University of California Press.

Rands, M. (1988). Changes in social networks following marital separation and divorce. In R. M. Milardo (Ed.), *Families and social networks* (pp. 127–146). Beverly Hills: Sage.

Raymond, J. G. (1986). *A passion for friends: Toward a philosophy of female affection.* Boston: Beacon Press.

Rook, K. S. (1989). Strains in older adults' friendships. In R. G. Adams & R. Blieszner (Eds.), *Older adult friendships: Structure and process* (pp. 166–194). Newbury Park, CA: Sage.

Rubin, L. (1985). *Just friends: The role of friendship in our lives.* New York: Harper & Row.

Savin-Williams, R. (1980). Social interactions of adolescent females in natural groups. In H. C. Foot, A. J. Chapman, & J. R. Smith (Eds.), *Friendship and social relations in children* (pp. 343–364). New York: John Wiley.

Smith-Rosenberg, C. (1975). The female world of love and ritual: Relations between women in nineteenth-century America. *Signs, 1,* 1–29.

Smith-Rosenberg, C. (1985). *Disorderly conduct: Visions of gender in victorian America.* New York: Knopf.

Tannen, D. (1990). Gender differences in topical coherence: Creating involvement in best friends' talk. *Discourse Processes, 13,* 73–90.

Walker, K. (1994). Men, women, and friendship: What they say, what they do. *Gender and Society, 8,* 246–265.

Wood, J. T. (1994). *Gendered lives: Communication, gender, and culture.* Belmont, CA: Wadsworth.

Wood, J. T., & Inman, C. C. (1993). In a different mode: Masculine styles of communicating closeness. *Journal of Applied Communication Research, 21,* 279–295.

Wright, P. H. (1988). Interpreting research on gender differences in friendship: A case for moderation and a plea for caution. *Journal of Social and Personal Relationships, 5,* 367–373.

FRIENDSHIPS AMONG MEN: CLOSENESS IN THE DOING

CHRIS INMAN

When morning broke and the first rays of the sun's light filtered in through the blinds of the bedroom in the house Jonathon and Tom shared, a sigh and a muffled groan were sufficient for each to know that their plan to rise at 7 A.M. was overly ambitious. Although they were eager to share time hunting, their bodies needed a respite after a hard week of studying. This day, even if it began later than planned, was rich with the promise of grace, beauty, and communion offered infrequently, but waiting for them to enjoy.

Tom and Jonathon are lifelong friends. One of Tom's earliest memories is of eating breakfast with Jonathon and his father at "Your House," a restaurant in their hometown that specialized in home cooking and that characteristically smelled like a mixture of strong coffee and "Old Spice." Jonathon and Tom are such a part of each other's life that they feel almost like family—in fact, they consider themselves even closer than family.

As Jonathon quickly showered, forgoing his morning shave for a more rugged, scruffy look, Tom started a pot of coffee and stumbled over Jonathon's dog, Tar, whose enthusiasm revealed she instinctively knew the events the day held. In a flurry of shiny, black hair, a wet, pink tongue, and a lethal tail, Tar bounded down the walk to retrieve the morning paper. The cold, dark waters and gray forbidding skies would put her to a truer test, but dove were in season, and Jonathon had trained her to retrieve them as easily as waterfowl, not to mention newspapers and an occasional athletic sock.

If you asked Jonathon, he would be hard pressed to choose between Tom and Tar as his best friend. Tom had helped him pick out Tar, a Christmas present from Tom's family to Jonathon's 8 years earlier. Since that time, Tar has been a constant in Jonathon's life, greeting him enthusiastically each morning and waiting for him every afternoon as school ended. When Jonathon went off to college his first year, he was unable to take Tar with him; pets were not allowed in dormitories on campus. Jonathon spent his first week trying to figure out how to live on his own and missing the comforts of home; then his mother called to say that Tar still sat in a chair in the dining room each afternoon to wait for his return from school. When Jonathon heard that, tears welled up in his eyes and tried to sneak down his cheeks, an impulse he resisted. Tom walked into the room just as Jonathon was hanging up the phone. Although each had seen the other upset over the years, these moments of frustration, anger, and sadness were not responses either welcomed in the other.

Despite the awkwardness of the moment, Tom tossed his books on his bed and sat down next to Jonathon on the floor. He put his arm around Jonathon's shoulder and fumbled for something to say, hoping that some flash of brilliance would rush over him and that he would be able to deliver just the right words. Tom finally decided on "I know and I don't know. And it's all right for us to try to figure it out together." The utterance wasn't particularly brilliant, but it communicated all that needed to be said in that moment. Those words drew them together and cemented their bond over the years and through many hurdles. The sentences carry more weight than either can explain, but again and again those words seem to do the trick when life becomes uncomfortably challenging or when one wants the other to know how deeply he cares. Much of the time a sincere look and a slight smile communicate the same sentiment and words aren't even necessary.

On the afternoon of the hunt, Tom and Jonathon eased the Jeep out of the driveway into the street in front of their house. It was almost impossible to see into the Jeep, as guns, vests, and collapsible stools blocked all light from reaching the inside of the truck. Packed into the front seats were Tom, Jonathon, and Tar, each a bit cramped and uncomfortable. Tom leaned his head out of the window, carefully playing the tension between the accelerator and the clutch while balancing a cup of coffee on his thigh and gracefully steering the Jeep into the open road. This was a moment neither would forget. As the distance increased between the Jeep and the crowds flocking toward town for the university's football game, Jonathon slid a tape into the cassette player. No words were necessary; in fact, words probably would have spoiled the moment. It was enough for Tom and Jonathon just to be together with some great music, a dog, and a host of memories.

FRIENDSHIP

The friendship Jonathon and Tom share is unique to these two men, yet it also displays marked similarities to close friendships of many men. In the pages that follow, we will explore the significance of friendship between men as well as some of the qualities that often characterize it. Interwoven throughout the discussion are examples drawn from the story of Jonathon and Tom's relationship and also from the experiences of five pairs of men who participated in a recent study on close male friendship.

What may surprise you in our discussion is that although men and women differ in how they express and create close friendships, we are similar in what we seek and value in friends. We all want close, meaningful connections with others with whom we share interests, values, or goals. Too often we overlook how much we share in our desires for close connections with friends. In 1990, Maya Angelou wrote:

> I note the obvious differences
> Between each sort and type
> But we are more alike, my friends,
> Than we are unalike.
> We are more alike, my friends,
> Than we are unalike (p. 5).

When you compare this chapter with Chapter 5 on friendships between women, you will find that men and women are more alike than they are unalike.

Although our commonalities are substantial, we also differ in how we form and sustain friendships. We use the word *friendship* as if it means one specific thing, yet actually friendships vary from person to person. Also, the variations in patterns of friendship reflect generalizable differences among groups of people. For instance, the meanings and roles of friendship in the United States differ from those in Taiwan; likewise, friendship patterns among members of the working class differ from those of the upper socioeconomic classes. In addition to issues of culture and class that affect expectations and experiences of individuals, friendship patterns differ systematically for women and men. Each sex seems to have generally preferred ways of expressing and experiencing close friendship. This chapter focuses on men's friendships—on what friendship means to men and how they create and express closeness in their relationships. These relationships represent strong and significant ways that men connect with other men.

WHAT IS MALE FRIENDSHIP?

Obviously close male friendship involves individuals who are biologically male. Little else about these relationships may be apparent, however. Few studies have examined friendships in terms of what they *mean* to men (for exceptions, see Inman, 1993; Swain, 1989). Indeed, some researchers paint a bleak picture of male friendship, asserting that the relationships are less intimate, less personal, and less rewarding than friendships between women (for example, Aukett, Ritchie, & Mill, 1988; Reisman, 1990; Williams, 1985).

For many men, close male friends provide a comfortable companionship that seems different from other relationships in their lives, both romantic and nonromantic. These male friendships often are built around activities enjoyed together, such as playing basketball and video games. Additionally, the importance of the friendships tends to be assumed, not discussed. Deeply personal self-disclosive conversation and intimate physical contact usually are not reported as dimensions of male friendships (Williams, 1985). Homophobia is one reason some men may be less physically and emotionally expressive with each other; friends fear closeness may be misinterpreted as a sign of sexual involvement.

In studies that lament the lack of close connections between men, researchers tend to define closeness very narrowly: Verbal sharing of deeply personal feelings, or self-disclosure, epitomizes closeness. Much of the work that denigrates men's friendships measures closeness by standards that do not recognize fully the many ways individuals enjoy and enact close relationships (Cancian, 1986; Swain, 1989; Wood & Inman, 1993). Rather than arguing over the occurrence of closeness in male friendship, this chapter assumes that men can and do have close friends. Further, the experiences of male friends may enlarge our understandings of the many different ways that we can be close to others in our lives, thus giving us more choices for ways to conduct our relationships.

Because I have been fortunate to enjoy a number of close male friendships, I have grown increasingly uncomfortable with descriptions of men's friendships as less intimate than those of women. Descriptions of men's friendships as impoverished do not fit with my own experiences. My male friends are important to me, and I value those relationships highly. So, too, do other men. A recent article in the *Wall Street Journal* (Sharpe, 1994) confirmed this conclusion. The article describes an entrepreneur in Atlanta, Mike Correll, who helps busy executive men find similar men for friendship. Presumably, the men using this service do not have sufficient time or opportunity to find male friends, yet each man wants male friends enough to pay up to $1,200 for Correll's services. This illustrates the importance of male friendships to men. Encouraged by conversations with men about our relationships, I set out to study closeness as it occurs in men's friendships. The story at the beginning of this chapter and other examples in the following pages challenge traditional conceptions of deficits in men's styles of relating to each other.

To study men's friendships, I interviewed five pairs of close male friends (Inman, 1993). By interviewing pairs of male friends, I could consider the experiences of both members of each pair, allowing insight into two perspectives on the same relationship. The 10 men interviewed were all either undergraduate students or recent graduates, and each friendship pair lived in the same city, thus giving the men frequent opportunities to interact. I discussed my findings with participants in the study to ensure that my perceptions fairly represented their experiences.

Although the experiences shared by men in this study may not be representative of all men's friendships, these self-defined "close" male friends described their relationships with the patterns discussed below. Thus the experiences shared here are the perceptions of a small sample of male friends of the closeness they have created and enacted in their relationships. Several of the themes discussed are similar to ones reported by female friends, illustrating that similarities exist between same-sex friendships that frequently are overlooked.

Let me briefly introduce the 10 men whose experiences supplement the story of Jonathon and Tom that opens this chapter. Gray and Nate are both varsity athletes at the university they attend. They met when they were in the seventh grade in New Jersey and have played baseball together on the same team ever since. The second pair, Marcus and Damian, are African American varsity athletes who play football. Marcus and Damian have known each other since Marcus started playing on the team his first year at college, 3 years prior to my study. Damian is one year older than Marcus. Mitch and Timothy, the third pair, live together in the same dormitory suite and have known each other for 3 years. The fourth pair, Mack and Jacob, met in the third grade and have lived in the same medium-sized southern town for most of their lives. They currently live together in a house off campus. Although they met at a young age, they did not consider themselves "close" until their sophomore year in high school. The final pair, Dan and Witt, are the only openly gay men in the study, though they have never been sexually involved with each other. Dan and Witt met in their college fraternity and together worked through the challenges of accepting their homosexuality, an experience that strengthened their bond.

From the interviews with these men, I discovered eight themes of closeness that male friends experience. Four themes—*continuity, perceived support and dependability, shared understandings*, and *perceived compatibility*—echo observations made elsewhere about men's relationships (Cancian, 1986; Sherrod, 1989; Swain, 1989; Wood & Inman, 1993). Four other themes represent dimensions of men's relationships that have not been acknowledged previously. These four themes, *self-revelation and self-discovery, having fun together, intermingled lives*, and *assumed significance*, build on other relationship research (Blumstein & Kollock, 1989; Duck, 1991; Swain, 1989; Winstead, 1986) but yield new insights into understandings of men's experiences. Each of these dimensions of closeness in male friendship is discussed in the pages that follow.

Finally, it is important again to note that many women report similar dimensions to these eight themes in their relationships, although variation often occurs in the ways similar experiences are described and the significance men and women attach to these ways of relating. As you read the descriptions and stories that accompany these themes, consider how well they characterize your relationships. I hope you will see consistencies between your relationships and the dimensions that were reported by the men in my study whether you are male or female. Even if you do not perceive similarities, I hope you will consider a range of ways to experience and appreciate your friends as illustrated in the following pages.

Continuity

One consistency reported across men's friendships involves a historical perspective. Continuity as a theme in men's friendship includes a shared past and an envisioned future. Tom and Jonathon have known each other since they were children. In fact, Tom remembers eating breakfast with Jonathon and his father at a local restaurant when they were only 3 years old. Other friends, such as Damian and Marcus, met in college and have built a relationship over several years. Whether the relationship began in college or during childhood, the history that these men share is important to their closeness. The shared past encourages a connection that leads these friends to envision a future where they will continue to be a part of each other's lives.

Dan described his relationship with Witt as providing a "living scrapbook" and added "it's nice to know someone who cares and who will remember things." In Dan and Witt's relationship, having been "outed" in their fraternity served to bring them closer together. As Dan said,

> Foxhole buddies who go through war together become close. Witt and I banded together in a way, sort of back to back, to defend ourselves against the world. And I think that created a lasting bond.

Other experiences discussed by friends are less dramatic than being "outed," and yet past events draw the friends together. Nate and Gray have played baseball together for 8 years, causing Nate to remark, "I guess being on the same team has a lot to do with it. You go through a lot on the field together."

The theme of continuity involves more than a shared history of events and experiences. The sense of continuity discussed by men in my study includes not only a past, but also a sense that the relationship will continue to be significant in the future. Neither Tom nor Jonathon can remember a time he did not know the other. Further, neither one can imagine a time when the other will not play a significant role in his life. Marcus offered this observation: "I don't really have time to make many friends, and Damian is somebody I feel I can trust. We'll probably be friends for the rest of our lives." For these men, friendship involves a shared past and anticipation of a continued connection over the years ahead.

In another study, Swain (1989) reported that a shared history makes friendships comfortable, providing a commonality that makes experiences more meaningful. The events endured and experienced in the past give men a sense that their relationship exists in a time frame that includes the past, the present, and the future. Dan reflected, "Witt provides a certain continuity that includes the past and the future." Each of the men interviewed shared a similar sense that his relationship will continue to be important.

Perceived Support and Dependability

The continuity that male friends experience leads them to believe they can rely on their friends for support and for a response to personal needs. Swain (1989, p. 80) discussed a similar notion as "reciprocity of assistance," which he suggested demonstrates interest and develops a balanced rather than a one-sided relationship. Participants considered here reported that they can count on their friend in a moment of crisis, for a personal favor, or for moral support when the need arises.

Gray observed that Nate is "someone who I know is always there for me—I know I can rely on him." Jacob expressed a similar conviction: "Basically, times when I really, really need somebody, Mack's always there for me." The men do not seem to question the strength of the relationship but rather feel certain that it can be counted on when needed. The support given by friends includes physical and emotional support. For instance, Witt recalled that when he and Dan were "outed," they provided "total moral support for each other, a protectiveness of each other, both mentally and physically."

The history the friends shared and the relationships developed allow special insight into ways men can meet each other's, needs. Marcus offered that when he had a disagreement with his family that distressed him, Damian started talking about a similar experience, making him feel better and also displaying an understanding of what Marcus needed at that moment. In Jonathon and Tom's friendship, Tom walked into their room while Jonathon was on the phone with his mother in a moment of personal crisis. Jonathon was depressed and scared, and he was upset. Tom decided how to respond to Jonathon in that moment, although he did not understand the reasons for the strong emotions displayed. In that instance, a few heartfelt words and a supportive embrace helped Jonathon through the trauma.

Male friends emphasize the ability to count on each other in a variety of circumstances. Friends perceive that they can depend on one another and know that support is always present. Marcus explained, "If Damian's there, I won't have to worry about a thing." Further, support is not taken for granted; it is an explicitly appreciated dimension of closeness. These men meet each other's needs; equally important, they say they know they can depend on each other to provide support.

Shared Understandings

For Tom and Jonathon, a set of words shared at one point in the relationship took on a special meaning in their friendship. Undoubtedly, the message "I know and I don't know, and it's all right for us to try to figure it out together" was what Jonathon needed to hear. But the expression took on a larger meaning for the friends, as it became part of their friendship's unique "dictionary." Swain (1989) referred to a shared "lingo" that gives close friendships a "covert" or hidden intimacy. Less important than the actual words are the meanings that they have for friends. Understandings range from jokes to more subtle exchanges that reveal a recognition and awareness of patterns in friends' interactions. These patterns often serve as nonverbal expressions of affection between partners, just as the example from Tom and Jonathon's friendship indicates. The words gain a much larger significance in their relationship and continue to be used to show support and affection.

Marcus and Damian, the varsity football players, periodically exchange secret fraternity signals that solidify their friendship. Confirming the importance of such gestures, Witt remarked, "Dan and I have our own nonverbal communication. We can be at a party, and with a nod of the head and a look of the eye, he'll know exactly what I'm saying and about whom." Other examples of shared understandings include verbal phrases. Dan allowed that "when he [Witt] does something really great, I tell him I hate him, which is like the ultimate compliment." To an observer outside a relationship, secret fraternity signals or the phrase "I hate you" might appear obscure or even rude. But these phrases and gestures carry meaning for the friends that reflect and solidify their connection.

In men's friendships, shared understandings are an important dimension of closeness. Other research noted that men are less likely than women to express caring verbally (Winstead, 1986). Thus, phrases, jokes, and gestures that carry subtle meanings of acceptance and understanding are significant expressions of affection. Not only do these expressions reveal depth in friendships, but they also cement a special bond between men.

Perceived Compatibility

The men I interviewed expressed an awareness of a "good fit" between individuals that attracts friends to each other and makes them compatible. Sometimes the compatibility results from a good deal of similarity, while at other times differences between men create complementarity. Interestingly, 8 of the 10 male friends have lived as roommates or suitemates. Only Marcus and Damian have not lived together for an extended period of time. Therefore, compatibility perceived between male friends seems to extend beyond an initial attraction into the ability, and perhaps desire, to live together.

In some cases, sports bring friends together. Damian and Marcus play football together, and Nate and Gray have played baseball on the same team for years. Video games, a passion for music, the movie *Star*

Wars, and a shared status as only children unite Mitch and Timothy. For Tom and Jonathon, hobbies like hunting and their parents' friendships supported their relationship. In other instances, friends indicated seeing things in another's life that they wished for in their own. Mack found Jacob's secure, well-established family attractive, since his family is less stable.

One aspect of compatibility involves friends' shared "maleness" (Swain, 1989). Mack offered, "It's the whole male thing; it's completely comfortable because he's male." He continued, "There are some things that you can tell a man that you can't tell a woman." The perceived compatibility creates a comfort that allows men to discuss almost anything and also to be more "natural" with each other. Timothy reported that he thinks Mitch is "really free and his true self with me. He doesn't hesitate one bit around me." Mitch boasted that he and Timothy can "talk to each other about anything and everything." Other participants echo these sentiments, reporting an ability to let barriers down. As Mack allowed, with Jacob "there's no shield up." Jacob confirmed that Mack creates "an environment for the two of us in which I am comfortable letting down barriers and sharing what I'm thinking and feeling, just about at all times." The compatibility in these relationships promoted a close connection between the friends.

Self-Revelation and Self-Discovery

Despite substantial research that questions men's ability and/or willingness to self-disclose (Winstead, 1986), the men I interviewed were neither unwilling nor unlikely to share personal information. In fact, 8 of the 10 participants in the study acknowledged disclosing intimate information about themselves with their male friend. The two participants whose interviews did not explicitly describe personal self-disclosure still displayed evidence of self-disclosure within the friendship. For example, although Nate's interview did not contain accounts of self-revelation, Nate's friend, Gray, shared a story of how Nate's disclosure of personal information brought the two closer together.

Not only did the friends share personal information with each other, but they also revealed that such disclosures created a vulnerability that required trust. Witt explained that sharing personal information creates a special intimacy: "It's sharing dreams, sharing anger, sharing ideas—things you might not tell other people because you'd be embarrassed if they knew what you were thinking or feeling." Witt went on to describe "coming out of the closet" as a "huge bonding thing" that required trust. These men do not take advantage of the insights gained from friends' openness. As Mack acknowledged, Jacob knows a lot of my insecurities, which leaves me wide open, but he doesn't take advantage."

The openness and trust described by these men establishes an environment that supports individual growth. Mack recalled a meaningful experience where personal feelings were shared: "There was some other-worldly connection. We were both discovering things about ourselves and each other." The openness in these relationships allows these men to feel comfortable exploring possibilities for their lives, enabling a process of self-discovery.

Having Fun Together

One consistency in research on men's friendships involves a focus on activities rather than talk. In fact, a frequently cited generalization describes men's friendships as "instrumental" or "side by side" and women's friendships as "face to face" (Wright & Scanlon, 1991). This emphasis on activities led Swain (1989, p. 77) to recognize a "closeness in the 'doing'"; that is, men feel close to each other by spending time doing things with each other. Each of the friendship pairs in the study reported a variety of activities they do together, including hunting (Tom and Jonathon), cooking dinner (Mack and Jacob), playing basketball (Nate and Gray), roller blading (Witt and Dan), throwing a cookout (Marcus and Damian), or going out to the bars (Timothy and Mitch). The friends emphasized that one of the benefits of an activity is the pleasure that time spent together allows.

Male friends reported enjoying "hanging out," "chillin'," or spending time that is "completely effortless." When questioned about such terms, Mack replied, "Men know what that means; women don't really know what 'hanging out' means." (Although Mack's statement that women don't understand "hanging out" reflects his perceptions, it should not be interpreted as a conclusion confirmed by this research.) Fun is an important result of time spent together, regardless of how the time is spent. Mitch said of his friendship with Timothy, "I guess you would call it a fun relationship. We don't always talk about stuff that's serious." Dan recalled that after seven years of knowing Witt, "I really enjoy his company."

Not only are activities enjoyable in their own right, but they often provide a context for discussions of more serious matters. That is, activities may encourage the type of serious conversation that men's relationships have been critiqued for not including (Williams, 1985). Jacob described his favorite evening of cooking dinner and drinking wine with

Mack as fun because "it's just pleasant to be engaged in an activity that we both thoroughly enjoy." After dinner they would "chill out, maybe watch a really cool movie, maybe read some poetry. An ideal evening would involve a great deal of communication because we enjoy each other's company." In activities there is involvement and fun, and there is also connection in lighthearted and sometimes significant ways.

Intermingled Lives

If we diverge from depictions of masculine autonomy and distance (Chodorow, 1978; Gilligan, 1982), we find that a profound sense of connection runs through close friendships between men. In contrast to stereotypes of the self-sufficient, distant male, the men I interviewed revealed that their lives are intermingled in significant ways. The interdependence (Blumstein & Kollock, 1988) reported includes behavioral, cognitive (for example, language and shared understandings), and emotional levels where friends' lives are woven together.

Nate offered stories of playing basketball with Gray, stating, "When we play, we know each other so well, it's like we don't even have to think about doing things [like making a pass or running a specific play]." Participants reported that their connection enables them to predict behaviors and allows insight into how a friend is feeling. Jacob explained that he and Mack "know each other well enough to know what particular mood the other person is in, or what the other person will do in a given situation." Marcus shared that his insights into Damian's life allow him to "tell when something's bothering him, and he can tell when something's bothering me."

The intermingling of lives creates a strong sense of connection between individuals. Although the level and type of connection experienced by friends varies from relationship to relationship, the friendships discussed include more interdependence than has been associated traditionally with male friendship. Far from being two completely independent individuals, these male friends report deep connections. As Mack stated, "Jacob has become a part of me. If he died, something would be missing forever. He's not a position in my life; he's a person."

Assumed Significance

Unlike women friends, men are more likely to engage each other in activities rather than in conversations about the relationship (Caldwell & Peplau, 1982; Swain, 1989). Rather than perceiving the lack of talk about the relationship as a weakness in the friendships, however, male friends indicate that they assume and understand their relationships are important. The unspoken bond (Rubin, 1985) does not require daily discussion or maintenance. Men know their relationships are significant, and they believe they can count on their friends, even if they do not express those feelings verbally. When I asked Mitch how Timothy knew that he liked him, Mitch responded, "Because we continually do stuff together. I guess he automatically knows that I like him." He went on to say, "Very rarely has there ever been any talk about the actual friendship itself. It's like a gift." Similarly, Dan quipped, "Oh, I think that Witt just knows that I like him." Although male friends seldom explicitly discuss their friendship or their feelings for each other, closeness exists—unspoken but strong.

Another aspect of assumed significance relates to the frequency with which the relationships are maintained. Busy lives often prevent friends from spending as much time together as they would like; even for roommates, schedules do not always permit frequent interaction. Timothy suggested, "I don't think you have to spend a lot of time with somebody to be a close friend; it's just important to stay in touch so that he knows you care." Gray observed that he and Nate "have a lot of background in our relationship, so we don't need to hang out with each other every day." Dan remarked, "I think it's a male thing. Males don't put that much emphasis on constantly making contact." Friends accept that periodically their lives do not allow as much interaction as they might wish; they assume relationships can and will withstand the absences.

CLOSING THOUGHTS

Because this chapter focuses in depth on friendships of a select group of men, it provides a detailed picture of men's friendships as experienced by some, but not all, men. Several of the men introduced in the preceding pages may be similar to you and your friends, and others may be radically different. Despite the diversity of backgrounds and characteristics of participants, these men's words reveal common dimensions of closeness in their relationships. It is hoped that the themes of closeness offered here open up possibilities for you to appreciate aspects of your relationships, whether with friends or family, men or women.

It is easy to focus on what appear to be dramatic differences in men's and women's relationships. Men do tend to have more "active" friendships, talking about and playing sports more frequently. And women do seem to want to talk more in and about their relationships. But it is important to look below the surface of our behaviors to consider what the relationships and their patterns *mean* to us. As experienced by the men introduced here, male friendship provides acceptance, support, and comfortable companionship. Friends meet our basic need for close, meaningful connection with others (Baxter, 1990).

Recent reports on men, women, and friendship assert that more similarities characterize our friendships than differences (Duck & Wright, 1993; Walker, 1994). When asked very general questions about relationships, participants responded in stereotypical ways—men focused on activities and women on conversations. Looking at those same relationships more closely revealed that popular conceptions of friendships were not always accurate. Men shared more feelings and women shared fewer feelings than we typically assume (Walker, 1994). The friendships, further, had more in common than initial responses and popular notions indicate. Although it may simplify matters to characterize our relationships in stereotypical and extreme ways, we probably experience many of the same things in our relationships, though we may not be conscious of the dimensions or we may call them by different names.

Instead of emphasizing ways relationships of men and women are different, better, and worse, perhaps it would be more useful to consider how we meet our common needs in diverse ways. Although it is important to recognize differences among us, it is also crucial that we not overlook basic similarities (Connell, 1985). One fundamental human need we share is connection with others. Our needs for connection may vary and our ways of experiencing meaningful relationships may be diverse, yet we are alike in our desires to form, sustain, and enjoy relationships. We can learn a good deal from each other, not only about diversity of experience, but also about similarity of needs. *"We are more alike, my friends, than we are unalike."*

QUESTIONS FOR REFLECTION AND DISCUSSION

1. Are men less close in their friendships than women because men are less emotionally expressive?
2. Why don't men want to talk about their friendships?
3. Are there differences between "talking about" and "doing" things within friendships with respect to how these behaviors feel to friends? What do activities and conversation provide for friends within their relationships?
4. What do you need within your friendships to feel close to and appreciated by friends? How do you show your friends you care about them?

REFERENCES

Altman, I., & Taylor, D. A. (1973). *Social penetration: The development of interpersonal relationships.* New York: Holt, Rinehart, and Winston.

Angelou, M. (1990). Human family. In *I shall not be moved.* New York: Random House.

Aries, E. J., & Johnson, F. L. (1983). Close friendship in adulthood: Conversational content between same-sex friends. *Sex Roles, 9,* 1183–1196.

Aukett, R., Ritchie, J., & Mill, K. (1988). Gender differences in friendship patterns. *Sex Roles, 19,* 57–66.

Balswick, J. O., & Peek, C. W. (1976). The inexpressive male: A tragedy of American society. In D. S. David & R. Brannon (Eds.), *The forty-nine percent majority: The male sex-role* (pp. 55–57). Reading, MA: Addison-Wesley.

Baxter, L. A. (1990). Dialectical contradictions in relationship development. *Journal of Social and Personal Relationships, 7,* 69–88.

Becker, C. S. (1987). Friendship between women: A phenomenological study of best friends. *Journal of Phenomenological Psychology, 18,* 59–72.

Bell, R. R. (1981). Friendships of women and of men. *Psychology of Women Quarterly, 5,* 402–417.

Blumstein, P., & Kollock, P. (1988). Personal relationships. *Annual Review of Sociology, 14,* 467–490.

Buhrke, R. A., & Fuqua, D. R. (1987). Sex differences in same- and cross-sex supportive relationships. *Sex Roles, 17,* 339–352.

Caldwell, M. A., & Peplau, L. A. (1982). Sex differences in same-sex friendship. *Sex Roles, 8,* 721–732.

Cancian, F. M. (1986). The feminization of love. *Signs, 11,* 692–709.

Cancian, F. M. (1987). *Love in America: Gender and self-development.* Cambridge, UK: Cambridge University Press.

Chodorow, N. (1978). *The reproduction of mothering: Psychoanalysis and the sociology of gender.* Berkeley, CA: University of California Press.

Connell, R. W. (1985). Theorising gender. *Sociology, 19,* 260–272.

Davidson, L. R., & Duberman, L. (1982). Friendship: Communication and interactional patterns in same-sex dyads. *Sex Roles, 8,* 809–822.

Duck, S. W. (1991). *Understanding relationships.* New York: Guilford Press.

Duck, S. W., & Wright, P. (1993). Reexamining gender differences in same-gender friendships: A close look at two kinds of data. *Sex Roles, 28,* 709–727.

Fischer, C. S. (1982). What do we mean by "friend"? An inductive study. *Social Network, 3,* 287–306.

Gilligan, C. (1982). *In a different voice: Psychological theory and women's development.* Cambridge, MA: Harvard University Press.

Inman, C. C. (1993). *Experiences of closeness in male friendship.* Unpublished master's thesis, University of North Carolina, Chapel Hill, NC.

Jones, D. C. (1991). Friendship satisfaction and gender: An examination of sex differences in contributors to friendship satisfaction. *Journal of Social and Personal Relationships, 8,* 167–185.

Maltz, D. N., & Borker, R. (1982). A cultural approach to male–female miscommunication. In J. J. Gumperz (Ed.), *Language and social identity* (pp. 196–216). Cambridge, UK: Cambridge University Press.

Monsour, M. (1992). Meanings of intimacy in cross- and same-sex friendships. *Journal of Social and Personal Relationships, 9,* 277–295.

Register, L. M., & Henley, T. B. (1992). The phenomenology of intimacy. *Journal of Social and Personal Relationships, 9,* 467–481.

Reisman, J. M. (1990). Intimacy in same-sex friendships. *Sex Roles, 23,* 65–82.

Rubin, L. B. (1985). *Just friends: The role of friendship in our lives.* New York: Harper & Row.

Sharpe, A. (1994, May 9). How to find guys to hang around and do stuff with. *The Wall Street Journal,* pp. 1, 6.

Sherrod, D. (1989). The influence of gender on same-sex friendships. In C. Hendrick (Ed.), *Close relationships* (pp. 164–186). Newbury Park, CA: Sage.

Swain, S. (1989). Covert intimacy: Closeness in men's friendships. In B. J. Risman & P. Schwartz (Eds.), *Gender in intimate relationships* (pp. 71–86). Belmont, CA: Wadsworth.

Walker, K. (1994). Men, women, and friendship: What they say, what they do. *Gender and Society, 8,* 246–265.

Weiss, L., & Lowenthal, M. F. (1975). Life-course perspectives on friendship. In M. F. Lowenthal, M. Thurnher, & D. Chiriboga (Eds.), *Four stages of life: A comparative study of women and men facing transitions* (pp. 48–61). San Francisco, CA: Jossey-Bass.

Williams, D. G. (1985). Gender, masculinity–femininity, and emotional intimacy in same-sex friendship. *Sex Roles, 12,* 587–600.

Winstead, B. A. (1986). Sex differences in same-sex friendships. In V. J. Derlega & B. A. Winstead (Eds.), *Friendship and social interaction* (pp. 81–99). New York: Springer-Verlag.

Wood, J. T., & Inman, C. C. (1993). In a different mode: Masculine styles of communicating closeness. *Journal of Applied Communication Research, 21,* 279–295.

Wright, P. H. (1974). The delineation and measurement of some key variables in the study of friendship. *Representative Research in Social Psychology, 5,* 93–96.

Wright, P. H. (1982). Men's friendships, women's friendships and the alleged inferiority of the latter. *Sex Roles, 8,* 1–20.

Wright, P. H. (1988). Interpreting research on gender differences in friendship: A case for moderation and a plea for caution. *Journal of Social and Personal Relationships, 5,* 367–373.

Wright, P. H., & Scanlon, M. B. (1991). Gender role orientations and friendship: Some attenuation, but gender differences abound. *Sex Roles, 24,* 551–566.

CROSSING THE BARRIERS
TO FRIENDSHIPS BETWEEN
MEN AND WOMEN

LEE WEST
JENNIFER ANDERSON
STEVE DUCK

"Men and women can never be friends; the sex thing always gets in the way."

--BILLY CRYSTAL IN *WHEN HARRY MET SALLY.*

In *When Harry Met Sally,* a movie about friendship and love, Billy Crystal's character, "Harry," spends a great deal of time trying to determine the social rules that govern friendship between a man and a woman. Even after several amendments, such as the notion that "potential friends" would have to be either unattractive or else involved with other romantic partners, Harry concludes that basically, "You want to nail them too." Thus he returns to his original conclusion that men and women can never truly be "just friends."

The "Harry Question" usually sparks provocative discussion among people of all ages (Rawlins, 1994). Even researchers are puzzled by it, yet male–female friendship has received insufficient research attention (O'Meara, 1989; Werking, 1994a). When researchers have investigated cross-sex friendships, the primary questions include: Is sexual interest inevitable? How are cross-sex friendships different from romantic relationships? Are cross-sex friendships simply steps on the pathway to romance?

Such questions feed into several broad and important issues concerning the role of gender in relationships, the ways in which relationships embody gender expectations, and the fact that masculinity and femininity are themselves relational concepts. In this chapter, we explore the question of whether men and women can move beyond powerful gender prescriptions and heterosexual romantic scripts to obtain the elusive, but certainly worthwhile, goal of male–female friendship. First, we distinguish friendship from romantic love. Following this, we investigate the intersection between friendship expectations and gender, and examine friendships between men and women across the life-span. We conclude the chapter by looking at the barriers to, and advantages of, friendships between men and women.

As you are reading, we invite you to consider a variety of ideas. Think carefully about your own experiences with friends of the opposite sex. How did the friendship develop? Are there any special difficulties? What part does your gender identity play in your interactions with these friends? How are gender roles performed or reinforced in friendships between women and men? Do you agree with "Harry's" argument that men and women simply can't be "true friends"?

DEFINITIONS OF CROSS-SEX FRIENDSHIPS

Social-emotional support...self-disclosure...trust...jealousy...mutual obligation...loyalty...possessiveness...Do these characteristics describe your best friend or your mate? If you said these qualities describe either a friend or a romantic partner, your response is representative of how most people experience friends and lovers (Davis & Todd, 1982). Friendship has been defined as a "voluntary interdependence between two persons over time, that is intended to facilitate social–emotional goals of the participants, and may involve varying types and degrees of companionship, intimacy, affection, and mutual assistance" (Hays, 1988). Clearly, this definition could also serve for romantic relationships, and there lies a dilemma, since conceptually differentiating "friendship" from "romantic involvement" seems particularly important in the consideration of friendships between women and men.

A Friend Is a Friend Is a Friend?

When asked what a same-sex friend is, both men and women answer that a friend is someone who is supportive, caring, encouraging (Duck & Wright, 1993; Sapadin, 1988), trustworthy, and dependable; who shares intimacies; and who is fun to be with (Sapadin, 1988). If women and men look for the same qualities in a friend, then how, if at all, are friendships between the sexes different from friendships between same-sex friends? Many researchers suggest that although males and females share the same friendship ideal, they participate in friendships differently along gendered lines (O'Meara, 1989; Rubin, 1985). In other words, men and women differ in the way they express intimacy, trust, and acceptance. This suggests that friendships between the sexes are a unique blend of male and female styles of friendship.

Many researchers claim that men's and women's same-sex friendships are indeed very different from each other, and that this difference explains dissatisfaction in friendships between the sexes (Rubin, 1985; Wright, 1988). While men are more likely to view friendships with men or women as equally satisfying, women rate same-sex friendships as more gratifying (Sapadin, 1988; Wright, 1989). Although men state they give and get nurturing and acceptance in friendships with women, women identify same-sex friendships as more intimate and emotionally supportive than cross-sex friendships (Sapadin, 1988). On balance then, both men and women seem to find friendships with women more intimate.

However, the differences may tell us less about the quality of friendships than about the connotations of terms such as *intimate* and *caring*. Some relational scholars suggest that the ways in which we think about these terms have been engendered with feminine values (Wood, 1993). In limiting our definitions of intimacy and closeness to explicit displays of affection and personal disclosure, which are more typically feminine modes of expressing closeness, we implicitly value feminine styles over masculine modes of communicating closeness (Duck & Wright, 1993; Wood & Inman, 1993).

The gendering of friendship is reflected in the characterizations of same-sex friendships. Women's friendships are commonly characterized by researchers as "communal" or "expressive," while men's friendships are seen as "agentic" or "instrumental" (Duck and Wright, 1993). This implies female friends spend their time talking and being together and male friends spend their time doing things together. But how accurate is this picture? Duck and Wright (1993) found that for same-sex friendships, both men and women said the main reason to get together with a friend is "just to talk" (both women and men chose "activity or task" as the second most common purpose for meeting friends). It seems then, that same-sex friendships of both women and men include expressive and instrumental dimensions, although the sexes may differ in the kinds of talk and activities they prefer.

Does "Friends" Mean "No Sex"?

Defining a complex term like *friendship* is difficult to begin with; separating it from other abstract concepts such as *love* or *romance* is even more tricky. It is tempting to argue that love or romance involves sexual activity and friendship does not. In fact, sexuality and passion have generally been considered defining criteria for distinguishing friendship from romantic love (Davis & Todd, 1982). But what about friends who occasionally enjoy sexual sparks in their relationships, or married couples who describe their partners as their best friends? Must a relationship between a heterosexual woman and man be one or the other?

Don O'Meara (1989) maintains that it is not the absence or existence of sexual activity that defines a relationship, but rather the function that those elements serve. To put it another way, the occurrence of sexual activity per se is less important than the *meaning* that it has for the relationships (Duck, 1994).

In support of this argument, research suggests that some people do not clearly separate friendships from sexual activity. In one study (Sapadin, 1988), 76% of the males and 50% of the females responded affirmatively to the statement "I like flirting and sexual teasing." Sixty-two percent of the males and 50% of the females agreed to the statement "Having a sexual relationship adds deeper feelings and closeness to friendship." Males responded to all of the statements about friendship and sexual activity with higher percentages than women (Sapadin, 1988). Montgomery (1986) reported that for women, flirting and sexual teasing are distinct, and that flirting indicates friendliness. For men the distinction is less clear.

Cultural Emphasis on Heterosexuality

Part of the difficulty of distinguishing friendship from romance is a pervasive cultural assumption that all personal relationships between socioeconomically compatible women and men must have been sparked by physical attraction. What follows is an expectation that the couple will become primarily romantic/sexual. Rawlins (1994) argues that our society is guilty of sexism in the sense that sexual potential and activity are constantly emphasized and privileged as the basis of close relationships. This "sexual lens" for viewing male–female interaction has also been referred to as a "heterosexual subschema" (O'Meara, 1989). Several researchers argue that this undertone of sexuality is due to a cultural emphasis on the gendering of identity (Rawlins, 1994; Wood, 1994). For instance, one of the central components of masculinity in our culture is an interest in sexual activity (Rawlins, 1994; Simon &

Gagnon, 1986). The traditional masculine identity is "programmed" to perceive women in terms of sexual potential. Research shows that men attribute more sexual meaning to heterosexual interactions than do women (Shotland & Craig, 1988). Rawlins (1993) suggests that the proclivity of men to view cross-sex interactions as potentially sexual may be due to men's tendency to view women uniformly, regardless of the romantic or platonic nature of the relationship. On the other hand, women's perception of men is more closely tied to specific relationships. In other words, men are more likely to use a "sexual lens" as opposed to a "relational lens" as they perceive and interact with women. Interestingly, this "sexual lens" is less problematic for androgynous individuals, or for those who adopt flexible sex-role orientations (O'Meara, 1989). Bell (1981) reported that nonconventional males and females were more likely to treat sexual attraction as secondary to a primary emphasis on friendship. Nontraditional participants also reported believing that their friendships were less threatened by the possibility of sexual interaction.

Personal Emphasis on Meaning

Specific relationships are defined and negotiated by the individuals involved, yet they are also framed by social norms and expectations about relationships. Heterosexual mates who emphasize emotional commitment, sexual exclusivity, and the intertwining of resources in their relationship are generally considered to be romantically involved. This does not mean that they are not friends, but that they have chosen a romantic emphasis for their relationship. A man and woman who concentrate on the voluntary, mutual, and platonic enjoyment of each other's company can be said to be friends, since they have adopted an emphasis on friendship—even if they are married!

Although relationships are formed and defined by those involved, they are not wholly private endeavors. Our ideas about the nature of relationships, as well as our ideas of what it means to be a "man" or a "woman," are drawn from social and cultural norms, assumptions, and expectations. Social order and private experience draw on and affect one another. Thus it would be naive to think we "enter" into relationships. Instead, they are constantly re-created in interaction (Duck, 1994). In studying friendships, we must look to the manner in which our interactions are framed by, reproduce, or transform existing relational norms and gendered identities.

There is one final note of caution. It is tempting to think of cross-sex friendships as *failed* romantic encounters. This view is reinforced by the fact that often a woman or a man will attempt to disengage from a romantic attachment, or avoid one altogether, by suggesting, "Let's just be friends." Yet friendship is itself a worthy accomplishment, rather than simply a means to an end, or a relationship of last resort. The cultural emphasis on sexuality devalues platonic interactions when it sees them as mere stepping stones (Duck, 1991; Rawlins, 1993) to "more rewarding" romantic interactions (Gaines, 1994). Even the phrase *"just friends"* suggests something is lacking from the relationship.

DEVELOPMENT OF FRIENDSHIPS BETWEEN MEN AND WOMEN

One meaning of the phrase *development of friendships* focuses on the manner in which relationships are initiated, maintained, and/or terminated. Yet development also means growth and change associated with age. In looking at friendships between men and women, development over the life span is particularly important because of the influence of gender expectations and gender identity, which are tightly woven into our experience of age. Fuller understanding of how friendships between women and men develop, therefore, requires looking at these friendships at various stages during our life span.

Childhood

Gender has been described as a primary role, "a central or major classifier of people within a culture" (Intons-Peterson, 1988, p. 2). It is arguably our first, and therefore strongest, means of classifying people, including ourselves, and depicting the kinds of relationships that we may have with them. In learning gender, we develop expectations of each sex, and as such, weave gender beliefs into our sense of self. One of the ways in which children enact gendered identities is in preferences for gender-typed toys. By the time children are 2 years old, they are more likely to choose for themselves—and to assign to another child—a toy that is gender stereotypical (Intons-Peterson, 1988). We are not suggesting that children play only with gender-specific toys, or do not play with children of the other sex because of their gender orientation to toys. We are pointing out that gender identities have already been incorporated into children's own identity and their expectations of others' gender by the age of 2.

Gender distinctions are reinforced in schools where children have chances to play with others of the same and of the other sex, yet tend to form same-sex groups as their sense of their own and others' gender emerges. Teachers' tendencies to separate boys and girls also promote sex segregation (Thorne, 1993). Following adult leads, children also frequently segregate by sex in free-time playground activities (Thorne, 1993). When children do interact with members of the other sex, they are often accused of romantic intentions, or of gender-inappropriate identities ("sissy" or "tomboy") (Shapiro, Baumeister, & Kessler, 1991). One study (Clark, 1994) looked at 10- to 16-year-olds' preferences for same or opposite sex peers when faced with either the desire to be "cheered up" or the need for help in coping with a specific problem. Although the study did not claim to be looking at children's friendships, the procedure required the children to respond to a series of scenarios by thinking of a specific person their age, with whom they would most like to talk if faced with the described dilemma. The 10-year-old children were the least likely to choose an opposite sex person, regardless of the type of problem. It would appear that one of the "lessons" of childhood is learning to separate and segregate others according to their sex.

Adolescence

Friendships between the sexes increase during adolescence (Buhrmester & Furman, 1987). In the study described above (Clark, 1994), children in 6th and 8th grades showed progressively more inclination to choose opposite-sex peers for interaction, a trend that held steady through the 10th grade. Interestingly, in all grades, boys showed a slight preference for girls, but not vice versa. Also, the nature of interaction influenced preference for a particular gender. Both boys and girls at all grades chose a male as a conversational partner for joking and telling stories. For 8th and 10th graders, girls were the preferred partner for cheering, advice on how to persuade someone, or suggestions on how to explain a complicated idea (Clark, 1994).

In addition to these changes in preference for friends, adolescence is marked by a movement away from the family and toward peers, with a focus on sharing feelings through self-disclosure (Berndt, 1982). One explanation for the increase in interaction between the sexes could be that the focus on self-disclosive talk renders gender less important than age. Additionally, there is a cultural expectation that adolescent girls and boys will begin to display overt heterosexual interest. (This is a source of stress for gay and lesbian adolescents.) This is usually the time of "going steady," first "mixed parties," and dating. Although the increased interest in the other sex is sometimes described as "merely hormones," this period of time also reflects shifting perceptions of gender, as both sexes display less rigid gender segregation and seek each other out as friends and romantic partners.

Adulthood

The tendencies of adolescents continue into adulthood. Men more frequently choose women for conversational partners than women choose men (Reisman, 1990), and men report higher satisfaction with friendships with women than vice versa (Sapadin, 1988). The preference for male storytelling, which also continues, may be because joking and storytelling are more common in men than in women (Maltz & Borker, 1983), so males may be more skilled in that communication genre. Women, however, are generally perceived as having better interpersonal communication skills than men (Clark, 1993; Duck & Wright, 1993), being more sensitive monitors of interaction, and being more expressive of personal and emotional involvement (Duck & Wright, 1993).

Although "adulthood" is often taken to mean life after 21 years of age, common sense tells us that life at 25 is typically very different than at 35, and both are very different from life at 60. In the following sections, we identify social forces and structures that affect specific elements of adult friendships between women and men.

Early Adulthood.   The highest occurrence of friendships between the sexes occurs among college students (Werking, 1994b). In one study, college students reported having three or more cross-sex friends (Buhrke & Fuqua, 1987). While another researcher found that most college students had at least one cross-sex friend, the majority of respondents stated they weren't interested in cross-sex friendships because of the difficulties in forming and maintaining these relationships (Rose, 1985). Additionally, men identified physical attraction as an important element for friendship with women. College students said they used humor and positive support as maintenance strategies for both same- and cross-sex friendships, but were more likely to self-disclose and share activities with friends of the same sex (Afifi, Guerrero, & Egland, 1994). Interestingly, the male students in this study tended to be more positive and supportive in cross-sex friendships than in same-sex friendships, while women showed a reverse trend. If men's friendships are characterized by fewer expressions of support, then in friendships with women, males may respond to and reciprocate the more demonstrative supportiveness characteristic of women's relating style.

In light of the above, what can we conclude about college students' gender expectations and gender identities? Intons-Peterson (1988) reported that personal and cultural descriptions of gender greatly diverged. Even as participants concurred on the general accuracy of cultural descriptions of gender, the gender attributions they offered of themselves varied widely from those definitions. Further, it was common for college students to make different gender attributions for themselves and others *of the same sex*. It would seem that cultural beliefs about gender are maintained while our understanding of who *we* are is much less rigidly defined.

Middle Adulthood. Marriage, or a similar committed relationship, and full-time employment are two major factors in the middle years of adult life, and both influence friendships between women and men.

Heterosexual marriage, or serious commitment, is most commonly identified as a reason not to have friendships with members of the other sex (Werking, 1994b). In fact, romantic relationships in general appear to be accepted as a self-evident reason not to have a friend of the opposite sex. In her study of cross-sex friendships, Werking (1994b) writes that one women responded, "I have a husband; enough said!" and a man said, "I can't do that (because of marriage)." Although people often say they believe husbands and wives should be able to have friends of the other sex, they also often feel it would be inappropriate for *their* spouse to have a close friend of the opposite sex (Lampe, 1985). One researcher suggested that there is a strong cultural message that spouses are supposed to be best friends (Rose, 1985), a position reflected by one of Werking's participants who stated, "As a married woman, it seems to be inappropriate for me to have a male friend that I confide in, aside from my husband." Blieszner and Adams (1992, p.102) state, "Being married, more than age, inhibit[s] the development of cross-sex friendships."

It is important to keep in mind that friendships are more difficult to maintain after marriage (Rubin, 1985; Werking, 1994b). Especially in the early stages of building a new family, a young couple is preoccupied with consolidating the new union and reassuring each other and themselves that their new family comes first (Rubin, 1985). Additionally, many of us agree that family takes priority, even when we are the friend who is left by the wayside once our friends marry. A common response of "That's the way it is" indicates an acceptance of the cultural expectation that romantic commitment overshadows friendship (Rubin, 1985). Some committed romantic partners do continue friendships, but they are significantly less likely to be members of the other sex, and initiation of such friendships is extremely rare (Werking, 1994b).

Couple friendships involve two couples developing a friendship, or a couple sharing a friend. Couple friendships do not threaten relational partners, and they provide social support and validation for the couple's commitment. When a couple "shares" a friend, the person is usually male, and typically has been the friend of the husband (Bendtschneider & Duck, 1993). Although women may identify this man as a "shared" friend, and hence a friend of the other sex, the friendship usually does not continue in the absence of the husband (Adams, 1985). One final way in which families affect friendship is parenthood, which has received little research attention. One study (Shulman, 1975) reported that in comparison to single and child-free couples, parents saw their friends least often because of parenting responsibilities.

Adulthood is also characterized by full-time employment. The demands of a job or career not only decrease the amount of time available to spend with friends, but typically do not offer the opportunity for initiating and maintaining friendships between the sexes (O'Meara, 1994). Many occupations are still firmly sex-segregated, particularly in terms of socioeconomic class. Because blue-collar work is labor-intensive, it continues to carry the cultural stereotypes of strength and, therefore, masculinity. There are women plumbers, electricians, and construction workers, but they are outnumbered by men. Similarly, there are male nurses, clerics, and waiters, but again, significantly fewer than women. Often men and women are employed in a given field or company, but the work they do (hence their coworkers and the place they work) will most often be assigned according to their sex. Thus, men and women are more likely to work, and thus form friendships, with members of the same sex.

Even when women and men work in close physical proximity, they are typically separated by the sex-stratified character of most occupational structures. Males typically occupy higher positions than women (Dillard & Miller, 1988), and unequal status poses an additional barrier to friendship (Zorn, 1995). Further, Western culture's sexualization of relations between men and women inhibits such friendships in the workplace.

Older Adulthood. Friendships between older women and men are rare (Chown, 1981; Wright, 1989). Most such friendships are extensions of work-related relationships, or as noted earlier, involve a "couple friend." Also, retirement typically leads to men and women terminating friendly relations previously based in the workplace. One study found that older women were particularly concerned about avoiding negative gossip associated with having a male as a friend (Adams, 1985).

What conclusions can we draw about gender expectations and gender identity from this review of friendships between men and women throughout the life span? Perhaps most striking is that our sense of *self*, although originating in a sense of being gendered, is not tied to social prescriptions for gender. Strikingly, however, our expectations of *others*, including both sexes, remain framed by cultural stereotypes of gender. As Intons-Peterson (1988, p.159) writes, "People appear to share quite similar ideas about what their culture says about the two sexes; they differ mainly in the extent to which they are incorporating this information into their own personal constructs."

Take a moment and make a short list of the gender characteristics attributed to your sex, and then evaluate whether those attributes define you. Do you identify with some and not others? Are there some with which you can identify given a particular set of circumstances, but not without this qualification? How closely do you think the men and women you know follow this gender prescription?

BARRIERS TO FRIENDSHIP BETWEEN MEN AND WOMEN

A recurring point is that friendship between women and men is constrained by a number of social barriers. These include the lack of social support for such relationships, as we have already noted (that is, teasing, suspicion, and gossip), and also the persistent belief that such friends are either lying about sexual involvement or blind to its inevitability. Two further barriers include a lack of cultural example and the social inequalities between the sexes.

A number of researchers have suggested that our culture offers few role models for enduring friendships between women and men (Pogrebin, 1989; Rawlins, 1993). Think for a minute about examples of female–male couples (in history, literature, or media) whose primary relationship has been and continues to be one of friendship. Harry (Billy Crystal's character) clearly proves his own point that men and women can't be "continuing" friends by developing a romantic attachment and marrying Sally at the end of the movie. Just a few television examples of cross-sex friends who eventually develop romantic relationships include Sam and Diane (and Rebecca) of "Cheers," and David and Maddie of "Moonlighting." More recently, but in a reverse direction, the characters Jerry and Elaine, from the show "Seinfeld," were originally romantic partners but have settled into a platonic friendship.

As a result, we have few cultural scripts or rules to guide us in forming and sustaining friends of the other sex (Chown, 1981; Lampe, 1985; O'Meara, 1989). Much like a movie script, cultural scripts tell us what to expect and how to behave in certain situations (Abelson, 1981). Lacking guidelines for male–female friendship, couples may follow scripts for other types of relationships. For instance, some people might fall back on same-sex friendship scripts (Rose, 1985). As discussed earlier, researchers have reported some differences in the workings of female–female and male–male friendships; thus, a reliance on same-sex scripts may lead to conflict or misunderstandings. For instance, a woman using a female–female friendship prototype may expect substantial expressions of intimacy and emotional support from a male friend, and may feel disappointed and confused if he fails to follow this particular friendship script.

Other women and men seeking friendships may resort to romantic scripts. Because interactions between men and women are culturally prescribed to involve romantic and/or sexual interaction, friends may find themselves pushed down the courtship path despite their intentions to be "just friends."

A further difficulty associated with friendships between the sexes surrounds the notion of equality, which many regard as essential to friendship (Hays, 1988). Pogrebin (1989) argues that men and women simply can't be friends because of social inequality. Other researchers confirm that there is less symmetry in cross-sex friendships than in same-sex friendships, as men demand more attention, response, and support than they give (Wood, 1994). May and Strikwerda (1992) argue that male interaction patterns, which usually dominate in cross-sex friendships, "perpetuate debilitating gender patterns" where women do all the emotional/relational work. Thus women get "the task of rescuing men" emotionally (O'Meara, 1989). As mentioned earlier, men describe friendships with women as closely resembling friendships with men, but women report that male friends provide less acceptance and less intimacy than women friends. Rose (1985) suggests that it is possible that women are willing to tolerate less emotional support in return for the increased status and resources they might gain from having a male friend. Yet the reward of status may be in tension with the inequality it reflects.

A variety of other explanations exist for the relatively small numbers of friendships between women and men. One argument maintains that we are culturally programmed to be "gender loyalists" in all interactions except those involving love and sex. This same-sex social tendency makes same-sex friendships more comfortable (Pogrebin, 1989). Another theory suggests that because sex segregation is encouraged early in life, men and women develop separate speech communities that foster separate interaction styles and communication rules, which can create misunderstandings and awkwardness (Johnson, 1989; Wood, 1994). Finally, many people, especially women, simply prefer friends of their own sex (Rose, 1985). Werking notes that individuals in her 1994b study who claimed preference for same-sex friends were often fairly critical of the opposite sex as these examples demonstrate:

> I have decided to forgo having any type of meaningful friendships with men. In the past I have attempted to maintain relationships with men, but I have been disappointed time and time again by their lack of depth, understanding, and compassion. (woman, age 20)

> Most of the females that I've ever known have been cheap, self-centered, money-hungry snobs. In the past, I've tried to have female friends and they have always lied and stabbed me in my back, and been two-faced to me and my other friends. (man, age 21)

ADVANTAGES TO FRIENDSHIPS BETWEEN MEN AND WOMEN

Despite these formidable barriers to the formation of friendships between men and women, such friendships do exist, and many of us want them in our lives (Swain, 1992). Susan Ambrose (1989) argues that cross-sex friendships are very rewarding and worth the extra effort. To balance our discussion so far, we conclude by exploring some of the rewards of friendships between the sexes.

Social support researchers generally regard close personal friendships as a valuable resource that provides a number of beneficial consequences ranging from emotional support to reduced vulnerability to illness (Hays, 1988). Logic suggests that inclusion of the opposite sex as potential friends doubles a person's opportunities. Vast human potential and sharing can be lost to the limitations created by sexism and sex segregation.

Ambrose (1989) maintains that friendships between men and women lead to happier and healthier lives for a variety of reasons. One of the most often cited advantages is the opportunity for insight into the psychological and social orientations of each sex (Swain, 1993; Werking, 1994b). As each partner represents his or her own sex, "expert" advice can be offered on cross-sex interactions, romantic or otherwise (Wood, 1994). Women and men who are friends might offer their "insider's perspective" to help each other cope with what might otherwise seem like inexplicable behavior of romantic partners. In addition, friendships between the sexes can provide an opportunity to try out new ideas before interactions with romantic partners. For instance, you might tell your opposite-sex friend that you hate your job and you want to quit. A friend might be more likely to discuss the possibility more openly than a romantic partner who might immediately evaluate the relational implications of such a decision.

Ambrose (1989) argues that because women and men complement each other, friendships between them can be especially rich. Although males may be socialized to provide more instrumental support, and females may tend to emphasize emotional responsiveness, the two create a nice blend of resources. Ambrose maintains that sexual attraction simply adds "spice" to the friendship and is a clear indication of the special chemistry that exists between women and men.

Considering the issues we have raised, and your own experiences with friends of the other sex, how would you respond to the "Harry Question"?

QUESTIONS FOR REFLECTION AND DISCUSSION

1. How do you and your friends define cross-sex friendship? What elements usually characterize this type of relationship?

2. In your experience, how common are cross-sex friendships? Are people more or less likely to have cross-sex friends these days?

3. Are there particular circumstances or conditions that make cross-sex friendships more likely or more difficult?

4. The authors argue that our culture doesn't provide scripts for male–female friendships. Compose a script for friendship between the sexes. In your script, explain rules about what activities, kinds of talk, feelings, and so forth are appropriate and inappropriate for friendships between men and women.

5. As the authors note, people differ in how they interpret sexual sparks between women and men who are friends. Some individuals think these sparks add spice and interest to a friendship. Others believe sexual sparks make friendships between men and women dangerous. Where do you stand on this issue?

REFERENCES

Abelson, R. P. (1981). Psychological status of the script concept. *American Psychologist, 36,* 715–729.

Adams, R. G. (1985). People would talk: Normative barriers to cross-sex friendships for elderly women. *The Gerontologist, 25,* 605–611.

Afifi, W., Guerrero, L., & Egland, K. (1994, May). *Maintenance behaviors in same- and opposite-sex friendships: Connections to gender, relational closeness and equity issues.* Paper presented at the International Network on Personal Relationships Annual Conference, Iowa City, IA.

Ambrose, S. F. (1989). Men and women can be friends. In N. Bernards & T. O'Neill (Eds.), *Male/female roles: Opposing viewpoints* (pp. 207–212). San Diego, CA: Greenhaven Press.

Bell, R. R. (1981). Friendships of women and men. *Psychology of Women Quarterly, 5,* 402–417.

Bendtschneider, L., & Duck, S. W. (1993). What's yours is mine and what's mine is yours: Couple friends. In P. J. Kalbfleisch (Ed.), *Interpersonal communication: Evolving interpersonal relationships.* Hillsdale, NJ: Lawrence Erlbaum.

Berndt, T. J. (1982). The features and effects of friendship in early adolescence. *Child Development, 53,* 1447–1460.

Blieszner, R., & Adams, R. G. (1992). *Adult friendship.* Newbury Park, CA: Sage.

Buhrke, R. A., & Fuqua, D. R. (1987). Sex differences in same- and cross-sex supportive relationships. *Sex Roles, 17,* 339–351.

Buhrmester, D., & Furman, W. (1987). The development of companionship and intimacy. *Child Development, 58,* 1101–1113.

Chown, S. M. (1981). Friendship in old age. In S. W. Duck & R. Gilmour (Eds.), *Personal relationships 2: Developing Personal Relationships.* London: Academic Press.

Clark, R. A. (1993). Men's and women's self-confidence in persuasive, comforting, and justificatory communicative tasks. *Sex Roles, 28,* 553–567.

Clark, R. A. (1994). Children's and adolescents' gender preferences. *Journal of Social and Personal Relationships, 11,* 313–319.

Davis, K. E., & Todd, M. J. (1982). Friendship and love relationships. In K. E. Davis & T. Mitchell, (Eds.), *Advances in descriptive psychology* (pp. 79–122). London: JAI Press.

Dillard, J. P., & Miller, K. I. (1988). Intimate relationships in task environments. In S. W. Duck (Ed.), *Handbook of personal relationships.* Chichester: John Wiley.

Duck, S. W. (1991). *Understanding relationships.* New York: Guilford.

Duck, S. W. (1994). *Meaningful relationships: Talking, sense, and relating.* Thousand Oaks, CA: Sage.

Duck, S. W., & Wright, P. H. (1993). Re-examining gender differences in same-gender friendships. *Sex Roles, 28,* 1–19.

Gaines, S. O. (1994). Exchange of respect denying behaviors among male–female friendships. *Journal of Social and Personal Relationships, 11,* 5–24.

Hays, R. B. (1988). Friendship. In S. W. Duck (Ed.), *Handbook of personal relationships* (pp. 391–408). John Wiley.

Intons-Peterson, M. J. (1988). *Children's concepts of gender.* Norwood, NJ: Ablex.

Johnson, F. L. (1989). Women's culture and communication: An analytical perspective. In C. M. Lont & S. A. Friedley (Eds.), *Beyond boundaries: Sex and gender diversity in communication* (pp. 301–316). Fairfax, VA: George Mason University Press.

Lampe, P. E. (1985). Friendships and adultery. *Sociological Inquiry, 55,* 310–324.

Maltz, D. N., & Borker, R. A. (1983). A cultural approach to male–female miscommunication. In J. A. Gumperz (Ed.), *Language and social identity.* New York: Cambridge University Press.

May, L., & Strikwerda, R. (Eds.). (1992). *Rethinking masculinity: Philosophical explorations in light of feminism.* Lanham, MD: Rowan & Littlefield.

Montgomery, B. M. (1986, July). *Flirtatious messages.* Paper presented to the Third International Conference on Personal Relationships, Herzlia, Israel.

O'Meara, J. D. (1989). Cross-sex friendship: Four basic challenges of an ignored relationship. *Sex Roles, 21,* 525–543.

O'Meara, J. D. (1994). Cross-sex friendship's opportunity challenge: Uncharted terrain for exploration. *Personal Relationship Issues, 2,* 4–7.

Pogrebin, L. C. (1989). Men and women cannot be friends. In N. Bernards & T. O'Neill (Eds.), *Male/female roles: Opposing viewpoints* (pp. 213–217). San Diego, CA: Greenhaven Press.

Rawlins, W. K. (1993). Communication in cross-sex friendships. In L. Arliss & D. Borisoff (Eds.), *Women and men communicating.* Fort Worth, TX: Harcourt Brace Jovanovich.

Rawlins, W. K. (1994). Reflecting on (cross-sex) friendship: De-scripting the drama. *Personal Relationship Issues, 2,* 1–3.

Reisman, J. M. (1990). Intimacy in same-sex friendships. *Sex Roles, 23,* 65–82.

Rose, S. M. (1985). Same- and cross-sex friendships and the psychology of homosociality. *Sex Roles, 12,* 63–74.

Rubin, L. B. (1985). *Just friends.* New York: Harper & Row.

Sapadin, L. A. (1988). Friendship and gender: Perspectives of professional men and women. *Journal of Social and Personal Relationships, 6,* 387–403.

Shapiro, J. P., Baumeister, R. F., & Kessler, J. W. (1991). A three-component model of children's teasing: Aggression, humor, and ambiguity. *Journal of Social and Clinical Psychology, 10,* 459–472.

Shotland, R. L., & Craig, J. M. (1988). Can men and women differentiate between friendly and sexually interested behavior? *Social Psychology Quarterly, 51,* 66–73.

Shulman, N. (1975). Life-cycle variations in patterns of close relationships. *Journal of Marriage and Family, 37,* 813–821.

Simon, W., & Gagnon, J. H. (1986). Sexual scripts: Permanence and change. *Archives of Sexual Behavior, 15,* 97–120.

Swain, S. O. (1992). Men's friendships with women: Intimacy, sexual boundaries, and the informant role. In P. M. Nardi (Ed.), *Men's friendships.* Newbury Park, CA: Sage.

Thorne, B. (1993). *Gender play: Girls and boys in school.* New Brunswick, NJ: Rutgers University Press.

Werking, K. J. (1994a). Hidden assumptions: A critique of existing cross-sex friendship research. *Personal Relationship Issues, 2,* 8–11.

Werking, K. J. (1994b). *Barriers to the formation of close cross-sex friendship.* Paper presented at the 1994 International Network on Personal Relationships Conference, Iowa City, IA.

Wood, J. T. (1993). Engendered relations: Interaction, caring, power and responsibility in intimacy. In S. W. Duck (Ed.), *Understanding Relationship Processes, 3: Social context and relationships* (pp 26–54). Newbury Park, CA: Sage.

Wood, J. T. (1994). *Gendered lives: Communication, gender, and culture.* Belmont, CA: Wadsworth.

Wood, J. T., & Inman, C. C. (1993). In a different mode: Masculine styles of communicating closeness. *Journal of Applied Communication Research, 21,* 279–295.

Wright, P. H. (1988). Interpreting research on gender differences in friendship: A case for moderation and a plea for caution. *Journal of Social and Personal Relationships, 5,* 367–373.

Wright, P. H. (1989). Gender differences in adults' same- and cross-gender friendships. In R. G. Adams & R. Blieszner (Eds.), *Older adult friendships.* Newbury Park, CA: Sage.

Zorn, T. (1995). Bosses and buddies: Constructing and performing simultaneously hierarchical and close friendship relationships. In J. T. Wood & S. W. Duck (Eds.), *Understanding Relationship Processes, 6: Off the beaten track* (pp. 122–147). Thousand Oaks, CA: Sage.

PART
THREE

GENDERED
ROMANTIC
RELATIONSHIPS

GENDER AND THE EXPERIENCE OF HETEROSEXUAL LOVE

CLYDE HENDRICK
SUSAN HENDRICK

Do men and women experience romantic love in the same ways? How are their experiences similar? How do they differ from one another? In this chapter, we explore romantic love within the context of gender, focusing on how men and women are similar and different in approaches to and experiences of romantic love. Gender issues in styles of loving in this chapter may be compared with gender issues in styles of sustaining relationships in the following chapter by Julia Wood.

REAL MEN DON'T TALK MUCH

John and Amy met at a party and were immediately attracted to one another. John took the initiative and asked for Amy's phone number; the next day he called and asked her for a date. John was tall and handsome. He was not very talkative; indeed, in many respects one might call him the "strong, silent type." He liked to talk about activities and things that he intended to do, but he never talked about his inner feelings, his fears, or his joys. As a man, John felt it would be inappropriate to show much emotion, and certainly he would not cry. John was very attracted to Amy, but as with previous girlfriends, he was a little concerned that she might want to get too emotionally close too fast. John wanted to have a good time, but he didn't want to become "committed" to anyone at this stage in his life. He was particularly suspicious of the possibility that Amy might make a lot of demands on his time and prevent him from doing some of the activities that he enjoyed with the guys.

Amy was a beautiful young woman. Although somewhat shy, generally she was open with her close friends. She also was quite expressive when she was with John. Although she hoped to prepare for a career while in college, her fondest hope was to meet "Mr. Right" and get married. She enjoyed small children and wanted to have a large family. In fact, she daydreamed about how she might someday be a contented wife and mother. Amy was very attracted to John and, in spite of herself, soon began to think about him constantly. She wanted to see him often and spent hours on the phone with him. John began to feel hemmed in, and he told Amy that he needed his own space and that she was crowding him. Amy sensed that their relationship was threatened, and she pleaded with him not to pull away. The more Amy pushed, the more withdrawn John became, and the more withdrawn he became, the more panicked Amy became, and so on.

Although we have described our couple in an exaggerated fashion, many of Amy's and John's behaviors are familiar. Their relationship could evolve in any one of several ways, but it is the process and not the outcome of their relationship that interests us here. John and Amy exemplify masculine and feminine orientations toward loving. Let's look a little more closely at these two basic concepts.

Masculinity and Femininity

Early in the century, gender differences were thought to be due to basic underlying personality or biological differences. Masculinity and femininity were viewed as opposite ends on a single scale of gender. That is, a person who was high on masculinity was assumed to be low on femininity. Thus, men and women were defined as representing opposite poles of a single personality dimension. Currently, masculinity and femininity are not viewed as a single dimension, but rather as two independent dimensions. This conception allows a person to be high on both dimensions, high on one and low on the other, or low on both. Scales have been developed to measure masculinity and femininity (Bem, 1974; Spence & Helmreich, 1978). Measurements show that many women and men are high on both masculinity and femininity. These people are called androgynous, and being high on both scales is generally considered desirable, since it allows individuals to exhibit the presumed strengths associated with both men and women.

Masculine and Feminine Relating

Perhaps you noticed in the story that John and Amy matched cultural ideals for the traits that a man and a woman supposedly should exhibit. Yet John and Amy seemed relatively unhappy together.

The question of what happens when masculine men are paired with feminine women was addressed by Ickes and Barnes (1978). These researchers matched pairs of men and women in such a way as to have either a traditional dyad, that is, a masculine man and a feminine woman, or other combinations, some of which included an androgynous member of the pair. Ickes and Barnes discovered that men and women in traditional couples did not like each other much and had less rewarding interactions than couples that included at least one androgynous member. It appears that the difference between the stereotypically masculine and feminine traits is large enough that partners don't enjoy interacting with each other.

The expectations of masculinity include some qualities that may not be helpful for affectionate relationships between men and women. In one study, Pleck, Sonenstein, and Ku (1993) correlated masculinity beliefs with a number of other questions in a national survey. Masculinity ideology was measured by eight items, such as "It is essential for a guy to get respect from others," and "A guy will lose respect if he talks about his problems." Men who subscribed strongly to the masculine ideology had more sexual partners in the previous year and a less intimate relationship in their last sexual intercourse with a current partner than men low in masculine ideology. Masculine ideology was also related to the belief that relationships between men and women are basically adversarial.

Given the discrepancies between traditional masculine and feminine ideologies, it may be surprising that women and men are similar on a variety of relationship-relevant attitudes. For example, Fehr (1993) found that when men and women were asked to rate the prototypical features of love, there were no gender differences. Similarly, Sedikides, Oliver, and Campbell (1994) found that in rating the costs and benefits of a romantic relationship, both women and men rated companionship, happiness, and feeling loved or loving another as important benefits in romantic involvement. However, men and women also differed, with women regarding intimacy, self-growth, self-understanding, and positive self-esteem as important benefits of a romantic relationship, and loss of identity and innocence about relationships as important costs. In contrast, men regarded sexual satisfaction as an important benefit, and monetary losses from dates as an important cost (Sedikides et al.,

1994). Thus, this study shows both gender similarities and gender differences in love and relationships, a pattern that we will find continually when considering the relationship between gender and the experience of love.

GENDER ROLES AND LOVE RELATIONSHIPS

So far we have discussed masculinity and femininity as personality dimensions of individuals, yet masculinity and femininity may also be thought of in terms of social roles. That is, masculine and feminine may be viewed not so much as inherent traits but as gender roles created and prescribed by a given society and socialized into individuals. Some notion of gender role is necessary to account for the change in the meanings of masculine and feminine over time. As Julia Wood pointed out in Chapter 1, the meanings of gender have changed, because what it means to be "masculine" or "feminine" today in Western culture is not the same as it was fifty years ago.

Love relationships may also be thought of as social processes. In the story of John and Amy, we saw that their relationship changed over time. Other relationships might change in different kinds of ways; they might "grow," "mature," "go stale," "be revived," "die," and so forth. These and other metaphors for relationships and their changes were captured in a delightful article by Duck and Sants (1983), who pointed out that relationships are processes that evolve over time. Yet relationships do not evolve in a vacuum. Instead, thinking of relationships as a set of processes can be useful; they grow and change within social structures or "society" (see Duck, 1993, for an extended discussion). For this reason, a love relationship is a set of interaction processes within social structures that affect partners' behaviors and expectations. With this beginning, understanding of love relationships as embedded in social life, we're now ready to ask what love itself is.

CONCEPTIONS OF LOVE

Poets, novelists, and academic researchers have all offered views of love. We'll overview current Western conceptions about love and then focus more specifically on a recent popular approach—attachment theory. We conclude our discussion with an extended exploration of the work with which we are most familiar: the love styles, or, as they are sometimes called, the "Colors of Love."

Some Theories of Love

Passionate and Companionate Love. Some years ago, two distinguished psychologists (Berscheid & Walster, 1978) proposed two distinct types of love, passionate and companionate (see also Walster & Walster, 1978). Passionate love might be called the "hothouse" type of love, and companionate love the everyday garden variety of love. Passionate love is often equated with "falling in love," and is the type of love about which movies are made and poetry is written. In contrast, companionate love is the quiet love that is left once the flames of passion die down.

The distinction between passionate and companionate love is valuable, although they may be phases more than absolute types of love. Movement from passion to companionship appears to be a process many men and women experience during the course of a romantic relationship. The strong feelings of passionate love have been sometimes compared to the feelings that people have on drugs—an amphetamine high (Liebowitz, 1983). Others have compared the quiet pleasure of companionate love to the effect of morphine, or the brain's own natural endorphins (Fisher, 1992). In any event, the distinction is one that most people recognize, even if they have not themselves experienced both. Hatfield[1] (1988) proposed that all people of any age, of any ethnic group, or of either gender are capable of passionate romantic love, defined as a state of intense longing for union with another person. Research to test these notions involved development of the Passionate Love Scale (Hatfield & Sprecher, 1986), as well as cross-cultural work (for example, Hatfield & Rapson, 1987), which indicated that there were no differences across ethnic groups in Hawaii on the Passionate Love Scale. There were also no differences between men and women across those ethnic groups, indicating that both genders experience passionate love with equal intensity. The comparability of people across diverse cultures suggests that the capability to experience passionate love may be part of our genetic heritage as human beings.

Sternberg (1986, 1987) has proposed that love consists of three basic components: intimacy, passion, and commitment. A person can be high or low on each component, so that all possible combinations would lead to eight types of love. These may range from nonlove, which indicates that a person is low in all three components, to consummate love, which indicates that a person is high on all three. Intimacy involves basic connectedness or closeness to another person; commitment is a desire to stay with that other person; and passion is a degree

---

[1] Elaine Hatfield formerly published under the name Elaine Walster.

of arousal that includes a desire for the other person, often but not always including sexual desire. Passion is a theme that appears in virtually every theory of love. Yet companionate aspects are important also, and Fehr (1993) argues convincingly that companionate features are central to people's conceptions of love, even romantic love.

Love as Attachment. Another theory of love is based on the quality of the first love relationship, which occurs when a child bonds with a parent or other adult. Human bonding, or attachment, was first discussed by Bowlby (1969), whose ideas provided the basis for Ainsworth, Blehar, Waters, and Wall (1978) to develop a typology of three types of infant–caregiver attachment: secure (confident infant, responsive mother), anxious–ambivalent (temperamental infant, inconsistent mother), and avoidant (undemonstrative infant and mother).

Hazan and Shaver (1987; see also Shaver & Hazan, 1988; Shaver, Hazan & Bradshaw, 1988) conjectured that the type of attachment pattern learned as an infant serves as the blueprint for adult relationships, particularly romantic relationships. The results of Hazan and Shaver's extensive research study suggested that the attachment style their adult participants selected was indeed related to remembered aspects of the participants' childhood. For example, adults who identified themselves as "secure" remembered their parents as having a warm relationship, and also recalled being treated warmly by their parents.

Early work by Hazan and Shaver (1987) did not find differences between men and women in attachment styles. Later work, however, suggests there are differences between the sexes. For example, Bartholomew and Horowitz (1991) reported a fourfold classification of attachment types: secure (somewhat comfortable with intimacy and autonomy), preoccupied (preoccupied with relationships), dismissing (dismissing of intimacy), and fearful (fearful of intimacy, socially avoidant). In our example of John and Amy, John had some characteristics of the dismissing type, since he seemed reluctant to establish a relationship, and Amy displayed qualities of the preoccupied type.

Later work by Scharfe and Bartholomew (1994) found that some men are more dismissive in interview and self-reports than women, and women are more preoccupied than men. This sex difference was also suggested in a longitudinal study by Kirkpatrick and Davis (1994), who followed a sample of romantic couples for approximately 3 years. They found that the couples in which both men and women were securely attached were most common. Also, they noted that there were no avoidant–avoidant pairs or anxious–anxious pairs. Presumably, such couples either would never get together or would break up immediately after getting together. There were, however, a few pairs in which one member was avoidant and the other member anxious. Relationships in which the man was avoidant or dismissing and the woman was preoccupied seemed relatively stable. In this case, both members of the pair were matching the cultural stereotype (as exemplified by John and Amy); therefore, even though they were not particularly happy in their relationships, they stayed within them because the relationships unfolded according to cultural expectations (see also Pietromonaco & Carnelley, 1994). Attachment theory suggests that securely attached individuals of both sexes form the best couples. It is also the case, however, that some number of stable pairings occur composed of avoidant men and preoccupied women. Avoidant women and preoccupied men are probably much less common, simply because they violate common cultural stereotypes.

The attachment perspective is particularly important because it reminds us that we learn how to love not only from our culture (as noted earlier), but also from individuals, especially those with whom we form our first love relationships. Yet theories and research that indicate *how* we may learn to love often do not tell us *what* we learn. Given this, it becomes important to ask, What styles of love do we learn? This question is addressed in the following section.

STYLES OF LOVE

There are many types of love; indeed, there may be many different types of *romantic* love. Earlier we discussed the difference between passionate and companionate love. In our example of John and Amy, it appeared that they may have experienced somewhat different types of love for each other. To study the different kinds of romantic love, Lee (1973) did a careful assessment of Western literature and developed an extensive interview called the Love Story Card Sort. With this sorting arrangement, he allowed research subjects to tell the story of their romantic loves—how those loves developed, unfolded, and sometimes ceased. An extensive analysis of his data revealed that there are indeed many types of love. In trying to order the types of love, Lee (1973) hit on the analogy of the color wheel as an ordering device, suggesting the name of his book, *The Colors of Love*. We developed our own research program around Lee's theory, and in the remainder of this chapter, we delineate some of that research with particular emphasis on gender issues. Most of our research has involved college students; thus, most of our conclusions apply to white, middle-class college students in the United States.

Six Love Styles

In our research, we worked with six different love attitudes or love styles. These love attitudes may be considered as pure types in a conceptual sense, although in the real world probably no one exemplifies any given style perfectly or is limited to any one style. The descriptions below give a flavor of the six major love styles.

Eros. Erotic lovers tend to fall in love at first sight, or at least rather quickly. They view love as one of the more important things in life, and are ready to give fully to the loved one. People high on eros have definite images of the kind of person who attracts them. The erotic lover seeks much contact; is open, honest, and sincere; wants the relationship to develop mutually; and enjoys intense emotion with the loved one. People with this love style often seek an early sexual relationship with the beloved, but sexuality is only one expression of erotic love. Intense intellectual, emotional, and/or spiritual connection may also exemplify erotic love (see Wood, 1995, for an extended discussion). Erotic lovers also tend to focus exclusively on each other, but tend not to be jealous or possessive of one another.

Ludus. The concept of ludus is that love is a game best played as a pleasant pastime. Apparently the notion of ludic love developed in the aristocratic courts in medieval western Europe; it survives today as a form of playfulness without serious involvement with another person. Ludics try to avoid too much intensity or a strong commitment to another person. They have an assortment of partners, no one of whom is of overwhelming importance. Ludic lovers tend not to be jealous or possessive and, indeed, may encourage a partner to have other relationships to help keep a delicate balance in their own relationship. Ludics tend not to have a definite preference with regard to physique, and consider sex as good fun, but neither sex nor committed relationships are the focus of life.

Storge. This love style may best be characterized as friendship love. Storge is "love without fever or folly, a feeling of natural affection, such as you might have for a favorite brother or sister" (Lee, 1973, p. 77). The basis for storge is solid friendship. In fact, people who are relatively pure storgic types may simply not understand the fire and passion of eros, and certainly would not appreciate the game playing of ludus. Storgic relationships are relaxed and unhurried, and partners love one another and disclose mutually. Interests and activities tend to be shared, and there may be considerable similarity, but there is not a strong focus per se on the relationship. Storgic lovers tend to assume that their relationship will unfold slowly and naturally. For them, love is not exciting, but it is solid, constant, and incorporated into the flow of life. Storgic love is similar to companionate love, which was discussed earlier.

Mania. Manic love is possessive, demanding, worried, and preoccupied. Throughout Western history, the notion of manic love has often been confused with "true love." Indeed, some mix of mania with eros is probably what most people think of in considering "romantic" love. Manics are often unhappy, however, because they yearn for union with the loved one but are often suspicious and jealous. They feel a loss of control over feelings and an inability to obtain the perfect happiness with the loved one that they so strongly desire. Mania is obsession. It is typified by calling the loved one time after time and panicking when no one answers the telephone. Manic love seldom ends well. Nevertheless, Lee (1973) discovered that mania is often a component of relationships and, on occasion, seems to characterize an individual's experience of love and romance.

Pragma. "Pragma is the love that goes shopping for a suitable mate, and all it asks is that the relationship work well, that the two partners be compatible, and satisfy each other's basic practical needs" (Lee, 1973, p. 124). This definition indicates that a pragmatic lover is looking for someone who matches a predetermined set of criteria. Stated otherwise, a pragmatic lover has a shopping list and goes searching for a mate who matches the list. Selection of a loved one is, indeed, a logical process. The pragmatic lover wants to avoid extremes, wants to get to know the partner well over time, and wants to ensure that the partner is compatible with his or her family. Pragma is practical, and the search for a lifetime mate must be taken seriously, but not obsessed over, as might be true for mania. Although pragmatic lovers may sound cold and unfeeling, they are not. They simply believe that selecting a lifetime love partner is a task worth doing carefully and well.

Agape. This love style emerged from the religious tradition of viewing God's love as totally selfless. It denotes concern for the partner's well-being without any self-interest. Lee said that he did not find any pure examples of agape, which is not surprising, given human nature. Agape is sacrificial in the sense that one's primary concern is the welfare of the loved one, rather than one's own welfare. Sexuality within agapic love would be something of a lofty sacramental act because agape tends to be more cognitive than emotional in orientation.

As you can see, these thumbnail sketches of the six love styles denote very different beliefs about the meaning and nature of love.

Measuring the Love Styles

The compatibility of partners' love styles likely influences how happy and stable couples may be. For example, imagine someone who is highly manic falling in love with someone who is very ludic. In our example of John and Amy, we have the semblance of such a mismatch. Amy appears to be moderately manic and John, as the strong silent type, may be moderately ludic. That combination could be disastrous for a developing relationship. Or consider an erotic lover falling in love with someone mostly pragmatic. These two people would frustrate each other, and the relationship might end early.

To study love styles and their implications, we conducted an extensive research program over the years, beginning with development of a Love Attitudes Scale (for example, Hendrick & Hendrick, 1986; Hendrick, Hendrick, Foote, & Slapion-Foote, 1984). The scale has 42 items, seven for each of the six love styles, and it has been revised to make all the items specific to a given love relationship (Hendrick & Hendrick, 1990). A short form of the Love Attitudes Scale is provided at the end of the chapter.

When we first devised the scale, we used the word *lover* in one way or another in the items in the scale. Over time, the word *lover* seemed both inappropriate and limiting. We wanted to develop the scale so that it suited not only young unmarried people, but also long-term couples living together and married couples. We eventually changed the terminology to refer to *partner.* This example illustrates that all relationships and rating scales that measure them tend to be culture-bound to some extent, because the meanings of terms shift and change over time.

We compared the Love Attitudes Scale to several other love scales and it held up well (Hendrick & Hendrick, 1989). We also developed a scale to measure sexual attitudes, and found some interesting relationships between love and sexual attitudes (for example, Hendrick & Hendrick, 1987a, 1987b). One of us (S. S. Hendrick, 1988) also developed a measure of relationship satisfaction, the Relationship Assessment Scale, in order to relate love and sex attitudes to relationship satisfaction.

Gender and Love Attitudes

We did not begin our research expecting gender differences to be a major aspect of the work. However, even in the first study, to our surprise, men and women differed on a large number of items (Hendrick et al., 1984). There were a few differences on eros; a substantial number on ludus, with men being more ludic in orientation; and notable differences on storge and pragma, with women generally being more storgic and pragmatic. In addition, women reported a more manic orientation than men reported.

Our studies lead us to conclude that men and women do not differ substantially on eros or agape. Across all studies, we have consistently found that men are more ludic than women (for example, Hendrick & Hendrick, 1987c). In most samples, women are more storgic and pragmatic than men, and in a number of studies women also are more manic. These gender differences have held up well over the past decade (Hendrick & Hendrick, 1995).

The differences between men and women on specific love attitudes need to be understood as part of a larger set of interpersonal attitudes. In other words, how does love relate to other aspects of relationships? To answer that question, we turn now to research on attitudes related to love styles.

Love Attitudes and Gender Role

In one study (Bailey, Hendrick, & Hendrick, 1987), we sought to determine whether gender role attitude was related to gender differences in the love styles. We classified a group of students into four categories, based on the Bem Sex Role Inventory (Bem, 1974). The participants were divided into the standard categories of masculine, feminine, androgynous (high on both feminine and masculine), and undifferentiated (low on both feminine and masculine). We found the usual gender effects for subjects, namely, that men were more ludic than women, and women were more pragmatic and manic than men on love attitudes. However, when we examined the data in terms of the Bem classification, some interesting results emerged. This classification ignores the actual biological sex of the subjects and simply looks at their gender role classification. We found that masculine subjects more strongly endorsed ludus, whereas feminine subjects were least endorsing of ludus. For mania, feminine subjects were most manic, differing significantly from masculine and undifferentiated subjects. For agape, androgynous and feminine subjects were the most endorsing, differing from masculine and undifferentiated subjects. For eros, androgynous subjects were the most endorsing, and undifferentiated subjects were the least endorsing. In general, the Bem classification in terms of gender role was independent of the actual sex of the subjects. Stated differently, there were no interaction effects between the sex of subjects and their

Bem gender role classification. These data indicate that the attitudes of masculinity and femininity may make as much or more difference in a person's love attitudes than is due to biological sex.

More About the Love Styles

A great many other studies have been conducted using the love styles. For example, Hendrick and Hendrick (1993) found that among many modern-day college students, lovers are indeed friends. In this study, participants provided written accounts of their love as well as ratings on the Love Attitudes Scale. We found that in the written accounts, storge, or friendship love, was the most frequently noted theme. Further, there was good correspondence between love themes in freeform accounts and the love style scores on the Love Attitudes Scale. In one study, we had participants generate accounts of their closest friendship. Almost half of the participants named their romantic partner as their closest friend. These results again suggest the importance of friendship (that is, storge) in the ongoing romantic relationships of many young men and women today (for example, Fehr, 1993).

We have also been interested in how people who are falling in love differ from people not currently in love. This question was explored in a paper entitled "Lovers Wear Rose Colored Glasses" (Hendrick & Hendrick, 1988). In that study, we compared people in love with people not in love, on many measures. We found that people currently in love were more erotic, more agapic, and less ludic than people not in love. There were also numerous other relationship-relevant differences for people in love as compared to people not in love. Perhaps it is indeed true, as noted earlier, that the experience of falling in love is somewhat like an amphetamine high (Liebowitz, 1983). Interestingly, there were few interaction effects for gender and being in love. In other words, women and men reacted similarly to being in love.

A number of other findings can be noted in passing. For example, the two of us (Hendrick & Hendrick 1987b) found a substantial relationship between love and sex attitudes and self-disclosure to a lover or friend. S. S. Hendrick (1981) also found that among married couples, women were significantly more self-disclosing than men. Working with Nancy Adler (Adler, Hendrick, & Hendrick, 1987), we found very few differences between male heterosexuals and male homosexuals in their love attitudes. Thus, we tentatively conclude that gay and straight men are similar in love styles.

Clearly, there are some gender differences, not only on the love styles, but on other closely related relational concepts. However, we must balance awareness of these differences with acknowledgment of similarities between women and men's way of loving. For example, Fehr (1993) found women and men to be similar in rating the prototypical features of love, and we (Hendrick & Hendrick, 1987c) found men and women to be similarly passionate and altruistic in their love styles. It strikes us that, overall, the genders show more similarities than differences, but that the differences do exist. Only future research will enable us to determine if the differences are themselves changing and shifting as the culture changes.

SUMMARY

The romance of John and Amy illustrates that extreme masculinity and femininity, whether conceived as personality traits or as gender roles, do not necessarily lead to an ideal relationship between a man and a woman. The traits and interpersonal styles society prescribes for masculinity and femininity appear to be too different to allow the easy rapport desired by intimates. Thus, we cannot rely on our culture for all (or perhaps even most) of our messages about love.

The attachment perspective underlines the importance of our early relationships with significant others, and the propensities toward love that may be a product of our evolutionary heritage are too numerous to discuss. The convergence of cultural, social learning, and biological forces are then transformed by individuals' personal life histories, so that ultimately our individual abilities to love are a mixture of prototypic features and unique, idiosyncratic ones.

On balance, there clearly are gender differences between men and women, at least in terms of tendencies toward various love styles; however, the structure of women's and men's belief systems about love and relationships appears to be roughly similar. Whether the similarities and differences we've discussed in this chapter remain constant over time is a question only further research can answer.

QUESTIONS FOR REFLECTION AND DISCUSSION

1. Consider the most successful romantic relationship that you know about (either heterosexual or homosexual). How would you describe the relationship partners in terms of gender role ideology—masculine, feminine, or androgynous? What impact might gender-role preferences have on this relationship's success?

2. Discuss how aspects of gender roles might be implicated in the fairly consistent findings that men are more game playing in love than women are, whereas women are more friendship-oriented, practical, and possessive/dependent than men are. Are these findings of gender differences in love preferences consistent with your own relationship experience? Why or why not?

3. Read the "Personals" ads in you local or regional paper. List the charateristics most sought after by women seeking a romantic partner, and then list those sought by men who are looking for a partner. How are these characteristics different? How are they similar?

SHORT FORM OF THE LOVE ATTITUDES SCALE

Listed below are several statements that reflect different attitudes about love. For each statement fill in the response beside the statement that indicates how much you agree or disagree with it. The items refer to a specific love relationship. Whenever possible, answer the questions with your current partner in mind. If you are not currently dating anyone, answer the questions with your most recent partner in mind. If you have never been in love, answer in terms of what you think your responses would most likely be.

For each statement:

1 = Strongly disagree with the statement
2 = Moderately disagree with the statement
3 = Neutral—neither agree nor disagree
4 = Moderately agree with the statement
5 = Strongly agree with the statement

Eros

___ 1. My partner and I were attracted to each other immediately after we first met.

___ 2. My partner and I have the right physical "chemistry" between us.

___ 3. Our lovemaking is very intense and satisfying.

___ 4. I feel that my partner and I were meant for each other.

___   = TOTAL

Ludus

___ 5. I try to keep my partner a little uncertain about my commitment to him/her.

___ 6. I believe that what my partner doesn't know about me won't hurt him/her.

___ 7. I have sometimes had to keep my partner from finding out about other partners.

___ 8. I could get over my affair with my partner pretty easily and quickly.

___   = TOTAL

Storge

___ 9. It is hard for me to say exactly when our friendship turned into love.

___10. To be genuine, our love first required *caring* for a while.

___11. I expect to always be friends with my partner.

___12. Our love is the best kind because it grew out of a long friendship.

___   = TOTAL

Pragma

___13. I considered what my partner was going to become in life before I committed myself to him/her.

___14. I tried to plan my life carefully before choosing my partner.

___15. In choosing my partner, I believed it was best to love someone with a similar background.

___16. A main consideration in choosing my partner was how he/she would reflect on my family.

___   = TOTAL

Mania

___17. When things aren't right with my partner and me, my stomach gets upset.

___18. If my partner and I break up, I would get so depressed that I would even think of suicide.

___19. Sometimes I get so excited about being in love with my partner that I can't sleep.

___20. When my partner doesn't pay attention to me, I feel sick all over.

___   = TOTAL

Agape

___21. I try to always help my partner through difficult times.

___22. I would rather suffer myself than let my partner suffer.

___23. I cannot be happy unless I place my partner's happiness before my own.

___24. I am usually willing to sacrifice my own wishes to let my partner achieve his/hers.

___   = TOTAL

Note: The names of the love styles are shown for the six sets of items. In a research study, participants are not told that there are six love attitudes, nor are they able to add up their scores.

REFERENCES

Adler, N. L., Hendrick, S. S., & Hendrick, C. (1987). Male sexual preference and attitudes toward love and sexuality. *Journal of Sex Education and Therapy, 12(2)*, 27–30.

Ainsworth, M. D. S., Blehar, M. C., Waters, E., & Wall, S. (1978). *Patterns of attachment: A psychological study of the strange situation.* Hillsdale, NJ: Lawrence Erlbaum.

Bailey, W. C., Hendrick, C., & Hendrick, S. S. (1987). Relation of sex and gender role to love, sexual attitudes, and self-esteem. *Sex Roles, 16*, 637–648.

Bartholomew, K., & Horowitz, L. M. (1991). Attachment styles among young adults: A test of a four-category model. *Journal of Personality and Social Psychology, 61*, 226–244.

Bem, S. L. (1974). The measurement of psychological androgyny. *Journal of Consulting and Clinical Psychology, 42*, 155–162.

Berscheid, E., & Walster, E. (1978). *Interpersonal attraction* (2nd ed.). Reading, MA: Addison-Wesley.

Bowlby, J. (1969). *Attachment and loss: Vol. 1. Attachment.* New York: Basic Books.

Duck, S. (Ed.). (1993). *Social context and relationships.* Newbury Park, CA: Sage.

Duck, S. W., & Sants, H. K. A. (1983). On the origin of the specious: Are personal relationships really interpersonal states? *Journal of Social and Clinical Psychology, 1*, 27–41.

Fehr, B. (1993). How do I love thee? Let me consult my prototype. In S. Duck (Ed.), *Individuals in relationships* (pp. 87–120). Newbury Park, CA: Sage.

Fisher, H. E. (1992). *Anatomy of love: The natural history of monogamy, adultery, and divorce.* New York: Norton.

Hatfield, E. (1988). Passionate and companionate love. In R. J. Sternberg & M. L. Barnes (Eds.), *The psychology of love* (pp. 191–217). New Haven, CT: Yale University Press.

Hatfield, E., & Rapson, R. L. (1987). Passionate love: New directions in research. In W. H. Jones & D. Perlman (Eds.), *Advances in personal relationships (Vol. 1,* pp. 109–139). Greenwich, CT: JAI.

Hatfield, E., & Sprecher, S. (1986). Measuring passionate love in intimate relationships. *Journal of Adolescence, 9,* 383–410.

Hazan, C., & Shaver, P. R. (1987). Romantic love conceptualized as an attachment process. *Journal of Personality and Social Psychology, 52,* 511–524.

Hendrick, C. (1988). Roles and gender in relationships. In S. Duck (Ed.), *Handbook of personal relationships: Theory, research and interventions* (pp. 429–448). London: John Wiley.

Hendrick, C., & Hendrick, S. S. (1986). A theory and method of love. *Journal of Personality and Social Psychology, 50,* 392–402.

Hendrick, C., & Hendrick, S. S. (1988). Lovers wear rose colored glasses. *Journal of Social and Personal Relationships, 5,* 161–183.

Hendrick, C., & Hendrick, S. S. (1989). Research on love: Does it measure up? *Journal of Personality and Social Psychology, 56,* 784–794.

Hendrick, C., & Hendrick, S. S. (1990). A relationship-specific version of the Love Attitudes Scale. *Journal of Social Behavior and Personality, 5,* 239–254.

Hendrick, C., Hendrick, S. S., Foote, F. H., & Slapion-Foote, M. J. (1984). Do men and women love differently? *Journal of Social and Personal Relationships, 1,* 177–195.

Hendrick, S. S. (1981). Self-disclosure and marital satisfaction. *Journal of Personality and Social Psychology, 40,* 1150–1159.

Hendrick, S. S. (1988). A generic measure of relationship satisfaction. *Journal of Marriage and the Family, 50,* 93–98.

Hendrick, S. S., & Hendrick, C. (1987a). Love and sex attitudes and religious beliefs. *Journal of Social and Clinical Psychology, 5,* 391–398.

Hendrick, S. S., & Hendrick, C. (1987b). Love and sexual attitudes, self-disclosure and sensation seeking. *Journal of Social and Personal Relationships, 4,* 281–297.

Hendrick, S. S., & Hendrick, C. (1987c). Multidimensionality of sexual attitudes. *Journal of Sex Research, 23,* 502–526.

Hendrick, S. S., & Hendrick, C. (1993). Lovers as friends. *Journal of Social and Personal Relationships, 10,* 459–466.

Hendrick, S. S., & Hendrick, C. (1995). Gender differences and similarities in sex and love. *Personal Relationships 2,* 55–65.

Ickes, W., & Barnes, R. D. (1978). Boys and girls together—and alienated: On enacting stereotyped sex roles in mixed-sex dyads. *Journal of Personality and Social Psychology, 36,* 669–683.

Kirkpatrick, L. A., & Davis, K. E. (1994). Attachment style, gender, and relationship stability: A longitudinal analysis. *Journal of Personality and Social Psychology, 66,* 502–512.

Lee, J. A. (1973). *The colors of love: An exploration of the ways of loving.* Don Mills, Ontario: New Press.

Liebowitz, M. R. (1983). *The chemistry of love.* Boston: Little, Brown.

Pietromonaco, P. R., & Carnelley, K. B. (1994). Gender and working models of attachment: Consequences for perceptions of self and romantic relationships. *Personal Relationships, 1,* 63–82.

Pleck, J. H., Sonenstein, F. L., & Ku, L. C. (1993). Masculinity ideology: Its impact on adolescent men's heterosexual relationships. *Journal of Social Issues, 49*(3), 11–29.

Scharfe, E., & Bartholomew, K. (1994). Reliability and stability of adult attachment patterns. *Personal Relationships, 1,* 23–43.

Sedikides, C., Oliver, M. B., & Campbell, W. K. (1994). Perceived benefits and costs of romantic relationships for women and men: Implications for exchange theory. *Personal Relationships, 1,* 5–21.

Shaver, P. R., & Hazan, C. (1988). A biased overview of the study of love. *Journal of Social and Personal Relationships, 5,* 473–501.

Shaver, P., Hazan, C., & Bradshaw, D. (1988). Love as attachment: The integration of three behavioral systems. In R. J. Sternberg & M. L. Barnes (Eds.), *The psychology of love* (pp. 68–99). New Haven, CT: Yale University Press.

Spence, J. T., & Helmreich, R. L. (1978). *Masculinity and femininity: Their psychological dimensions, correlates, and antecedents.* Austin: University of Texas Press.

Sternberg, R. J. (1986). A triangular theory of love. *Psychological Review, 93,* 119–135.

Sternberg, R. J. (1987). Liking versus loving: A comparative evaluation of theories. *Psychological Bulletin, 102,* 331–345.

Walster, E., & Walster, G. W. (1978). *A new look at love.* Reading, MA: Addison-Wesley.

Wood, J. T. (1995). *Relational communication: Change and continuity in personal relationships.* Belmont, CA: Wadsworth.

SHE SAYS/HE SAYS:
COMMUNICATION, CARING,
AND CONFLICT IN
HETEROSEXUAL RELATIONSHIPS

JULIA T. WOOD

Erica and Carlos spent 2 hours arguing heatedly about whether to move to Atlanta where he has a great job opportunity but her career prospects are unclear. Although they finally agreed to visit Atlanta and check out job possibilities for Erica, both still feel tense and distant. When Carlos suggests they make love, Erica is infuriated. How can he want sex when the fight created such distance between them? Before being intimate, she needs to talk to restore closeness.

Phyllis is angry. Her roommate, Yolanda, is a slob, and their room looks like a pigsty. Worse yet, Phyllis can't study or sleep with Yolanda's stereo blaring. When she sees her boyfriend, Ray, Phyllis starts telling him how frustrated she is. He advises her to lay down the law to Yolanda. Phyllis shrugs and resumes talking about how upset she feels, so Ray tells her to move out. She shakes her head and plunges back into describing her feelings. Ray then says she should get the resident advisor to pull Yolanda into line. Finally, Phyllis explodes at Ray: "Quit telling me what to do! I didn't ask for advice. I just want a little support." Ray is baffled. He thought he was *supporting her.*

Andrea and Josh have been dating seriously for 2 years. She knows he really cares about her and in most ways they're compatible, but she feels he never listens to her. Whenever she's talking to him, he just sits silently and looks at her until she's through. Her best friend, Leah, always nods and says "um hmm" and "yeah," to show she's listening. Josh stays mum. If he loves her, why doesn't he really listen like Leah?

If these scenarios seem familiar, you already have experiential knowledge of gendered dynamics in heterosexual relationships. Men and women sometimes misinterpret and hurt each other because they don't use communication in the same way. Fern Johnson (1989) claims that the differences are so great that the sexes live in distinct communication cultures. In this chapter, we explore reasons for differences in women's and men's interaction styles, and we consider ways to translate each other's communication so that misunderstandings are less likely.

Years ago, sociologist Jesse Bernard (1972) noted disparities in men's and women's styles of relating. In any marriage, she said, there are actually two marriages—his and hers. To follow up on Bernard's insight, we want to examine the distinct ways women and men communicate and deal with conflict. We'll first discuss gender cultures that teach women and men gendered ways of communicating. We'll then trace the implications of gender socialization to see how differences in communication styles surface—and sometimes clash—in heterosexual relationships.

GENDER COMMUNICATION CULTURES

If you've ever watched children at play, you've probably noticed differences in the games girls and boys play and the ways they interact. Maltz and Borker (1982) systematically studied childhood play and discovered it is actually serious business. Games socialize children into understandings of how, when, and why to talk. The researchers concluded that boys and girls tend to learn markedly different rules for communicating, and these promote misunderstandings when the sexes interact with each other.

Since Maltz and Borker's (1982) classic study, scholars have developed the theory that males and females are socialized into separate gender communication cultures (Coates, 1986; Coates & Cameron, 1989; Johnson, 1989; Kramarae, 1981; Tannen, 1990; Wood, 1994a, 1994b). A communication culture exists when a group of people share understandings about how to communicate (Labov, 1972). Members of a communication culture have common ideas about the goals of communication, ways to achieve the goals, and how to interpret one another. They acquire these common views as a result of interacting with other members of their culture. Although not all girls and boys are socialized into, respectively, feminine and masculine communication cultures, the majority of us are. Because children's activities tend to be sex-segregated, gendered patterns of interaction are learned early and may persist throughout life.

Masculine Communication Culture

Young boys tend to play games such as soccer, baseball, and war, which share common features. First, each of these games requires a number of players, so boys learn to interact in large groups. Second, the games are structured by goals and rules, so little talk is needed to organize relationships among team members. Instead, talk is used to negotiate for power, position, and influence—who calls plays, who has key positions on the team. Third, boys' games are highly competitive not only between teams, but also within teams. An individual boy's status depends on being better than other players—being the MVP (most valuable player). Finally, the bond that develops among players results from doing something together—working as a team to achieve a goal. These qualities of boys' games teach three rules about communicating.

Use Communication to Achieve Instrumental Goals. Boys' games emphasize winning as the goal. The point of a game is to beat the other side—to achieve a concrete result. The outcome, or goal, is the reason for playing. Thus, the games don't teach boys to use communication to work out personal relationships and to express feelings. Instead, they use talk to assert their identities, solve problems, plot strategy, and argue points of view. Because they must *do* things to be valued by a team, boys learn to view talk as a means to achieve instrumental goals.

Use Communication to Establish Individual Status and Authority. Boys learn early that each player has to establish his own status on the team. Although teammates work together, each player is responsible for himself and must not depend on others. The boy who scores the most points soars in prestige; the one who offers the best argument for his idea wins respect; the one who conceals his vulnerabilities evades attack. The goal of earning status teaches boys to use communication to assert individual identity and to gain standing. Thus, they come to see talk as a way to demonstrate knowledge, expertise, and superiority; conversation is an arena for asserting themselves and winning respect. Further, because their games are generally played side by side, boys aren't encouraged to tune into subtle clues about others' feelings.

Use Communication to Compete for Attention and Power. Most games favored by boys are competitive. The point is to win. You win a football game by scoring more points than the other team, and you win in conversation by gaining more attention and power than others. From masculine games, boys learn how to hold their own in the rough and tumble of conversation. They learn to use words to block others, win arguments, and defend themselves. Viewing communication as a competition for attention and power, boys learn to interrupt, intimidate others, reroute topics, fend off challenges, and dominate the talk stage. In addition, boys learn to conceal weaknesses and vulnerabilities, which others could use to defeat them. This promotes guardedness, which may explain why some men are uneasy talking about their feelings and personal problems.

In sum, socialization in masculine communication cultures emphasizes doing things together as the basis of relationships and closeness. Masculine culture is defined by activities—by doing things together and by exchanging favors (Swain, 1989). Players learn to count on one another—on the basketball court the point guard has to set up the play, on the football field the offensive line protects the zone and gives the backfield time to execute a play. As adults, men often form profound bonds during war when they rely on each other for safety, courage, and a sense of community in a foreign land (Rubin, 1985). Whether on the football field or in the trenches, closeness in masculine culture arises more from shared experiences than from personal talk (Cancian, 1987; Wood & Inman, 1993).

Feminine Communication Culture

Games such as "house" and "school," which young girls often play, also share common features. First, they involve few people—usually two or three is enough to play. Second, there aren't clear-cut, external goals and rules. There's no parallel in house or school for the touchdown or the home run. Instead, the purpose of the games is to be together—to enjoy each other's company and learn about one another. Thus, girls use talk to work out relationships and interpersonal dynamics. Third, girls' games tend to be more cooperative than competitive. Unlike soccer or war, house has no opposing team. Also, because girls' games center on relationships, they involve less competition among members of the group. Cooperativeness supports the goal of having fun together. Finally, girls develop closeness primarily through talking, while activities are merely a backdrop for communication. The features of girls' games impart three rules for communication.

Use Communication to Build Connections with Others. The purpose of house or school is not to win by scoring touchdowns or annihilating the enemy, but to form and sustain relationships. To play house or school girls have to talk to decide who will have each role and how time will be structured. This gives girls practice in using talk to create relationships. Within feminine culture, communication functions to build and sustain harmonious relationships by talking about expectations and feelings and working out problems)

Use Communication to Include Others. The relationship focus that is typical of girls' games places priority on including others. Because there are few players and everyone must be satisfied for a game to continue, girls become skillful at discerning others' feelings, needs, and moods. To include others, girls learn to ask questions and avoid put-downs. In fact, when there is conflict, girls are more likely to stop the game than to risk hurting each other (Fox, Gibbs, & Auerbach, 1985). Relationships generally take priority over instrumental goals.

Use Communication to Cooperate, Respond, Show Interest, and Support Others. The cooperative and interpersonal character of girls' games requires that they respond to others' requests and support others' feelings. Because their games are played face to face, girls learn to maintain eye contact, notice subtle clues of others' feelings, give feedback, and show interest in what others say. In addition, they learn to share their own thoughts and feelings with others.

· (The rules of feminine communication culture emphasize communication as the basis of relationships and closeness. Because their games pivot on talk, girls often feel that intimacy grows out of talking about personal issues and feelings.) Becker (1987) has termed this "closeness in dialogue," meaning that girls and, later, women weave their lives together by talking.) As Fern Johnson points out in Chapter 5, women friends share the details of their worlds and their feelings through an ongoing dialogue that continually enriches closeness (Aries, 1987; Aries & Johnson, 1983; Rubin, 1985). In general, women regard communication as the crux of relationships. It isn't just a means to other, instrumental goals, but is a key way to build and express closeness. In other words, women see communication as a goal in its own right.

Childhood games, of course, are only one of many influences on individual development. In addition, we are socialized as we interact in families and schools and as we participate in social life generally. These contexts, like childhood play, encourage girls to follow feminine communication rules and boys to follow masculine ones. Other chapters in this book clarify how specific relational contexts reinforce separate gender cultures, and additional research also demonstrates this (Belenky, Clinchy, Goldberger, & Tarule, 1986; Chodorow, 1978, 1989; Epstein, 1988; Janeway, 1971; Miller, 1986). In the next section, we trace the implications of gendered socialization for dynamics in communication in heterosexual romantic relationships.

GENDERED DYNAMICS IN HETEROSEXUAL COMMUNICATION

So far, we've seen that masculine and feminine communication cultures instill different views of how to create and express closeness. Whereas doing things with and for one another builds closeness in masculine cultures, personal talk is a key foundation in feminine ones. This difference paves the way for substantial misunderstandings between heterosexual partners. We'll discuss six gendered dynamics that often complicate communication between women and men.

Topics of Talk

Men and women sometimes talk about different things and don't understand what is important to one another. In general, women enjoy discussing feelings and personal issues, since this is a primary way they develop intimacy (Aries, 1987; Miller, 1986; Riessman, 1990; Wood, 1993a). Masculine cultures, however, do not emphasize personal talk, so most men are less interested and skillful at it than women (Swain, 1989). Men typically prefer to talk about politics, sports, and other topics that don't expose personal feelings.

Compounding the difference in preferred topics of talk are the sexes' misinterpretations of each other. Women may be inclined to see men's lower interest in personal talk as a rejection of intimacy, and men may not understand that talking about feelings is a primary way women create and express closeness. In *Men Are from Mars, Women Are from Venus,* John Gray (1992) points out that many women freely discuss their feelings, confusions, and problems with others, but many men feel they might lose control and others' respect if they express their feelings openly.

For those socialized in masculine cultures, doing things together is the primary path to intimacy (Swain, 1989; Wood & Inman, 1993). Thus, when men want to create or express closeness, they are likely to prefer a shared activity to personal talk. This is the source of misunderstanding between Carlos and Erica, the couple in the scenario that opened this chapter. After an intense argument, both of them feel distant and want to restore intimacy. For Erica, talking about their feelings and the fight they experienced is the way to rebuild closeness. For Carlos, however, the way to rebuild intimacy is to enjoy an activity such as sex together.

Marital therapists report that a recurrent problem for couples is different views of what sex means (Bergner & Bergner, 1990). Many men view sex as a way to restore closeness in order to talk about feelings. Reversing this sequence, women are likely to see talk as a way to become intimate enough to make love. Sam Keen (1991, p. 78), a scholar of men's studies, explains:

> It is not that men are only interested in sex, but that we have been so conditioned to curtail our natural needs for intimacy that only in sex do we have cultural permission to feel close to another human being. [Men] often use sexual language to express their forbidden desires for communion.

A second gendered dynamic surfaces in topics of talk. More than most men, women tend to enjoy sharing details of their daily lives and activities (Becker, 1987). Thus, to tell her partner about her day, a woman may itemize who was present at a meeting, what each person said, what food was served, and so forth. Women share specifics to weave the intricate fabric of connection with others. However, because masculine culture sees talk as a means to achieve clear results, many men regard detailed descriptions as superfluous or even boring. In general, men do not understand that in sharing details, women are trying to share themselves. On the other hand, men's tendency to discuss only big events and to skip the details often frustrates women, who may feel men are not sharing themselves and their lives.

Discussing the Relationship

"Let's talk about us" probably creates more misunderstanding between women and men than any other single phrase. The misunderstanding results from radically different views of what communication does. Because feminine communication cultures regard talk about relationships as a way to create closeness, women tend to find interpersonal dynamics continuously interesting and important. From this perspective, talking about a relationship is a way to intensify intimacy (Acitelli, 1988; Beck, 1988; Riessman, 1990). Masculine communication culture, however, regards the purpose of talk as instrumental. Thus, men tend to think that talk about relationships is needed only if there are problems. "Can we talk about us?" may imply to a man that a problem exists. If nothing's wrong, then men often see no point in talking about relationships, since, unlike women, they generally don't regard talk as the basis of intimacy (Beck, 1988; Riessman, 1990). From a feminine perspective, men's lack of interest in talking about relationships may be misinterpreted as a signal that they don't care about relationships.

Showing Support

We all look to intimates for support and comfort, but women and men differ in what they consider supportive. That difference is the source of tension between Phyllis and Ray in the second scenario that opened this chapter. Frustrated with her roommate, Phyllis talks to Ray to vent her feelings. She wants him to understand how she feels and to empathize with her. Instead, he offers advice, which Phyllis finds unhelpful and unsupportive. He is following the rules of masculine communication culture, which stress using communication to do things—solve problems, give advice. Seeing her unhappiness, Ray tries to help in the only way he knows how, but his responses lead Phyllis to feel he doesn't understand or care about her. When people they care about have problems or are upset, men often try to fix things, not realizing that women often value feeling connected more than resolving problems. This misunderstanding also works conversely: When men express problems or frustrations, they may appreciate pragmatic help more than empathic responses.

Listening Styles

Linguist Deborah Tannen (1990) coined the term *listening noises* to describe women's tendencies to give visible and audible feedback when others are speaking. Because they are socialized to pay attention to others, women learn to show interest and involvement by nodding their heads, keeping eye contact, using facial expressions, and giving continuous vocal noises such as "um hmm," "right," and "I know what you mean." Women tend to use such clues to signal that they are listening and involved. The side-by-side style of boys' play doesn't emphasize ongoing responsiveness to others. Instead, most boys learn to keep their feelings and responses to themselves in order to retain independence and control (Beck, 1988; Hall, 1987).

This explains why Andrea felt Josh didn't listen to her in the third scenario that opened this chapter. She wanted "listening noises" like her girlfriend Leah provides, but Josh wasn't taught to provide them. More hurtful than distinct listening styles is what we may assume they mean. Andrea thinks Josh isn't listening and doesn't care because he listens differently than she and Leah do. Josh probably does listen and care, but Andrea can't translate his communication style.

Conversational Maintenance

Another gendered communication dynamic concerns communication used to maintain conversations. Although typically we're not aware of it, a lot of work is required to keep a conversation going: We ask questions, probe what others say, show interest, give responses, and so on. Without maintenance work, conversations flounder and fail. Research (Beck, 1988; Fishman, 1978) indicates that women generally exceed men in maintaining communication. They invite others to speak, ask questions about topics others initiate, encourage elaborations, and respond to what others say. In addition, women use nonverbal behaviors more than men to signal interest and involvement (Noller, 1980). As a rule, men engage less in conversational maintenance and may deter others from talking by interrupting, failing to respond, or shifting to topics of their own when another has initiated a topic (DeFrancisco, 1991).

Differences in maintenance work reflect gendered socialization. Feminine culture emphasizes including others, responding, and sharing the talk stage. On the other hand, masculine culture stresses competing for status and attention. The masculine emphasis on independence leads many men not to tune into others or feel responsible for including them in conversation. By extension, men, in general, feel no need to invite others to talk because they assume others will speak up if they have something to say. This masculine assumption is at odds with the feminine inclination to actively encourage others to join in conversations. Consequently, women may be hurt if men don't ask how they feel or how their day went. Men, meanwhile, assume that individuals introduce topics when they have something to say. Conversely, men may resent being asked to talk about themselves and their activities when they haven't initiated these topics.

Gendered Responses to Conflict

Conflict is disagreement or tension between people, and it is part of close relationships. From your own experience, you may have discovered that women and men respond to relationship conflict in dissimilar ways. Research confirms this observation and clarifies the differences typical of the sexes. Caryl Rusbult (1987) has conducted a series of studies that reveal four basic responses to conflict. *Loyalty* is a response of remaining quietly committed to a partner and a relationship without actively doing anything to resolve problems. *Voice* is a more active response, which involves overtly addressing the sources of conflict and encouraging discussion of problems. The response of *neglect* denies problems exist or downplays their importance. Finally, the *exit* response involves leaving a relationship either literally or psychologically when conflict surfaces.

Rusbult (1987) reports that women and men, in general, differ in their responses to conflict. Women, both heterosexual and lesbian, generally adopt either loyalty or voice strategies. Consistent with feminine socialization, both responses prioritize a relationship and assumes its continuation. In addition, the voice response relies on communication—talking about tensions—to restore intimacy. Both gay and heterosexual men tend to respond to conflict by neglecting or exiting. Reflecting the independence of masculine communication cultures, both exit and neglect place one partner's perceptions ahead of the bond: Either there is no problem (even if the other partner feels one exists) or the problem can't be solved so it's time to leave. Neither neglect nor exit uses communication to address and resolve tensions.

Adding to Rusbult's findings are those from other researchers. A number of investigations have shown that men are more likely than women to withdraw from conflict (Christensen & Heavey, 1990; Gottman, 1993; Wood, 1986, 1994b). Further, there is limited evidence (Falbo & Peplau, 1980; Howard, Blumstein, & Schwartz, 1986) that women are more likely than men to rely on indirect strategies for influencing what happens during conflict. This makes sense, since feminine cultures teach women not to criticize others overtly. Also, indirect strategies may reflect the fact that women generally have less power than men. Consistent with this picture, investigations also indicate that women are more likely to regard the source of tension as interpersonal dynamics, whereas men are more prone to fault partners or external circumstances (Wood, 1986, 1994b). Women more than men compromise, accommodate, defer, and submit in order to preserve relationships and harmony between partners. Men, on the other hand, more frequently bully their partners to get their way or to end discussion when they become uncomfortable (Belk & Snell, 1988; Howard et al., 1986; White, 1989).

When gendered patterns of dealing with conflict are carried to extremes, violence may erupt. Violence is also a gendered phenomenon with women being disproportionately the victims of violence from intimates (French, 1992; Goldner, Penn, Scheinberg, & Walker, 1990; Thompson, 1991). In 1994, the Center for Disease Control released the grim fact that domestic violence is now the leading cause of injury for women between the ages of 15 and 44 (Lazarus, 1994). Recently, a major study reported that 7% of all women, a total of 4 million women, had been physically abused by their partners in a 1-year period, and as many as 4,000 of these women are battered to death (Hunt, 1994). Jacquelyn White and Barrie Bondurant explore gendered violence in detail in Chapter 12.

SUMMARY

Gendered socialization teaches men and women different understandings of relationships and communication. We've seen that masculine communication cultures emphasize instrumental action, competition for status, and self-assertion and that they emphasize doing things together as a primary route to closeness. Feminine communication cultures, in contrast, prioritize relationships by emphasizing inclusion, cooperation, and responsiveness, and they regard personal communication as a principal path to intimacy.

Women and men who have been socialized into their respective gender cultures often misunderstand one another because they bring dissimilar assumptions, expectations, and interpretations into relationships. Among the ways in which gendered dynamics infuse communication between heterosexual partners are six that we discussed: topics of talk, talk about relationships, expression of support, listening styles, conversational maintenance, and responses to conflict. In these and other ways, women and men may speak different languages, which suggests that becoming bilingual is important for building satisfying and healthy relationships in which partners understand and can talk each other's language.

What we've covered in this chapter certainly doesn't unravel all of the mysteries that are part of the frustration and pleasure of relationships between women and men. Perhaps, however, our discussion promotes better understanding of distinct styles of communication that women and men use. If so, that understanding may lessen misunderstandings between the sexes and enrich the possibilities for meaningful communication in our romantic lives.

QUESTIONS FOR REFLECTION AND DISCUSSION

1. Think back to the games you played as a child. Did you engage in ones typical for your sex or not? Can you see how the games you played shaped your orientation toward interaction?

2. Compare the gendered communication dynamics identified in this chapter against your own experience. How many of the issues discussed in this chapter have surfaced in your relationships with members of the other sex?

3. With others in your class watch a recent film or segment of a popular prime-time drama. Analyze how the gendered communication

dynamics discussed in this chapter show up in interaction between characters. Do any of the characters fail to follow gender patterns? If so, what happens as a result?

4. Gain permission from a day-care center to observe children who are 4 to 6 years old while they are playing. Notice what kinds of games they play and the extent to which their games reflect features identified in Maltz and Borker's (1982) study. Do you see differences between the games and the interaction patterns in same-sex and mixed-sex play? Have a class discussion about observations you and others make.

REFERENCES

Acitelli, L. (1988). When spouses talk to each other about their relationship. *Journal of Social and Personal Relationships, 5,* 185–199.

Aries, E. (1987). Gender and communication. In P. Shaver & C. Hendricks (Eds.), *Sex and gender* (pp. 149–176). Newbury Park, CA: Sage.

Aries, E. J., & Johnson, F. L. (1983). Close friendship in adulthood: Conversational content between same-sex friends. *Sex Roles, 9,* 1183–1196.

Beck, A. (1988). *Love is never enough.* New York: Harper & Row.

Becker, C. (1987). Friendship between women: A phenomenological study of best friends. *Journal of Phenomenological Psychology, 18,* 59–72.

Belenky, M., Clinchy, B., Goldberger, N., & Tarule, J. (1986). *Women's ways of knowing.* New York: Basic Books.

Belk, S. S., & Snell, W. E., Jr. (1988). Avoidance strategy use in intimate relationships. *Journal of Social and Clinical Psychology, 7,* 80–96.

Bergner, R. M., & Bergner, L. L. (1990). Sexual misunderstanding: A descriptive and pragmatic formulation. *Psychotherapy, 27,* 464–467.

Bernard, J. (1972). *The future of marriage.* New York: World.

Cancian, F. (1987). *Love in America.* Cambridge: Cambridge University Press.

Chodorow, N. (1978). *The reproduction of mothering: Psychoanalysis and the sociology of gender.* Berkeley, CA: University of California Press.

Chodorow, N. (1989). *Feminism and psychoanalytic theory.* New Haven, CT: Yale University Press.

Christensen, A., & Heavey, C. (1990). Gender and social structure in the demand/withdraw pattern in marital conflict. *Journal of Personality and Social Psychology, 59,* 73–81.

Coates, J. (1986). *Women, men, and language: Studies in language and linguistics.* London: Longman.

Coates, J., & Cameron, D. (1989). *Women in thier speech communities: New perspectives on language and sex.* London: Longman.

DeFrancisco, V. (1991). The sounds of silence: How men silence women in marital relations. *Discourse and Society, 2,* 413–423.

Epstein, C. F. (1988). *Deceptive distinctions: Sex, gender, and the social order.* New Haven, CT: Yale University Press.

Falbo, T., & Peplau, L. A. (1980). Power strategies in intimate relationships. *Journal of Personality and Social Psychology, 38,* 618–628.

Fishman, P. (1978). Interaction: The work women do. *Social Problems, 25,* 397–406.

Fox, M., Gibbs, M., & Auerbach, D. (1985). Age and gender dimensions of friendship. *Psychology of Women Quarterly, 9,* 489–502.

French, M. (1992). *The war against women.* New York: Summit Books.

Goldner, V., Penn, P., Sheinberg, M., & Walker, G. (1990). Love and violence: Gender paradoxes in volatile attachments. *Family Process, 29,* 343–364.

Gottman, J. M. (1993). The roles of conflict engagement, escalation, or avoidance in marital interaction: A longitudinal view of five types of couples. *Journal of Consulting and Clinical Psychology, 61,* 6–15.

Gray, J. (1992). *Men are from Mars, women are from Venus: A practical guide for improving communication and getting what you want in your relationships.* New York: Harper Collins.

Hall, J. A. (1987). On explaining gender differences: The case of nonverbal communication. In P. Shaver & C. Hendricks (Eds.), *Sex and gender* (pp. 177–200). Newbury Park, CA: Sage.

Howard, J. A., Blumstein, P., & Schwartz, P. (1986). Sex, power, and influence factors in intimate relationships. *Journal of Personality and Social Psychology, 51,* 102–109.

Hunt, A. R. (1994, June 23). O.J. and the brutal truth about marital violence. *Wall Street Journal,* p. A15.

Janeway, E. (1971). *Man's world, woman's place: A study in social mythology.* New York: Dell.

Johnson, F. L. (1989). Women's culture and communication: An analytical perspective. In C. M. Long & S. A. Friedley (Eds.), *Beyond boundaries: Sex and gender diversity in communication* (pp. 301–316). Fairfax, VA: George Mason University Press.

Keen, S. (1991). *Fire in the belly: On being a man.* New York: Bantam.

Kramarae, C. (1981). *Women and men speaking: Frameworks for analysis.* Rowley, MA: Newbury House.

Labov, W. (1972). *Sociolinguistic patterns.* Philadelphia: University of Pennsylvania Press.

Lazarus, M. (1994, June 21). The "ongoing problem" is killing too many women. *Raleigh News and Observer,* p. 9A.

Maltz, D. N., & Borker, R. (1982). A cultural approach to male–female miscommunication. In J. J. Gumpertz (Ed.), *Language and social identity* (pp. 196–216). Cambridge: Cambridge University Press.

Miller, J. B. (1986). *Toward a new psychology of women* (2nd ed.). Boston: Beacon.

Noller, P. (1980). Misunderstandings in marital communication: A study of couples' nonverbal communication. *Journal of Personality and Social Psychology, 39,* 1135–1148.

Riessman, C. K. (1990). *Divorce talk: Women and men make sense of personal relationships.* New Brunswick, NJ: Rutgers University Press.

Rubin, L. (1985). *Just friends: The role of friendship in our lives.* New York: Harper & Row.

Rusbult, C. E. (1987). Responses to dissatisfaction in close relationships: The exit-voice-loyalty-neglect model. In D. Perlman and S. W. Duck (Eds.), *Intimate relationships: Development, dynamics, deterioration* (pp. 209–238). London: Sage.

Swain, S. (1989). Covert intimacy: Closeness in men's friendships. In B. J. Risman & P. Schwartz (Eds.), *Gender and intimate relationships* (pp. 71–86). Belmont, CA: Wadsworth.

Tannen, D. (1990). *You just don't understand: Women and men in conversation.* New York: William Morrow.

Tavris, C. (1992). *The mismeasure of woman.* New York: Simon & Schuster.

Thompson, E. H., Jr. (1991). The maleness of violence in dating relationships: An appraisal of stereotypes. *Sex Roles, 24,* 161–178.

White, B. (1989). Gender differences in marital communication patterns. *Family Process, 28,* 89–106.

Wood, J. T. (1986). Different voices in relationship crises: An extension of Gilligan's theory. *American Behavioral Scientist, 29,* 273–301.

Wood, J. T. (1993a). Engendered relations: Interaction, caring, power, and responsibility in intimacy. In S. W. Duck (Ed.), *Understanding relationship processes, 3: Social contexts and relationships* (pp. 26–54). Newbury Park, CA: Sage.

Wood, J. T. (1993b). Enlarging conceptual boundaries: Research in interpersonal communication. In S. Bowen & N. Wyatt (Eds.), *Transforming visions* (pp. 19–49). Cresskill, NJ: Hampton Press.

Wood, J. T. (1994a). Gender, communication, and culture. In L. Samovar & R. Porter (Eds.), *Intercultural communication: A reader* (7th ed., pp. 155–164). Belmont, CA: Wadsworth.

Wood, J. T. (1994b). Gender and relationship crises: Contrasting reasons, responses, and relational orientations. In J. Ringer (Ed.), *Queer words, queer images: The construction of homosexuality* (pp. 238–265). New York: New York University Press.

Wood, J. T. (1994c). *Gendered lives: Communication, gender, and culture.* Belmont, CA: Wadsworth.

Wood, J. T., & Inman, C. (1993). In a different mode: Recognizing masculine modes of communicating closeness. *Journal of Applied Communication Research, 21,* 279–295.

GENDERED DYNAMICS IN THE ROMANTIC RELATIONSHIPS OF LESBIANS AND GAY MEN

MICHELLE HUSTON
PEPPER SCHWARTZ

As children, many of us played "house" at one time or another. One of the first things to be decided when playing house was who would be the mommy and who would be the daddy. Once these roles were cast, the make-believe activities of "house" could run smoothly, with mommy staying home and cleaning and cooking, while daddy went to work and made money. But how would we have organized our "house" if we didn't have the preset social roles of mommy and daddy to play? Or what would we have done if there were two mommies or two daddies? This is a question many couples must answer, when "house" is no longer make-believe but instead the day-to-day reality of adulthood.

The interplay between gender and homosexuality is interesting, and it can be explored at several levels. A fair amount of research has looked at the gender (or gender orientation) of homosexuals on the individual level, while a much smaller body of literature has investigated the roles lesbians and gay men play within their relationships. The concept of "playing a role" is important, for it emphasizes the contextual nature of our behavior. That is, we often behave as our interpretation of the situation suggests we should, rather than out of some biological or psychological predetermination. From this perspective, "gender roles" are the behaviors and traits we think others expect of us as women or men. You can probably think of many things that our culture presumes men should or should not do or be: They shouldn't cry, they should work hard to support their families, and they should act as leaders. Conversely, women shouldn't be too aggressive, they should place the care of their children (and their husbands) ahead of their own careers, and they should be good at understanding other people. Notice that these roles help make the organization of heterosexual relationships more predictable and efficient. For example, women are expected to provide certain types of housework (cooking, laundry, and most child care), while men are expected to be responsible for other types (maintenance of the yard, cars, and plumbing). Between the two sets of roles, most (or all) tasks necessary for life are conveniently assigned to one partner or the other, with little need for negotiation.

When studying any couple, the question of gender involves both an individual's adherence to stereotypes the culture prescribes for his or her sex and the roles people play relative to one another. Gender dynamics are especially intriguing in the interaction of gay and lesbian couples. If Beth and Susan make a home together, who cares for the yard? If John and Steve are a couple, who cleans the bathroom? In traditional heterosexual relationships, these questions are not likely to arise. In homosexual couples, partners need to arrive at some solution so that the work gets done—but they can't rely on conventional notions of "women's work" or "men's work" to make that solution "obvious."

Traditional femininity and masculinity often shape heterosexual relationships in such a way that complementarity on a basic level is ensured. Gender roles assure that necessary tasks are taken care of in a two-partner, heterosexual partnership: Children are cared for primarily by the mother, while financial security is provided primarily by the father. Partners are also trained for separate spheres of responsibility for the relationship: She sees to its emotional needs by working hard at being a good listener, and a faithful reader of body language and other nonverbal cues, while he is responsible for sexual initiation and much of the large decision making (England & Farkas, 1986; Wood, 1994a). If there are disagreements, the male has the final say. In gay and lesbian relationships, however, this traditionally gendered division of labor cannot be assigned on the basis of the partners' sex(es).

There are also interesting dilemmas facing gay and lesbian couples because as women and men they are often socialized to lack (or have deficiencies in) certain components that are central to many relationships. If, for example, both women have internalized the norm that women should not be sexual initiators, and that an overt interest in sexual behavior is "wrong," then how do lesbians ever manage to have

Facts about
sexuality

a relationship have internalized the norm that men
otions related to fear, unhappiness, and uncertainty,
nen manage to communicate their apprehensions
imily, and all the other issues that arise for modern
learned (sometimes subconsciously) by members of
ationships can teach us a great deal about all men
out the options available to them in their own lives.
xually assertive, more emotionally revealing, and
'e are goals that might benefit all individuals and, by
uples. However, these goals revolve around the
d how individuals learn and relearn gender through

chapter is to introduce you to the many ways gays
and lesbians organize their romantic relationships, and to point out
how gender affects and is affected by this organization. Much of the
data on gay and lesbian relationships are limited. Until the 1960s, the
study of homosexuality focused on questions of etiology with an eye
toward "curing" the wayward soul. Although researchers have moved
away from this judgmental vein, it is still difficult to receive funding for
large-scale, in-depth studies. Therefore, our work is restricted to either
small samples for which statistical analyses would be impossible, or
large samples for which we can collect only the most cursory data.
While the HIV/AIDS crisis has focused public interest (and hence
research dollars) on the intimate lives of gay men, research on lesbians
is more rare.

We should also point out that sexuality is an often misunderstood
component of our lives. While some people spend their whole lives as
strictly homosexuals or heterosexuals, most people tend not to fit that
description. Many people who identify themselves as lesbians have had
sexual intercourse with men in their past and have sometimes married;
some gay men marry women. People who identify themselves as homosexual today may in the future find they are attracted to a person of
the opposite sex and act on that attraction. The converse is true of heterosexuals: Many will have some passing interest or even a sexual
encounter with someone of their own sex, and may or may not continue to consider themselves strictly heterosexual. Even people who
use a specific label for themselves may behave in ways that would seem
to make that label inappropriate. The majority (although by no means
all) of the research conducted about gays and lesbians uses self-identification as the primary determinant of who qualifies to participate in
the study, yet self-identification does not always predict behavior or
vice versa.

GENDER IN THE INTIMATE RELATIONSHIPS OF HOMOSEXUALS

We begin this section on relationships where the vast majority of modern American couples begin: dating and courtship. Although often a fun and exciting activity, finding a partner is rarely a completely pain-free process. The road to couplehood is often fraught with miscues, wrong turns, and dead-ends. Heterosexual men and women, however, have scripts that help make dating relationships a bit more predictable. For example, it is still the case that, in general, the man makes the "first move" by asking someone out, while it is up to the woman to turn him down or accept his offer. In general, it is still the man who attempts to increase the level of sexual intimacy with his sexual partner, and the woman who "puts on the brakes" (or not).

While some types of casual relationships are scripted in the world of gay dating, not all are, and not all aid the level of predictability in the situation, as we will soon see. The dating and courtship rituals of gay men and lesbians are, not surprisingly, affected by these "scripts," as well as by the gender identity of the individuals involved.

Although some stereotypes of gay men suggest otherwise, most lesbians and gay men report that they would like to "settle down" in a long-term relationship at some point in their life. However, the act of finding a permanent partner is not always easy. In isolated, rural areas (and some urban areas as well), gay and lesbian organizations and meeting places do not exist; hence, the most likely sources of finding others with similar sexual orientations and goals are not available. Furthermore, because homosexuals in isolated areas are more likely to be closeted because of the lack of any sort of gay community, even knowing who is gay and who is not is problematic. Even in those urban settings in which we find large gay populations, meeting potential partners is not always a simple process. A large number of people remain "in the closet," and finding partners in bars and gay-oriented meetings necessarily limits the population of potential partners to people who feel comfortable in such settings. Once a person decides to look for a partner, how does she or he do so, and is the process affected by gender?

The lesbian dating game can be tricky. Lesbian bars are not as common as gay bars, and hence women cannot always count on them as a way to meet potential partners. Furthermore, lesbian bars primarily serve as gathering places for already-established lesbian couples, and the norms governing the behavior that occurs within them generally favor socializing instead of overt, aggressive attempts to pick someone up. Because lesbians tend to go to bars in couples, finding unattached lesbians is unlikely. Therefore, lesbians tend to rely more on friendship circles, mutual acquaintances, and participation in lesbian and women's political groups for chances to meet prospective partners (Vetere, 1982).

Not surprisingly, gender has an impact on this process. For example, women who adhere to the traditional feminine role may find the thought of going to a lesbian bar very unattractive. They are required to go out at night, often to areas of the city that are not entirely safe for a lone woman (or even a group of women); furthermore, many people do not like the atmosphere of bars—they can be smoky, loud, and full of inebriated people. These women may also not feel comfortable in the realm of political activism, and thus may keep their distance from such organizations. Finally, the feminine gender role prohibits interest in same-sex behavior; in fact, norms surrounding female sexuality in general tend to put women in a reactionary role. In short, they are untrained and hence frequently uncomfortable making the first move toward a potential partner. This is one reason so many lesbian relationships develop from already existing friendships. It eliminates the necessity of straightforward romantic courting, although admitting and pursuing interest is no easy task even with a friend.

Although men may be socialized to handle the potentially ego-bruising chore of expressing interest (or at least more resigned to the task), and the culture of gay bars streamlines the process of finding a sexual partner, these two facts can also undermine long-term relationships. First, men are socialized to be the initiators, and taking the role of the one who is approached may seem foreign and undesirable to them—so much so that they may refrain from pursuing relationships in which they were the ones asked out. Furthermore, while the gay bar subculture has made finding a casual sexual partner relatively uncomplicated, it has also made finding a long-term companion rather difficult. Because male homosexuality has often included the endorsement of anonymous sex, the culture surrounding it has developed norms that tend to work against long-term relationships (Silverstein, 1981; Tuller, 1978). For example, most gay men pride themselves on their appearance, and tend to prefer partners who are also strikingly handsome (Deaux & Hanna, 1984). Although perhaps gratifying in the short-run, attractiveness is not a trait that ensures the durability of a relationship. Until recently, even those gay men who managed to form long-term relationships were not well supported within their communities. Singlehood was, and in most places still is, the norm.

MAINTAINING RELATIONSHIPS

Once the rocky road of courtship is navigated, the work of maintaining a relationship begins. Although a great deal can be said about homosexual couples, we will explore only those aspects of relationships that are affected by or reflect the element of gender identity and roles.

Theoretically, homosexual couples have several options in organizing their relationships. For example, individuals can choose partners whose gender typing complements their own, which is usually referred to as "butch–femme" role playing. In this arrangement, a feminine woman and a masculine woman partner, and each plays the traditional role corresponding to her gender identity. This sorting by preexisting gender identities, although often found in stereotypes, is not common in real life. Many studies find that over 90% of the lesbians questioned desire egalitarian relationships, a quality difficult to maintain in butch–femme arrangements because the notion of "butch" is tied into elements of power and control, while "femme" is akin to dependency and submission. Nonetheless, there remain some lesbians who are happy with relationships organized in this way, most of whom grew up in the first half of this century before the widespread feminist critique of gender roles.

Even for those women of more recent generations who have reclaimed some aspects of the feminine role (so-called "lipstick lesbians"), gender typing does not run deep. In fact, even when we know the gender identity of an individual who identifies as homosexual, we cannot accurately predict his or her sex-role behavior within the relationship (Blumstein & Schwartz, 1983; Cardell, Finn, & Maracek, 1981). This suggests that gender is fluid and often contextually situated: The woman who wears the lipstick might also be the one to change the oil in the car or take out the trash.

We know even less about this type of relationship among gay men. However, we would suggest that again there may be a cohort effect, with much older men being more likely to arrange their lives in this manner. Some gay couples also display some elements of "butch–femme" in that an older, established man trades his wealth, experience, and leadership for the youth and attractiveness of a much younger partner, whereby the older man is seen as the provider for the couple and displays the younger man's attractiveness and youth as a "prize." Of course, this type of couple is also found among heterosexuals.

Another option is to create nongendered roles after the couple is established. In this case, once a couple is formed, they organize their home life and relationship around a division of labor in which each partner has a fixed set of chores and duties for which he or she alone is responsible. Although not as confining as heterosexual norms, this style of organization can still benefit one partner over the other if one person gets stuck doing all the "dirty work."

Another way homosexual couples can deal with their freedom from gendered relationship roles is by creating new divisions of labor, in which each partner does what she does best, with the unwanted chores shared evenly between the two. These relationships tend to be more egalitarian, at least when power is measured by who bears responsibility for what household tasks. However, when we look at specific examples of role sharing, we find that some attempts are more successful than others. We now turn to these concrete examples of effective communication, division of housework, and sexual relations.

Organization of Communication

Many people, including several authors in this book, have suggested that men and women communicate differently: Women are taught to nurture conversation, to listen well, and to support their conversational partner, while men are taught that conversation is a way to display their own importance, to achieve status, or to arrive at definitive conclusions by following the rule "might makes right." Research on the communication styles of men and women in conversation with one another pinpoints different elements of conversation that can be defined as part of either a "masculine" or a "feminine" style of communicating. For example, men tend to interrupt their partner more (which is one way to retain the privilege of putting forth their own ideas), they tend to talk more, and they tend to fill lulls in the conversation with noncommittal "uh-huhs" (called minimal responses), which signal their disinterest in what the other person is saying. Women, on the other hand, tend to interrupt less, respond more to others, and use tag lines, which are questions at the end of their own statements that invite the other person to interject her or his own opinion.

Some theorists have suggested that different communication styles are a result of psychological differences between men and women, while others have pointed to the idea that men and women are raised in different cultures: one of power and privilege, another of powerlessness and servitude (Wood, 1994a). Other scholars have suggested that it may not be just gender that influences conversational style; it may be that power mediates the effects of gendered communication styles (Kollock, Blumstein, & Schwartz, 1985; Lakoff, 1990). In other words,

it could simply be that men traditionally have more power in their relationships (both intimate and professional) than women, and this power
allows them to communicate in a direct, confident way. One way to
control for this factor is to study relationships in which power differ-
entials occur, but in which sex (and by extension, gender to some
degree) is held constant. Gay and lesbian relationships provide such an
opportunity.

Women are often the caregivers in their relationships—they are
taught to feel responsible for the well-being of those relationships
(Wood, 1994b). Usually women develop skills that help them in this
endeavor: They are good listeners, and they learn to "read" subtle communication cues that help them interpret and predict the needs of their
companions. By and large, lesbians have learned these skills well, and
their conversational style reflects this fact. They tend to avoid challenging one another (Clunis & Green, 1988; Tannen, 1990), they do not
interrupt as often as other couples (Kollock et al., 1985), and the less
powerful partner uses fewer tag questions.

However, because lesbians tend to use communication as a way to
achieve emotional intimacy, this goal often supersedes other functions
of conversation, such as solving problems or reaching agreements about
disputed issues. Because confrontation and dominance tend to work
against the main goal of augmenting intimacy, and because they are not
emphasized in feminine speech cultures, lesbians sometimes suffer from
an inability to deal constructively with problems (Becker, 1988; Clunis
& Green, 1988). They find it difficult to express discontent or ask for
change. Hence, while lesbian communication tends to be warm and
supportive, it may not always be effective for resolving painful differences of opinion or creating change. Partners may also feel suffocated
if conversations return again and again to matters of emotional intimacy and to how each person feels about the relationship.

Communication between gay men is often influenced by the speech
patterns common to most men, gay or straight. This is particularly true
when the couple is trying to resolve a problem or talk over an issue
about which the partners disagree. These "discussions" can take on
great symbolic meaning, turning into a battlefield on which each partner tries to win the upper hand and assert or display his own dominance (Blumstein & Schwartz, 1983). If this is the case, winning is more
important than resolution, and simple disagreements can evolve into
serious arguments for which there seem to be no answers that satisfy
both men's desire to dominate. One gender difference that remains even
after controlling for power is that men resist others' attempts to interrupt them. Powerful gay men have a very low rate of successful inter-

rupting, which suggests that their less powerful partners will not yield the floor even when the other person tries to take it by conversational force (Kollock et al., 1985). Consequently, gay men in couples have to work hard to build trust and intimacy because at least one of the traditional routes through which emotional closeness is formed (that is, communication) is problematic.

Power and the Organization of Housework and Decision Making

The vast majority of lesbians and gay men espouse an ideology of equality: They want their relationships to be based on an egalitarian model in which both partners have equal say in decision making, assume equal responsibilities for housework, and share the privileges and rights generated in the relationship. In most heterosexual relationships, power imbalances are an expected part of life: The man, by virtue of his greater earning power (and usually greater earnings) and also simply by convention, tends to have the "upper hand" in decision making, and is exempt from most of the responsibility for housework and child care. Gays and lesbians make concerted efforts to avoid such an imbalance; however, they are not always successful.

Lesbians are more likely to succeed at maintaining egalitarian relationships than gay men (Kurdek, 1993). In part, this could be due to the fact that women are not taught to measure their own worth by the amount of money they make, and do not apply that criteria to other women. It could also be related to the depressed, and hence more similar, earning power of women; in short, they are more likely than gay men to have incomes close to one another. Even when a large gap between incomes occurs, money is not correlated with power in lesbian relationships (Blumstein & Schwartz, 1983; Lynch & Reilly, 1985/86). Gay men, however, do measure power by income, and the partner who earns more tends to have more say in decision making and does less housework than his partner. This can become problematic when the partner making less money believes he should have as much influence as his partner in making decisions, or when he feels financially dependent on his partner. This is especially true when the more wealthy partner's income allows a luxurious lifestyle to which the poorer partner can contribute little.

In general, gay men and lesbians do not allocate household chores along the same lines as heterosexuals, that is, with the bulk of the work being assigned to one partner. Instead, gay men tend to divide the number of chores they do evenly between the two—carving out "separate but equal" domains based on preference and ability. Lesbians, on the other hand, are likely to share all the tasks relatively equitably—either taking turns or doing the chore together (Kurdek, 1993). For example, gay men might settle on an arrangement in which one is primarily responsible for preparing meals while the other cleans up afterward. Lesbians are more likely to cook the meal together and both clean up, or trade the jobs back and forth. Interestingly, while household labor is associated with elevated levels of psychological distress among married women, housework is negatively associated with distress for lesbians, perhaps because the context in which lesbians perform these duties is one in which they had some say and their partners also do housework. Wives, on the other hand, are traditionally expected to perform these chores with little or no recourse for change and with little, if any, help from partners (Hochschild with Machung, 1989; Kurdek, 1993).

In heterosexual relationships in which children are present, the mother is usually the primary caretaker of those children (despite the growing number of fathers who are trying to be more involved in their children's lives). The role of caretaker is extremely understudied in gay and lesbian relationships, probably because it was assumed for a long time that homosexuals did not have children. However, a large minority of lesbians are also parents, as are some gay men. For the most part, these children were conceived during heterosexual marriages, before the person "came out."

Very little is known about the way in which gay men and lesbians divide child-rearing tasks. Among lesbians, children—and the chores that come with them—are often wanted by both partners. The biological mother in lesbian couples often has greater power than her partner when it comes to making large decisions and is less dependent on the relationship (Moore, Blumstein, & Schwartz, 1994). This element of the division of labor is ripe for study, and few (if any) researchers have explored the mechanisms by which child-care responsibilities are allocated.

Organization of Sex

While for some people sex can be a simple, uncomplicated act, most people discover that it is often bound tightly to emotions. What happens during sex can carry over into the rest of the relationship, or reflect the relationship's strengths and weaknesses in a microcosm. Furthermore, because men and women are usually raised with different understandings of the meanings and purpose of sex, gender has a profound impact on the organization of sex in the intimate relationships of lesbians and gay men.

In fact, we see the least amount of equality for lesbians in the organization of sex. Most lesbians espouse the ideal of equal right of initiation and refusal, usually because of their conscious rejection of "male" behaviors—including those associated with being sexually aggressive and passionate. However, few couples achieve this balance. Most couples tend to fall into patterns in which one person generally takes the role of sexual initiator, which can cause a variety of problems. Even the women comfortable in this role may grow to resent the responsibility of it, and wish their partners would shoulder some of the burden and risk of expressing interest. Conversely, the noninitiating partner may become dissatisfied with her role and with the obligation of having the final say about having sex (often hurting the initiator's feelings unintentionally). Interestingly, the more emotionally expressive partner (hence, by many tests, the more "feminine" one) tends to take responsibility for making sexual overtures (probably because lesbian sex usually starts with displays of affection), and it is usually the more powerful partner who refuses (Blumstein & Schwartz, 1983).

Gay men are not exempt from issues surrounding gender roles and sex, although their problems differ from those of lesbians. Men are trained to be initiators, but this leads to potential problems when both partners think that they should be the one to make the advance, and that by not making the advance they're somehow surrendering part of their masculinity. Furthermore, refusing sex can become a power play by which one partner tries to assert his own dominance of the situation (or the relationship). However, this is a less satisfying position to be in because refusing sex is not a sanctioned part of the male sexual role. If these issues are not resolved, sex can become a highly significant and symbolic battleground on which the partners spar for control, and more distantly, for the assertion of their own masculinity.

Specific sex acts can also take on symbolic meaning, although these meanings differ from one man to another. For example, some men who perform oral sex say it makes them feel powerful and in control, while other men say they feel most masculine and dominant while *receiving* oral sex. As with lesbians, reciprocity of oral sex is expected; if men do not rotate this responsibility, resentment can arise. Anal intercourse is a bit less ambiguous. Although there exists no evidence to suggest that sexual position (being the penetrator or penetratee) is related to overall gender identity, most men report that they feel differently, depending on the role they are taking during that moment of intercourse. Men report that they tend to feel more feminine and more passive when receiving anal sex, and more dominant and in control when they are the penetrators. Thus, power and masculinity can be implicated in sexual position and can have greater import than one might think (Blumstein & Schwartz, 1983).

Implicit in the discussion above is the notion that gender identity is influenced by context. For gay men, playing a given role during anal intercourse will connote certain feelings of maleness or femaleness that are not a part of their everyday routine. A similar phenomenon is found among lesbians. Rosenzweig and Lebow (1992) found that only a small part of their sample could be classified as "feminine" using a conventional measure of gender identity in a global context. However, when they used the same scale to measure gender identity within the specific context of sexual activity, nearly half the sample fell into the "feminine" category, and most of the rest were classified as "androgynous" (which means they scored above the mean for the measure of masculinity and the measure of femininity). The authors suggest that this migration toward femininity when it comes to matters of sex could be due to the restrictive and heavily sanctioned nature of the norms surrounding female sexual behavior. However, they have found evidence that a "feminine" style of sex (which emphasizes a caring, gentle, sensitive approach to lovemaking) is more rewarding and satisfying. More research is necessary in this area before any definitive conclusions can be made, however.

CONCLUSION

In conclusion, while gay men and lesbians are freed from many of the conventional ways of organizing relationships because sex does not automatically prescribe roles, they must also bear the responsibility of creating their own schemes for deciding how to divide responsibilities and rights within relationships. Often, they must also form ways of dealing with the deficits that socialization into one gender role produces. Although not impossible, this often presents challenges.

We can all learn from how these challenges are met. Those who wish to establish more egalitarian heterosexual relationships can use those models developed by gay men and lesbians, which demonstrate that equitable division of labor is not only rewarding, but also possible. Two gay men, both of whom work full time, still manage to keep their toilets clean and the dishes done. If they can do it, so can husbands and male partners of heterosexual women. Beyond applying the lessons learned from gay men and lesbians to relationships, we might learn something about the contextual nature of gender. While each individual's upbringing undoubtedly differs, we are all part of a culture that holds rather strict notions about what it means to be men and women. Many lesbians and gay men demonstrate that it is possible to overcome that socialization and to learn new ways of looking at ourselves, our relationships to intimate partners, and our relationship to the larger society. Women can learn to be independent, assertive, and self-confident without giving up their ability to nurture and feel empathy for others. Men, too, can maintain those traits valued most in the traditional masculine role while developing capacities to foster and express intimacy, compassion, and responsiveness. While we do not contend that these new models of relationships and gender would be satisfying for everyone, they nonetheless provide a place to start—and a glimmer of hope—for those who wish to change the current power imbalances prevalent in many heterosexual relationships.

QUESTIONS FOR REFLECTION AND DISCUSSION

1. What can heterosexual couples learn from the organization of homosexual couples?
2. What can individual men and women learn from the fluid aspect of behavior that was once considered gender-specific?
3. Why are lesbians and gay men not likely to be in "butch–femme" relationships? Why would this kind of organization be appealing? Not appealing?
4. Given what you now know about homosexual relationships, how do you think gay men and lesbians decide who will be responsible for child care?
5. Imagine being in a relationship with someone very much like yourself. Say, for example, you both liked to cook, but neither of you liked to wash the dishes. How would you resolve the obvious problem (that is, making sure you had clean dishes)? What other areas of couplehood might become problematic if you and your partner were very much alike? Would the same type of solution work for all situations?

REFERENCES

Becker, C. S. (1988). *Unbroken ties: Lesbian ex-lovers.* Boston, MA: Alyson.

Blumstein, P., & Schwartz, P. (1983). *American couples.* New York: William Morrow.

Cardell, M., Finn, S., & Maracek, J. (1981). Sex-role identity, sex-role behavior, and satisfaction in heterosexual, lesbian, and gay male couples. *Psychology of Women Quarterly, 5*(3), 488–494.

Clunis, D. M., & Green, G. D. (1988). *Lesbian couples.* Seattle, WA: Seal Press.

Deaux, K., & Hanna, R. (1984). Courtship in the personals column: The influence of gender and sexual orientation. *Sex Roles, 11*(5/6), 363–375.

England, P., & Farkas, G. (1986). *Households, employment, and gender: A social, economic and demographic view.* Hawthorne, NY: Walter deGruyter.

Hochschild, A., with Machung, A. (1989). *The second shift.* New York: Avon Books.

Kollock, P., Blumstein, P., & Schwartz, P. (1985). Sex and power in interaction: Conversational privileges and duties. *American Sociological Review, 50,* 34–46.

Kurdek, L. A. (1993). The allocation of household labor in gay, lesbian, and heterosexual married couples. *Journal of Social Issues, 49,* 127–139.

Lakoff, R. (1990). *Talking power: The politics of language.* New York: Basic Books.

Lynch, J. M., & Reilly, M. E. (1985/86). Role relationships: Lesbian perspectives. *Journal of Homosexuality, 12,* 53–69.

Moore, M., Blumstein, P., & Schwartz, P. (submitted 1994). The power of motherhood: A contextual evaluation of family resources. Submitted to *Journal of Marriage and the Family.*

Rosenzweig, J., & Lebow, W. (1992). Femme on the streets, butch in the sheets? Lesbian sex-roles, dyadic adjustment, and sexual satisfaction. *Journal of Homosexuality, 23*(3), 1–20.

Silverstein, C. (1981). *Man to man: Gay couples in America.* New York: William Morrow.

Tannen, D. (1990). *You just don't understand: Women and men in conversation.* New York: Ballantine Books.

Tuller, N. R. (1978). Couples: The hidden segment of the gay world. *Journal of Homosexuality, 3,* 331–343.

Vetere, V. A. (1982). The role of friendships in the development and maintenance of lesbian love relationships. *Journal of Homosexuality, 8,* 51–65.

Wood, J. T. (1994a). *Gendered lives: Communication, gender, and culture.* Belmont, CA: Wadsworth.

Wood, J. T. (1994b). *Who cares: Women, care, and culture.* Carbondale, IL: Southern Illinois Press.

BEING SEXUAL IN THE
SHADOW OF AIDS

SHERYL PERLMUTTER BOWEN
PAULA MICHAL-JOHNSON

At least 1 in 500 (Gayle et al., 1990), and perhaps 1 in 200, college students is infected with the human immunodeficiency virus (HIV), the virus that causes acquired immunodeficiency syndrome (AIDS). More than 400,000 people have been diagnosed with full-blown AIDS. Most of them have died.

As a man or a woman coming of age in the 1990s, you face a challenge that no other generation has experienced in exploring and enjoying sexuality. HIV/AIDS is a constant and deadly threat to women and men who went through puberty in the early 1980s, much as the nuclear holocaust hung over the heads of adolescents in the 1960s. Defining events for you might be the end of the Cold War, the *Challenger* disaster, the Persian Gulf War, the aftermath of the Rodney King verdict, and the AIDS epidemic (Levine, 1993). HIV/AIDS is different from other sexually transmitted diseases (STDs) like herpes, gonorrhea, syphilis, or chlamydia that hounded sexually active people of other generations. With these diseases, doctors were able to prescribe a medication and the disease dissipated. With HIV/AIDS, it is unlikely that a cure will be found in this century.

We (Sherry and Paula, the authors of this chapter) became concerned about the impact of HIV/AIDS on our students when we began working together in 1987. We conducted several studies of college students and their talk about AIDS, and we worked with an urban African American AIDS education and prevention organization. Through our university AIDS task force, we trained peer educators and student performers to help raise awareness at our university, and we brought the NAMES Project Quilt, which memorializes those who have died of AIDS, to our campus. We care a great deal about this issue—it has permeated our teaching, our research, and our service to our campus, community, and nation. Perhaps general publicity or HIV/AIDS prevention activities at your school have alerted you to the disease. In this chapter, we tell you some of what we know about how HIV/AIDS is affecting college students and how you can more effectively deal with the challenges that HIV/AIDS poses for us all.

In our work, we found that women and men do not always deal with HIV/AIDS information in the same ways. Gender is an issue in how people understand the sexual situation and plays a part in people's willingness to practice safer sex. The physiological risks of contracting HIV for men and women may even be different. These differences deserve to be discussed. Our goals in writing this chapter are to help you (1) understand the forces in your own social milieu that might place you as a college student at highest risk for HIV infection, and (2) think through the research findings about how gender affects women's and men's tendencies to follow prevention advice offered by health care professionals.

In this chapter, we focus primarily on heterosexual encounters and relationships because that is where the majority of research on college students has focused. We acknowledge that the issues relating to homosexual encounters and relationships may be similar in many ways, and different in others, but we lack the research to advance information about lesbian women and gay men. We have restricted our focus here to sexual transmission and have excluded attention to perinatal transmission or transmission through blood contact by exchange of needles.

HOW REAL IS THE RISK OF HIV INFECTION ON COLLEGE CAMPUSES?

The statistics on how many people are infected with HIV can be misleading. Most states are not able to monitor people who test positive for antibodies to the virus, and the cases reported by the Centers for Disease Control are only for people who have full-blown AIDS. As you may know, individuals can harbor the virus for 10 years with no symptoms, and through exchange of semen, blood, or mother's milk, they pass on the infection to others. The long dormancy phase makes

HIV/AIDS particularly frightening. Cases of full-blown AIDS in the 20-to 24-year age group are rising, and it is likely that the infections for most 25- to 35-year-olds with AIDS were acquired when they were in their late teens and early 20s (Butcher, Manning, & O'Neal, 1991).

College students are particularly vulnerable to HIV infection for several reasons. First, college students are often involved in sexual experimentation. When combined with high alcohol use, the level of sexual activity is estimated to be very high, with 75 to 85% of college students reporting they are sexually active (DiClemente et al, 1990). The students at highest risk are the 10 to 12% who tell researchers that they have multiple sexual partners, while 15 to 25% of college students are abstinent, placing them at least risk. Young men tend to be sexually active at an earlier age and have more partners than women. Second, the typical college student is quite optimistic, and believes that she or he is invulnerable (van der Pligt, Otten, Richard, & van der Velde, 1993). College women and men do not believe that they will become infected with HIV in spite of their high rates of sexual activity. Women take health threats more seriously than men (Cochran & Mays, 1990; Darling & Davidson, 1986; Linville, Fischer, & Fischhoff, 1993; Spees, 1987; Sprecher & McKinney, 1993), but they are still at risk for HIV.

HIV risk is heightened by the exponential growth of STDs. Eighty-six percent of all STDs occur among 15- to 29-year-olds (Grimley, Riley, Bellis, & Prochaska, 1993). STDs are considered a co-factor for HIV transmission because herpes, chlamydia, genital warts, pelvic inflammatory disease (PID), gonorrhea, and syphilis create lesions, allowing the HIV virus to enter the system.

We know that HIV/AIDS has affected how some young adults think about sexual behavior. Research consistently shows that college students have accurate knowledge about HIV/AIDS (Butcher et al., 1991; Cochran & Mays, 1990; O'Leary, Goodhart, Jemmott, & Boccher-Lattimore, 1992; Oswalt & Matsen, 1993; Williams et al., 1992). This knowledge, however, is not often translated into action. In our own research of college students' talk about AIDS (and corroborated by others' research), we found that a minority report actually changing their behavior. Those who do change typically say that they don't have one-night stands anymore; they are more selective in choosing partners; they check out potential partners through their friends or by "scoping" them before they go out with them; and they attempt to know the other person well before having sex. These are good precautions, yet they do not eliminate risk. It is almost impossible for your knowledge of a partner to be 100 percent accurate. The partner may not know that he or she is infected or that any previous partners were carriers of the virus. (There is a 6-week to 6-month lag before HIV antibodies show up in tests.) Behavior and appearance are just as vulnerable to erroneous judgments.

There are major differences in the ways that men and women frame their thinking and behavior about their own risk of becoming infected. In our data from five colleges and universities, and from studies of college students by other researchers, we find that in general, men report less fear or concern about HIV than women (Cochran & Peplau, 1991; Gray & Saracino, 1991). Men were more likely to report having enough information already or being saturated with information. Men's attitudes also reflect higher levels of homophobia, which may interfere with their ability to hear HIV information (Cline & McKenzie, 1994; Cochran & Peplau, 1991; Goodwin & Roscoe, 1988; Metts & Fitzpatrick, 1992; Stiff, McCormack, Zook, Stein, & Henry, 1991). In part, many men retain the false notion that AIDS affects only gay men. (We are not implying that all men think in these ways, just that studies report these tendencies for men in general.) We know, of course, that AIDS is spreading among heterosexuals, so AIDS prevention is relevant for all sexually active people and for those who put themselves at risk through other means of transmission.

Women, on the other hand, are more open to hearing HIV information (Gray & Saracino, 1991; Moore & Rosenthal, 1991). But why? We know that women typically take responsibility for health issues in their families, and that contraception is more salient for women; therefore, their higher degree of attentiveness is not surprising. Also, women place more importance than men on finding and keeping monogamous relationships as a way of protecting themselves (Gray & Saracino, 1991). Women are also more inclined to talk about HIV in their relationships (Bowen & Michal-Johnson, 1990; Cline, Freeman, & Johnson, 1990; Gray & Saracino, 1991; Sprecher, 1990). For the most part, women see themselves as the initiators of talk about AIDS protection in their sexual liaisons. This suggests that gender may be an important factor in HIV/AIDS risk. Even so, *less than 50% of college women studied report talking about HIV/AIDS in their relationships* (Bowen & Michal-Johnson, 1990; Cline, Freeman, & Johnson, 1990), and only 35% of men discuss it with their partners (Bowen & Michal-Johnson, 1990).

We are beginning to understand that there are no pat answers to protecting ourselves from HIV infection. "Just Saying No," for example, is an effective strategy for celibate students, but not for sexually active ones. Passion and personal needs may propel sexual activities as conventional wisdom flies out the window.

WHAT INFLUENCES WHETHER A PERSON WILL HAVE SEX?

We first need to understand some of the influences that lead to sexual activities. These include *situational or contextual* variables, such as alcohol use, the length of a relationship, and the trajectory or path of a relationship. Whether students date in dyads (where relationships evolve) or socialize in more anonymous group settings also affects how or whether sex happens. *Personal characteristics,* including body type, weight, and biological sex, among others, also influence how sexual encounters unfold. *Individual differences* in communication style (for example, open, passive, dramatic, friendly, or assertive) and cognitive processing (for example, intelligence, inferencing, and decision-making processes) further influence behaviors surrounding sexual activity. Our scripts and metaphors for sexuality also guide our plans and actions regarding sex.

Cultural Groupings

Cultural groupings based on ethnicity (for example, African American, Hispanic, or European American), sexual orientation (for example, straight, gay, lesbian, or bisexual), social group or class (for example, college students, or working class), religious affiliation (for example, Catholic, or Christian Fundamentalist), and recreational activities (for example, biking, bowling, surfing) entail differing norms about what is typical and/or acceptable for sexual and relational partners (Blumstein & Schwartz, 1983). The cultural groupings of each partner influence what happens between them. These influences affect how we understand sexual activity as well as our efforts to prevent HIV infection (Michal-Johnson & Bowen, 1992).

As you may already realize, sexual arousal changes how we make decisions. Some decisions are strategic, and some are far less deliberate and conscious (de facto decisions). De facto decisions are made without overt discussion, and without a hyperrationalism that may characterize other sorts of decisions (for example, deciding whether to do your assignment and read this chapter). Instead, sexual choices are a product of verbal *and* nonverbal behaviors that are manifest in a heightened physiological state of arousal that adds an urgency and immediacy that isn't typical of other activities. In addition, messages that suggest "yes, yes!" and "no, no!" may occur simultaneously in an episode (Edgar & Fitzpatrick, 1990). Ambiguity in the form of innuendo, conflicting verbal and nonverbal messages, and token resistance to preserve one's image may become part of sexual episodes. We will now focus on alcohol use, the mind-set of the individual, and gender differences as keys to managing risk of HIV infection.

Alcohol

Alcohol use undermines the ability to make self-protective decisions or to negotiate safer sex. Alcohol has been referred to as a "social lubricant," since many students feel that drinking helps them deal with awkward circumstances, cope with stress, and reduce fear. Drinking, like sex, is also associated with "adult behavior." Both men and women are heavy users of alcohol on college campuses. While studies consistently show that white men drink more, and more often, than women, the number of women drinking to get drunk has tripled since 1977 (Commission on Substance Abuse, 1994). Further, the rate of heavy drinking by college women is double the rate of their noncollege peers (Commission on Substance Abuse, 1994). The consequences of drinking are greater for women than for men—they get sicker faster, and they can become addicted faster.

The students with whom we have worked tell us that "hooking up" (that is, pairing off) is more common after drinking (also see Corcoran & Thomas, 1991). Interestingly, men report that both partners are sexiest when both parties are drinking beer, while women give their lowest rating of sexuality in that condition (Leigh, Aramburu, & Norris, 1992). Between 35 and 70% of college students report some type of sexual activity primarily as a result of alcohol (Commission on Substance Abuse, 1994). O'Leary et al. (1992) found that men reported being more likely than women to have sex under the influence, and white students were more likely to do so than African Americans. Seventy-six percent of unmarried, sexually active students in their New Jersey sample reported engaging in risky behavior. Nonetheless, 60% of college women diagnosed with an STD were drunk at the time of infection (Commission on Substance Abuse, 1994), pointing up the incredible risk for college women. In addition, college women who are binge drinkers are more likely to engage in unplanned sex (Weschler & Isaac, 1992).

Alcohol also affects the likelihood that partners will practice *safer* sex (Boyer & Kegeles, 1991). When they are drunk, at least one out of five college students abandon the safer sex practices they would normally engage in (Commission on Substance Abuse, 1994). According to some estimates, 30% of college students never use condoms under any conditions (Butcher et al., 1991), and at least 40% use condoms only half of the time they have sex (Oswalt & Matsen, 1993). The number of people using condoms after heavy drinking is unlikely to be high (Freimuth, Hammond, Edgar, McDonald, & Fink, 1992). Hingson, Strunin, Berlin, and Heeren (1990) found that among the Massachusetts adolescents they sampled who drink and use drugs, 16% used condoms less often after drinking, and 25% less often after drug use.

Using alcohol and/or drugs, then, interferes with normally cautious individuals' attention to precautions against HIV/AIDS. Some students in our research admit they became too drunk to bring up AIDS or condom use. Being intoxicated alters expectations, including those surrounding the scripts and metaphors people have in their heads as they negotiate in sexual situations.

Scripts/Metaphors

When we ask our college students what happens at a party, we usually hear that there is beer and music, and men and women begin to pair off for sexual interludes. They can easily describe what happens first, next, and afterward. This might work as a rough script of "hooking up," as our students refer to it. The label *hooking up* is conveniently ambiguous, since it can include anything from kissing to intercourse.

Scripts are "cognitive representations of temporally ordered sequences of behaviors. People are actors and scripts include their qualities, [their] motives for behavior and their verbal and nonverbal activities" (Miller, Bettencourt, DeBro, & Hoffman, 1993, p. 97). When college students were asked to describe the typical sequence of events that leads to sex between strangers, they were able to pinpoint the following consistent pattern (Edgar & Fitzpatrick, 1993): First, when couples meet in a public setting, they engage in initial exchanges, verbal and nonverbal, and they proceed to dancing and complimenting, perhaps allowing them to touch one another in a social way. As the physical contact continues, intimate touching and kissing occur. Then, they move from the public to the private setting. "Foreplay" occurs when they arrive at a private setting (an apartment or room), get comfortable, and decide that intercourse is going to happen (whether or not initial resistance occurs). The final sequence of behaviors culminates with an act of intercourse.

Sexual scripts may vary based on how well the partners know each other, but the predictability of the script suggests that people have a sense of what steps lead to sexual intercourse. There are cues that men and women look for to acknowledge that a sexual sequence is a "go." Unfortunately, negotiating or using condoms is not yet a well-defined part of the script for those who choose to have sex. The level of predictability can be useful in identifying ways to circumvent the pattern or operate more safely within it.

Metaphors, unlike scripts, can give us insight into the key mind-sets individuals carry into an encounter. As ways of understanding experience, metaphors can be the same or different for partners contemplating sex. To the extent that the same metaphor is used by both partners, it is easier to talk about how their script plays out. A number of different metaphors men and women may use in relationships are also appropriate to understanding their thinking about their own sexual behavior (Borisoff & Hahn, 1993). As you look over the following list of metaphors (most of them from Bowen & Michal-Johnson, 1995), pay attention to the use of power and control, relationship expectations, rewards, and seduction inherent in each metaphor. It also may be helpful to acknowledge that individuals may enact more direct metaphors as they attempt to persuade partners to have sex and more indirect metaphors as they persuade partners to avoid having sex (McCormick, 1979). People can shift or combine metaphors based on how events unfold. Finally, a range of different power dynamics also can be present as men and women influence one another to use or not use condoms.

> *Hunting:* The hunter goes out, looking for prey; he has the proper equipment for disabling the target, and he takes it home as a trophy.
>
> *Caveman:* He is big and strong; he claims his woman, and she submits. Very traditional, perhaps primitive sexual stereotypes are used.
>
> *Ensnaring:* The captor strategically sets a trap for the unwitting or hapless captive.
>
> *The fairy tale:* The metaphor requires traditional stereotypes of the prince who will rescue and take care of the damsel in distress.
>
> *The dance:* This may be a learned dance step with leaders and followers or a free-form activity where individuals respond to the music and enact their own dance.
>
> *The game:* Established rules govern how players who are *winners* or *losers* take turns to attempt to outsmart the other.
>
> *Go with the flow:* This metaphor has a wait-and-see process that presumes that either participant can stop the flow whenever he or she chooses.
>
> *The barter:* This presumes that both parties interact as long as they believe they are experiencing rewards and will cease to interact when rewards diminish.

Play: Participants toy with each other in creative ways that allow each player to suspend "reality" for a time; each is free to take on roles different from the normal persona.

Out of my head: This assumes that individuals bear no responsibility for their own actions and are free of guilt. Being under the influence of a substance "made me do it."

Raging hormones: The biological drive of the species is to reduce the physical tension created by sexual desire and excitement.

Tricking: One of the participants uses his or her superior cunning to outwit the other.

Big brother/big sister caretaking: The responsible party ensures that all avenues of protection have been explored and that everyone is safe.

Virgin Mary: The person, usually female, stops short of vaginal intercourse, although she engages in other types of sexual behavior.

In addition to all of these ways that sexual encounters can be influenced, being male or female also plays a significant role in how sexual activity is perceived. In the metaphors, look for those you would describe as being used by a "typical" male, by a "typical" female, or by either sex. Your expectations probably reflect cultural socialization that promotes different standards and views of sex for men and women. Even in the way they are labeled, some seem to be more masculine (for example, hunting, caveman) or feminine (for example, Virgin Mary or fairy tale). Particularly in heterosexual encounters, partners probably have differing perspectives on acceptable verbal and nonverbal behavior, the meaning of sex within a relationship, and even the meanings of safer sex and condoms.

TEST YOUR ABILITY TO TROUBLESHOOT

As you watch Jen, a first-year student at her first fraternity party, observe the particular forces that propel the situation. Ask yourself which metaphors she and Chad play out. Assess Jen and Chad's risk of contracting HIV in this encounter. What particular verbal and nonverbal cues are they sending that place them at risk? What elements of this scene would be different if Jen and Chad were from different cultures, if the social norms for using alcohol and drugs were different, or if it had not occurred in the fraternity house? At what points in this scene could different strategies have been used? Will this experience yield a relationship for Jen and Chad?

Jen had dreamed of this moment for years. All the hassles of getting into college were behind her. Here she was at her first fraternity party. If her friends from Jones High could see her now. She hadn't ever seen so many great-looking guys—they all looked like models. Whew! The guy with the Yacht Club jacket was coming over to her. "Looks like your mug's empty. Want a refill?" he asked. (Oh, he's talking to me, Jen realized.) "Uh, uh, sure! What kind of beer is this?" "The cheapest we could find from our distributor. What's your name?" "Jen, I'm from Long Island. How about you?" "Chad. Senior from Jersey." After an hour of joking about Jersey and New York and the recollections about freshman orientation, Jen began to feel the beer catching up to her. Chad was still making sure her glass was full. He leaned over and gave her a brief kiss on the neck. (Not bad, she thought. Actually pleasant!) The next thing she knew he was holding her close with his arms around her waist. It looked like they were dancing, but his hands kept slowly wandering below her waist, stopping, then moving back up to her waist. She wished she hadn't worn the tube top. Chad was pressing her so hard that it kept sliding down, revealing her breasts. When she stopped to adjust her top, Chad said, "It's a little hot here. I have an air conditioner in my room; wanna go?" She looked around for her suitemates, but didn't see them. Well it was hot, and air conditioning sounded pretty good. "Oh, sure why not. Just for a little while. You wouldn't take advantage of me, would you?" she asked, giggling and slurring her words.

As they walked past others on the stairs, Chad guided her to his room. "Yeah, it is cooler in here. Do you have any music?" Looking through his tapes she found one of her favorites and put it on. There were trophies on shelves, posters of the university sports teams, fraternity photos. So this is what a senior's room is like, she thought. Not bad.

Chad had gone to get more beer for them. She could stay a little while. Here he comes. Such a nice guy. He really seemed interested in what she had to say. He was a finance major; she was undecided. She started looking through the Blue and White *and saw pictures of Chad in his fraternity photo. Definitely one of the best-looking guys here. As she closed the yearbook, she looked up. Chad was kneeling on the bed, and he began to tease the nape of her neck with her french braid. Then he used his tongue to tickle her near her earlobes. It felt good. The next thing she knew, he had swiveled her around, and his tongue had found her lips. Not bad; a little kissing couldn't hurt. Then she felt herself leaning back onto his pillows. Her hands found his shoulders, pressing them to her. He slowly slipped her tube top down and began to feel her breasts. She could feel the excitement. He was so strong. This is pretty fast, but I can stop him. Then he was loosening her shorts and sliding his off. He put on the condom by his bed and continued to tease her gently. In a giant surge they were kissing each other deeply as he penetrated her. Oh, well, she thought as she dozed off to sleep, he was wearing a condom.*

The next morning, she opened her eyes slowly and saw where she was. It took a few minutes for her to take it all in. He must have pulled the sheet over her; she didn't remember being under the covers. What should she say to this guy? How could she get home to her dorm? Where's his phone?

Better call and let her roommates know where she was. Was this thing a mistake? Her head kept throbbing, and the room swirled around from time to time. What if the condom had broken? What would he say to the other guys in the house? She'd better be careful of her reputation. Not good to get pegged that way. Her suitemates were going to kill her. But where were they? Did she dare just walk out now? She just wanted out! Did she talk to him? Would he remember anything? They were pretty loaded. She hoped she wouldn't run into anybody downstairs. She scribbled Chad a note and walked home.

When she got home, Lauren her sophomore suitemate, howled, "Oh, not Chad. Jen, this guy is a predator. He sees freshmen and makes his move. There's no telling where his thing has been."

Although it may seem that this "just happened," the truth is that Jen and Chad made choices. See if you can identify the choices that each made. Sexual intercourse and other sexual acts are neither automatic nor inevitable. There are a number of junctures in this case where Jen or Chad could have changed the direction of the episode. We get an even clearer view of how gender plays into the kinds of decision making men and women encounter around sex and HIV prevention in the next section.

PREVENTION ADVICE AND GENDER

Because AIDS destroys the lives of college students, AIDS educators on college campuses have focused on prevention efforts, such as counseling students to abstain from sex or to use condoms. Posters on campuses and peer education sessions exhort college students to "Wait for the Right One," to "Know Your Partner," and to "Practice Safer Sex." In the following section, we encourage you to compare the responses from college students across the country with your own reactions. In some places, we are going to deviate from the descriptive tone used in the rest of the chapter in order to provide advice on how you might put into practice what you've learned from your reading.

Know Your Partner

The most prevalent piece of preventive advice given to college students, and indeed to any sexually active person, is to "know your partner." In an ideal world, this advice might be easy to follow. However, in the real world, it's fraught with difficulties. The big question is *how* do you go about knowing your partner? One way is to gather information about a potential partner from friends and acquaintances. (Is he or she wild?

Does she or he sleep around? Does he or she hang out in "safe" places with people who are "just like me"? Does she or he dress in ways that telegraph safety or risk?) Another strategy is to talk with a partner until you are convinced that the person poses no risk to you. We will walk through some of the research findings that describe how American college students respond to the advice "Know your partner."

Selection of Safe Partners. Perhaps the "most popular prophylactic" is the selection of a noninfected sexual partner (Maticka-Tyndale, 1991). People choose partners from within friendship networks and presume that others are trustworthy and safe. They assume (falsely) that it is possible to tell "unsafe" people by looking at them, for example, by their style of hair and dress (Bowen & Michal-Johnson, 1989). They assume someone with HIV will look sick, which is not the case at all, since many people infected with HIV live more than 10 years before showing symptoms of the virus.

There are differences in responses to this advice by men and women. No studies have shown a significant increase in use of condoms, the single most effective tool to fight the sexual spread of HIV. The greatest change men report regarding AIDS is in being "more cautious" in selecting partners (Carroll, 1991; Cline, Johnson, & Freeman, 1992). Women report being more willing to refrain from sexual activities they see as "unsafe" (Gray & Saracino, 1991). As mentioned earlier, women seem to be more worried than men about AIDS, perhaps because of women's generally greater concerns about health and contraception practices (Cochran & Peplau, 1991). Cochran and Peplau found that women's sexual histories, such as previously having a sexually transmitted disease and having a number of previous partners, were the causes of worry linked to their concern about AIDS. Men's perceptions of personal vulnerability and homophobia determined their level of concern.

Determining whether you are in a mutually monogamous relationship is a sequel to the "know your partner" adage. College women appear to be caught in a confusing set of assumptions about using monogamy as an HIV prevention strategy. Many AIDS education specialists fear that college women trust the notion of monogamy and are less likely to question the fidelity of partners (Cline et al., 1992). Women admit to guessing about the safety of partners (Gray & Saracino, 1991). Hernandez and Smith (1990) indicate that significantly more college women than men claim to have monogamous relationships, while Moore and Rosenthal (1991) suggest that women take greater risks in relationships they presume are monogamous. In addition, many women don't differentiate between monogamy and serial monogamy (one partner at a time), where HIV risks may be greater. Some college women reported not using protection when they become involved in a relationship they saw as intimate (Cline et al., 1992; Moore & Rosenthal; 1991). Only mutual monogamy (that you and your partner are with only one another as long as you are together) is effective if both partners start out HIV-free.

Talking about HIV/AIDS with a partner. Women are more likely than men to attempt discussion of the disease, because women are socialized to talk more about intimate topics (Cline, 1989), while men may not be as willing to initiate, and perhaps participate in, such talk. In some cases, however, women substitute AIDS talk for safer sex; that is, they think that if a man is willing to talk about HIV with his partner, then surely he is not the type to have the virus, and therefore, condoms are unnecessary (Cline et al., 1990). While talk about HIV/AIDS can promote a healthier relationship that involves open and honest communication, talking alone will not prevent the spread of HIV/AIDS.

Some men are reluctant to talk about HIV/AIDS because they fear it might derail a relationship and reflect poorly on their character (Cline et al., 1990). For instance, men in one study saw talk as a sign of harming the relationship, breaking taboos, and building mistrust (Cline & McKenzie, 1994). Men also believed that AIDS talk would make the partner suspicious, possibly suggesting that they were bisexual or homosexual. Women were more likely to be honest in their interactions with partners, yet we cannot assume that all partners are honest with one another (Cline & McKenzie, 1994; Cochran, 1989). Men and women both reported not telling partners about one-night stands. As Cline and McKenzie (1994) note, these findings reframe the choice to talk about HIV/AIDS with a relational partner as possibly in conflict with the goal of making a good impression and furthering the relationship.

Condom Use and Negotiation

The second piece of HIV preventive advice given if abstinence is not practiced is to use a condom. We know, however, that condom use is sporadic at best. Oswalt and Matsen (1993) reported that 44% of their respondents used condoms only 50% of the times they had sex. As the number of partners increased, condom usage became less frequent, thus increasing the potential for STD infection. A variety of issues come into play in the sexual scene—self-esteem, degree of loneliness, peer pressure, perceptions of how a partner is likely to react, and the influence of alcohol, to mention just a few.

Because of differences in the ways that men and women typically communicate and think about sex, condom negotiation can be troublesome. This may be true in part because the process of sexual seduction is both emotionally and physiologically "volatile." Introducing a rational and unromantic topic like HIV protection is not easy. This volatility partly results from verbal and nonverbal seduction strategies. Women may verbally seduce by hinting (teasing, giving compliments, using code words, using sexy romantic talk), and men may seduce by deception (promising a deeper relationship than they intend to pursue) (Edgar & Fitzpatrick, 1990). Each of these strategies adds an additional layer of interpretation for each partner. Believing that sex should be mysterious and spontaneous may encourage men, especially, to see talking as a way to reduce the chance of "success." Nonverbal strategies, however, can be less direct and more ambiguous than verbal strategies. For instance, whispering, moving into closer physical proximity, using fragrances, wearing sexy clothing, escalating touching, and subtly changing one's appearance can signal a readiness to be pursued or resist. The ambiguity offers a safety net—a more graceful retreat and less loss of face.

Within this verbal and nonverbal milieu of seduction, it may be a surprise to men that women tend to have a positive view of condoms. Men see condom use as more embarrassing than do women, and think that introducing condoms threatens their own character and their relationship with their partner (Cline & McKenzie, 1994). Despite women's more positive view of condoms, and their tendency to feel more comfortable talking about AIDS in a general way, introducing a condom requires a level of assertiveness that may be more typical of males. The meanings each gender has for sex may account for some of the problems that arise. Women tend to equate sex with love and intimacy, while men are more likely to see sex as an end in itself (Christopher & Cate, 1985; Hatfield, Sprecher, Pillemer, & Greenberger, 1988; Lott, 1994; Sprecher, 1991). In a traditional sex-role script, the male is "sexually assertive and experienced, a lover who initiates the shy and inexperienced female to her first sexual experience" (Metts & Fitzpatrick, 1992, p. 13). A woman in this situation will have a difficult time insisting on condom use. This places her at great risk with a sexually experienced partner. Compounding this difficulty, straightforward, assertive arguments are not consistent with her sexual naivete. Asking for condom use encourages the traditional male to think of her as sexually promiscuous. Finally, to gain money, status, and so forth, some women will remain in a relationship even if a partner is reluctant to use condoms (Cochran, 1989).

In a study where respondents reported actual strategies they had used, women were more likely than men to say the following:

I'm really afraid of AIDS.

We should be responsible.

We should find out about safer sex measures.

We should talk about our past sexual experiences.

If we can't even talk about using condoms; maybe we aren't ready to have sex.

A condom protects both of us.

If you care, you'll use a condom.

This isn't a joke to me.

If you don't respect me enough to use a condom, then I'm with the wrong person.

There were no strategies men used more than women. These seem to reflect women's preference for talking, and their seeing condom use as a sign of caring and respect. They are further indications of the relational issues that women often focus on more than men. The next set of messages, which includes some different strategies, were more likely to be relayed by people who had used condoms. Gender did not seem important in this part of the analysis by Reel and Thompson (1994, p. 136).

I'm afraid I might get AIDS from you.

I practice safer sex.

We should talk about condoms to prevent pregnancy.

I'm scared of getting pregnant.

It's better to be safe than sorry.

We both aren't sure if we have AIDS, so I think we should use a condom.

I think we should use a condom.

Condoms provide double protection (pregnancy and AIDS).

Condoms protect both of us.

This isn't a joke to me.

These strategies are much more "rational" and direct. Again, we see that negotiating safer sex requires a move from subtlety toward straightforward communication about disease or pregnancy prevention.

We see many factors that work against women who want to initiate and insist on condom use. Women may have the desire to use condoms, but sometimes lack the personal security as well as the vocabulary to have frank discussions about safer sex in a way that might eroticize the act (Fine, 1988). Both women and men may need to suspend typical behaviors in order to prevent HIV transmission. First, you need to know what is typical for you, and what your ultimate goals and limits are in regard to sexual behavior. Then you can explore various means of reaching those goals. Women may need to bypass cultural teachings of seduction and indirectness to use clear and assertive messages with their partners. Men may need to let go of the strong, silent role; experiment with feelings of emotional vulnerability; and then figure out ways to remain safe while having fun.

We hope that reading this chapter has opened new avenues for evaluation and discussion of the sexual landscapes you are likely to encounter whether in marriage or before. From this discussion, it should be clear that being sexual persons places us in a complicated sphere where pleasure and safety exist in a constant and dynamic tension. This is compounded by the gendered dynamics of sexual interaction. The irony is that we expect that intimacy, romance, and mystery will spirit us away to a never-never-land where managing all of our goals occurs almost magically. Yet, as we've said throughout this chapter, intimacy, romance, and magic are best when they are safe. Taking responsibility for your own behavior can reduce the chance that you will ever be infected with HIV.

QUESTIONS FOR REFLECTION AND DISCUSSION

1. Identify your own approach to sexual relationships/encounters. Ask yourself the following questions: Which metaphors are typical of me? Do I choose different strategies with different partners? Do I sometimes change my mind-set within a sexual episode? Do I decide to regulate drinking? If I do, how? To negotiate safer sex, does it mean I have to cut across traditional norms for women or men? Do I see women as gatekeepers, and men as initiators?

2. Using the metaphors on pages 184 and 185, review your last intimate personal encounter with a romantic partner. Which metaphors can you say were operating in the episode? How would you describe the metaphors present in your partner's behavior? How do you define the relationship? Was it close? Short-lived? Was alcohol consumed and, if so, how did it affect your ability to plan behavior?

3. The research reported in this chapter indicates that "women in a relationship are more likely to talk about HIV." What does this suggest about the socialized gender roles of men in discussing intimate topics with a partner?

4. How would you negotiate abstinence with a partner? What refusal strategies would you use? Are they likely to be different?

5. A description of a typical script leading to intercourse is on pages 186 and 187. How would you fit condom negotiation or condom use into this script? Think about possible strategies that might be effective. (For some additional perspectives, you may want to read Adelman, M. B. [1992a]. Healthy passions: Safer sex as play. In T. Edgar, M. A. Fitzpatrick, & V. S. Freimuth [Eds.], *AIDS: A communication perspective* [pp. 69–89]. Hillsdale, NJ: Lawrence Erlbaum.)

REFERENCES

Blumstein, P., & Schwartz, P. (1983). *American couples: Love, sex, and money.* New York: Morrow.

Borisoff, D., & Hahn, D. F. (1993). Thinking with the body: Sexual metaphors. *Communication Quarterly, 41,* 253–260.

Bowen, S. P., & Michal-Johnson, P. (1989). The crisis of communicating in relationships: Confronting the threat of AIDS. *AIDS and Public Policy, 4,* 10–19.

Bowen, S. P., & Michal-Johnson, P. (1990, November). *Evaluating the validity of college students' strategies for HIV risk assessment with relational partners.* Paper presented to the Speech Communication Association Convention, Chicago, IL.

Bowen, S. P., & Michal-Johnson, P. (1995). HIV/AIDS: A crucible for understanding the dark side of sexual interactions. In S. Duck & J. T. Wood (Eds.), *Understanding relationship processes, 5: Relationship challenges.* Newbury Park, CA: Sage.

Boyer, C. B., & Kegeles, S. M. (1991). AIDS risk and prevention among adolescents. *Social Science and Medicine, 33,* 11–23.

Butcher, A. H., Manning, D. T., & O'Neal, E. C. (1991). HIV-related sexual behaviors of college students. *Journal of the American College Health Association, 40,* 115–118.

Carroll, L. (1991). Gender, knowledge about AIDS, reported behavioral change, and the sexual behavior of college students. *Journal of American College Health, 40,* 5–12.

Christopher, F. S., & Cate, R. M. (1985). Premarital sexual pathways and relationship development. *Journal of Social and Personal Relationships, 2,* 271–288.

Cline, R. J. W. (1989). The politics of intimacy: Costs and benefits determining disclosure intimacy in male–female dyads. *Journal of Social and Personal Relationships, 6,* 5–20.

Cline, R. J., Freeman, K. E., & Johnson, S. J. (1990). Talk among sexual partners about AIDS: Factors differentiating those who talk from those who do not. *Communication Research, 17,* 792–808.

Cline, R. J., Johnson, S. J., & Freeman, K. E. (1992). Talk among sexual partners: Interpersonal communication for risk reduction or risk enhancement. *Health Communication, 4,* 39–56.

Cline, R. J. W., & McKenzie, N. J. (1994). Sex differences in communication and the construction of HIV/AIDS. *Journal of Applied Communication Research, 22,* 322–337.

Cochran, S. D. (1989). Women and HIV infection: Issues in prevention and behavior change. In V. M. Mays, G. W. Albee, & S. F. Schneider (Eds.), *Primary prevention of AIDS* (pp. 309–327). Newbury Park, CA: Sage.

Cochran, S. D., & Mays, V. M. (1990). Sex, lies, and HIV. *New England Journal of Medicine, 322,* 774–775.

Cochran, S. D., & Peplau, L. A. (1991). Sexual risk reduction behaviors among young heterosexual adults. *Social Science and Medicine, 33,* 25–36.

Commission on Substance Abuse at Colleges and Universities. (1994). *Rethinking rights of passage: Substance abuse on America's campuses.* Center on Addiction and Substance Abuse. New York: Columbia University.

Corcoran, K. J., & Thomas, L. R. (1991). The influence of observed alcohol consumption on perceptions of initiation of sexual activity in a college dating situation. *Journal of Applied Social Psychology, 21,* 500–507.

Darling, C. A., & Davidson, J. D. (1986). Coitally active university students: Sexual behaviors, concerns, and challenges. *Adolescence, 21,* 403–419.

DiClemente, R. J., Forrest, K. A., Mickler, S., & Principal Site Investigators. (1990). College students' knowledge and attitudes about AIDS and changes in HIV-preventive behaviors. *AIDS Education and Prevention, 2,* 201–212.

Edgar, T., & Fitzpatrick, M. A. (1988). Compliance-gaining in relational interaction: When your life depends on it. *Southern Speech Communication Journal, 53,* 385–405.

Edgar, T., & Fitzpatrick, M. A. (1990). Communicating sexual desire: Message tactics for having and avoiding intercourse. In J. Dillard (Ed.), *Seeking compliance: The production of interpersonal influence messages.* Scottsdale, AZ: Gorsuch-Scarisbuck.

Edgar, T., & Fitzpatrick, M. A. (1993). Expectations for sexual interaction: A cognitive test of the sequencing of sexual communication behaviors. *Health Communication, 5,* 239–261.

Edgar, T., Freimuth, V. S., Hammond, S. L., McDonald, D. A., & Fink, E. L. (1992). Strategic sexual communication: Condom use resistance and response. *Health Communication, 4,* 83–104.

Fine, M. (1988). Sexuality, schooling, and adolescent females: The missing discourse of desire. *Harvard Educational Review, 58,* 29–53.

Freimuth, V. S., Hammond, S. L., Edgar, T., McDonald, D. A., & Fink, E. L. (1992). Factors explaining intent, discussion and use of condoms in first-time sexual encounters. *Health Education Research, 7,* 203–215.

Gayle, H. D., Keeling, R. P., Marcia-Tunon, M., Kilbourne, B. W., Narkunas, J. P., Ingram, F. R., Rogers, M. F., & Curran, J. W. (1990). Prevalence of the human immunodeficiency virus among university students. *New England Journal of Medicine, 323,* 1538–1541.

Goodwin, M. P., & Roscoe, B. (1988). AIDS: Students' knowledge and attitudes at a midwestern university. *Journal of American College Health, 36,* 214–222.

Gray, L. A., & Saracino, M. (1991). College students' attitudes, beliefs and behaviors about AIDS: Implications for family life educators. *Family Relations, 40,* 258–263.

Grimley, D. M., Riley, G. E., Bellis, J. M., & Prochaska, J. O. (1993). Assessing the stages of change and decision-making for contraceptive use for the prevention of pregnancy, sexually transmitted diseases, and acquired immunodeficiency syndrome. *Health Education Quarterly, 20,* 455–470.

Hatfield, E., Sprecher, S., Pillemer, J. T., & Greenberger, D. (1988). Gender differences in what is desired in the sexual relationship. *Journal of Psychology and Human Sexuality, 1*(2), 39–52.

Hernandez, J. T., & Smith, F. J. (1990). Inconsistencies and misperceptions putting college students at risk of HIV infection. *Journal of Adolescent Health Care, 11,* 295–297.

Hingson, R. W., Strunin, L., Berlin, B. M., & Heeren, T. (1990). Beliefs about AIDS, use of alcohol and drugs, and unprotected sex among Massachusetts adolescents. *Journal of American Public Health, 80,* 295–299.

Leigh, B. C., Aramburu, B., & Norris, J. (1992). The morning after: Gender difference in attributions about alcohol-related sexual encounters. *Journal of Applied Social Psychology, 22,* 343–357.

Levine, A. (1993). The making of a generation. *Change, 24*(4), 8–16.

Linville, P. W., Fischer, G. W., & Fischhoff, B. (1993). AIDS risk perceptions and decision biases. In J. B. Pryor & G. D. Reeder (Eds.), *The social psychology of HIV infection* (pp. 5–38). Hillsdale, NJ: Lawrence Erlbaum.

Lott, B. (1994). *Women's lives* (2nd ed.). Pacific Grove, CA: Brooks/Cole.

Maticka-Tyndale, E. (1991). Sexual scripts and AIDS prevention: Variations in adherence to safer-sex guidelines by heterosexual adolescents. *Journal of Sex Research, 28,* 45–66.

McCormick, N. B. (1979). Come-ons and put-offs: Unmarried students' strategies for having and avoiding sexual intercourse. *Psychology of Women Quarterly, 4,* 195–211.

Metts, S., & Fitzpatrick, M. A. (1992). Thinking about safer sex: The risky business of "know your partner" advice. In T. Edgar, M. A. Fitzpatrick, & V. S. Freimuth (Eds.), *AIDS: A communication perspective* (pp. 1–19). Hillsdale, NJ: Lawrence Erlbaum.

Michal-Johnson, P., & Bowen, S. P. (1992). The place of culture in HIV education. In T. Edgar, M. A. Fitzpatrick, & V. S. Freimuth (Eds.), *AIDS: A communication perspective* (pp. 147–172). Hillsdale, NJ: Lawrence Erlbaum.

Miller, L. C., Bettencourt, B. A., DeBro, S. C., & Hoffman, V. (1993). Negotiating safer sex: Interpersonal dynamics. In J. B. Pryor & G. D. Reeder (Eds.), *The social psychology of HIV infection* (pp. 85–123). Hillsdale, NJ: Lawrence Erlbaum.

Moore, S., & Rosenthal, D. (1991). Adolescent invulnerability and perceptions of AIDS risk. *Journal of Adolescent Research.* 6(2), 164–180.

O'Leary, A., Goodhart, F., Jemmott, L. S., & Boccher-Lattimore, D. (1992). Predictors of safer sex on the college campus: A social cognitive theory analysis. *Journal of the American College Health Association, 40,* 254–263.

Oswalt, R., & Matsen, K. (1993). Sex, AIDS, and the use of condoms: A survey of compliance in college students. Psychological Reports, 72, 764–766.

Reel, B. W., & Thompson, T. L. (1994). A test of the effectiveness of strategies for talking about AIDS and condom use. *Journal of Applied Communication Research, 22,* 127–140.

Seibold, D. R., & Thomas, R. W. (1992). *College students' interpersonal influence processes in alcohol intervention situations: A critical review and reconceptualization.* Paper presented to the International Communication Association, Miami, FL.

Spees, E. R. (1987). College students' sexual attitudes and behaviors, 1974–1985: A review of the literature. *Journal of College Student Personnel, 28,* 135–140.

Sprecher, S. (1990). The impact of the threat of AIDS on heterosexual dating relationships. *Journal of Psychology and Human Sexuality, 3*(2), 3–23.

Sprecher, S., & McKinney, K. (1993). *Sexuality.* Newbury Park, CA: Sage.

Stiff, J., McCormack, M., Zook, E., Stein, T., & Henry, R. (1990). Learning about AIDS and HIV transmission in college-age students. *Communication Research, 17,* 743–758.

van der Pligt, J., Otten, W., Richard, R., & van der Velde, F. (1993). Perceived risk of AIDS: Unrealistic optimism and self-protective action. In J. B. Pryor & G. D. Reeder (Eds.), *The social psychology of HIV infection* (pp. 39–58). Hillsdale, NJ: Lawrence Erlbaum.

Weschler, H., & Isaac, N. (1992). Binge drinkers at Massachusetts colleges. *Journal of the American Medical Association, 267,* 2929–2931.

Williams, S. S., Kimble, D. L., Covell, N. H., Weiss, L. H., Newton, K. J., Fisher, J. D., & Fisher, W. A. (1992). College students use implicit personality theory instead of safer sex. *Journal of Applied Social Psychology, 22,* 921–933.

GENDERED VIOLENCE IN INTIMATE RELATIONSHIPS

JACQUELYN W. WHITE
BARRIE BONDURANT

They had grown up together, and now they were college roommates. Very distraught, Janet revealed that Rob, the guy she had been dating for the last 3 weeks, had raped her. She kept blaming herself, wondering what she did wrong, and chastising herself for not being able to tell what he was really like. Sue, in seeking to comfort Janet, confided that the same thing had happened to her in high school. Her boyfriend, whom they all knew and believed to be a nice guy, had forced her to have sex with him. Until this moment, she had never told anyone, sure no one would believe her. She understood just what Janet was feeling. Sara then spoke up, assuring both that she understood, because she had been sexually victimized by her stepfather when she was 8 years old. In sharing their experiences, these friends came to see that what had happened to them was not unique. Girls and women of different ages are the victims of violence committed by men they thought they could trust.

In spite of images of loving, supportive families and caring, protective lovers, intimate relationships often are plagued by alarming levels of aggression and violence. In a wide array of nonintimate crimes, adult men are usually the perpetrators and the victims. In families, however, girls are more likely to be victims of sexual abuse than boys, and boys are more likely to be victims of physical abuse than girls (youth is defined as 0–18 years). In play groups, boys encounter more opportunities for physical aggression than girls. In intimate relationships, women are much more likely than men to be the victims of both emotionally and physically damaging violence at the hands of men they know and frequently trust. Women too commit acts of aggression and violence toward intimate partners, often as frequently as men, but usually with less serious consequences and for different reasons (Straus & Gelles, 1990; White & Koss, 1991). In this chapter, we explore the character of gendered violence. We first discuss historical and research influences on what is known about gendered violence and then trace the pattern of its occurrence from childhood through adulthood. Although the research discussed in this chapter focuses primarily on violence in relationships in the United States, violence against women is recognized as a worldwide problem (French, 1992).

THE CONTEXT OF RESEARCH ON GENDERED VIOLENCE

Research Biases

Most of the research in this chapter focuses on intimate heterosexual relationships for several reasons. First, strong emphasis is placed on heterosexuality in our culture. Friends, family, acquaintances, movies, and television programs all usually assume and expect individuals to have heterosexual interests. Researchers mirror this cultural prejudice by studying male–female intimate relationships, often assuming that "couple" refers to a man and a woman. This heterosexist bias has slowed research on violence in lesbian and gay relationships. A second reason for concentrating on heterosexual relationships is the low number of lesbian and gay male relationships. Although research indicates that 20 to 37% of men and 13 to 20% of women have had homosexual experiences (Hunt, 1974), the actual number of long-term homosexual relationships is lower. Even researchers who want to study lesbian and gay couples have difficulty locating research participants.

Along with a heterosexist bias, research on violence in relationships is limited by ethnic and class assumptions. Frequently, research is done on college students. As with heterosexual relationships, middle-class, white behavior has been assumed to characterize all human behavior or to represent "normal" behavior. Because people tend to study people with whom they are familiar, ethnic minorities are more likely to study ethnic minorities (Reid, 1993). However, few researchers belong to ethnic minorities. Furthermore, white, middle-class researchers have more difficulty accessing and gaining the confidence of poor or minority populations. These biases shape the nature of our knowledge just as other cultural factors shape our attitudes. Even though knowledge of violence in minority and gay and lesbian relationships is limited, we will discuss the information that is available.

Historical Setting

One cultural factor that may be important for intimate relationships is Americans' preoccupation with obsessive love and violent love. Violence is romanticized, as in Harlequin-type novels where the rugged, mysterious stranger simultaneously frightens and intrigues, then violently "seduces" (that is, rapes), the innocent young heroine. Violent relationships also are romanticized in film, with Scarlett O'Hara and Rhett Butler in *Gone with the Wind* being but one of many examples. Unfortunately, examples of violent relationships throughout history are not limited to fiction. The violent control of women has existed since the beginning of recorded history. In *The Creation of Patriarchy*, Gerda Lerner (1986) asserts that because of biological vulnerability in childbearing, more men than women filled the role of warrior. When neighboring tribes were conquered, the defeated men were killed, and their wives and children were enslaved. Rape was the most powerful mechanism to enforce the subjugation of the captured women. Thus, these women became property. Ironically, women of the victorious tribes also came to be viewed as property. Women and men began to realize that if their tribe were defeated, the women would become the property of the enemy. Hence, the women turned to their own men for protection from captivity by warring forces. Over time, men's power extended from controlling the strategies and tools of war to controlling most aspects of public and private life, including the treatment of women as men's possessions. Today, many feminists argue that fear of rape remains a powerful social tool that maintains men's control of women (Koss et al., 1994).

THE PERVASIVENESS OF GENDERED VIOLENCE

Women state that rape is the crime they most fear (Warr, 1985). The notion of a stranger lurking in shadows, poised to attack the unsuspecting victim, is a continuing fear of many women. However, as devastating as stranger rape is, it is not the most common crime women experience. Research has established that women are more likely to be the victims of violence committed by male acquaintances and intimates (Koss et al., 1994). This violence takes many forms, including incest, sexual abuse outside the family, emotional and physical abuse, dating violence, acquaintance rape, and marital abuse. All these forms of violence share in common the fact that they frequently are committed by men known to the girls and women. Unlike other crimes, they are crimes in which others, as well as the victim herself, tend to blame the victim for what happened. Thus, the social support that most victims of crime receive is missing for victims of gendered violence. Additionally, the consequences of sexual violence extend beyond the immediate violation and can be severe and long-lasting.

Gendered Violence in Childhood

The gendered nature of violence is evident early in childhood and establishes a framework for patterns of interactions between adult women and men. Children are at great risk for victimization because of their small physical stature and dependency on adults; they have little choice over with whom they live, and few opportunities to leave an abusive home. During childhood, boys have more experience with physical aggression and girls have more experience with sexual aggression (Finkelhor & Dziuba-Leatherman, 1994). Among older children, girls are at greater risk than boys, presumably because they are less physically able to defend themselves.

The types of messages about aggression and violence that children receive in the home are gender-specific. This is true in both normal and abusive homes. The majority of parents in American homes use verbal and physical aggression as disciplinary tactics, inadvertently teaching children that "might makes right." Murray Straus and Richard Gelles (1990) report that over 90% of children are spanked sometime in their youth, with many parents (62%) reporting physical aggression against their children; this aggression includes pushing, shoving, and slapping. Fewer parents (11%) reported using severe aggression, including hitting, kicking, beating, threatening, and using weapons against their children.

Punishment does not appear to be uniform, however; the sex of the child and the parent affect the pattern and the outcome (Strassberg, Dodge, Pettit, & Bates, 1994), as does the particular type of punishment used (Eron, 1992). Punishment can take many forms, some physical, such as spanking, and some psychological, such as withdrawal of love and approval. This distinction is important because research results may suggest different conclusions depending on what type of punishment or which aspect of child aggression is studied.

In a 22-year longitudinal study of 632 children, followed from the third grade to age 30, Eron (1992) reported conflicting tendencies in parents' attitudes and behaviors toward aggression. The parents generally saw aggression as an undesirable attribute for children, but viewed it as a desirable *masculine* bahavior; this was in spite of the fact that they physically punished boys more harshly than girls for aggression (a result confirmed by Perry, Perry, & Weiss, 1989). Girls, in contrast, were more likely to receive psychological punishment from their parents (Eron, 1992). These gender-related patterns of punishment were associated with boys being more aggressive than girls. Apparently, parents' behaviors teach boys to be more physically aggressive than girls, though giving mixed messages about the desirability of aggression in boys.

In a review of socialization practices, Lytton and Romney (1991) found that, at least in North American homes, parents are as likely to spank girls as boys. However, the effects of the spanking may be different (Strassberg et al., 1994). On the one hand, paternal spanking has been shown to lead to reactive aggression in both girls and boys (that is, angry retaliation in reaction to a peer's behavior); on the other hand, spanking by fathers has been associated with bullying aggression (unprovoked attacks on peers). Strassberg and his colleagues (1994) conclude that fathers' spanking of boys communicates a "gender-based approach to interpersonal disagreements, that of physical dominance,...explicitly transmitting gender-stereotypic notions" (p. 457). Such conclusions are consistent with social learning theory, which argues that male authority figures are modeled more than are female authority figures, and that within-gender modeling is more powerful than between-gender modeling (Hicks, 1968).

With regard to more severe punishment (that is, child abuse), at younger ages boys are at greater risk than girls, but the risk for girls increases during preadolescence and adolescence (Straus, Gelles & Steinmetz, 1980). This is presumably because of boys' increased ability to inflict harm as they physically mature. Children, especially those from abusive homes, have many opportunities to learn that the more powerful person in a relationship can use aggression to successfully control the less powerful person.

This lesson is also learned in a sexual context for a minority of girls and boys. It has been estimated that 10 to 30% of women and 2 to 9% of men are victims of child sexual abuse (Finkelhor, 1984), with approximately 95% of the abuse of girls and 80% of the abuse of boys being perpetrated by men (Russell, 1982). Boys are more likely to be sexually abused by someone outside the family; girls are more likely to be sexually abused by a family member or a man known to the family. Within the family, father–daughter incest (which includes stepfathers) is the most common form of sexual abuse (Russell, 1984).

Just as sexual abuse teaches children about the gendered nature of power, so do children's play experiences. Given that children often play in same-sex groups, it is not surprising that the forms of aggression expressed in these groups differ. For example, boys are more likely than girls to establish dominance physically (for example, by shouldering), whereas girls are more likely to use verbal persuasion (Charlesworth & Dzur, 1987). This leads boys to be the targets of physical aggression in play situations more often than girls. When children attempt to influence the other sex, boys are more successful than girls. Jean Block Miller (1986) has suggested that girls learn to protect themselves from boys' physical aggression by avoiding them. They develop a wariness that they carry into adolescence. Cultural prescriptions for gender also teach girls to be less direct in expressing aggression (Lagerspetz, Bjorkqvist, & Peltonen, 1988). Thus, women come to experience aggressive behavior as a loss of emotional control, whereas men find aggression rewarding and an effective way to control others (Campbell, 1993). These patterns explain why girls and women develop greater anxiety and feelings of guilt regarding aggressive behavior.

By the age of 6 or 7, boys and girls show definite preferences for gender-segregated play. The pressure for young boys to differentiate themselves from girls is strong at this age. Boys run from girls, tease each other about girls, and chase girls. In these ways, boys define girls as different and inferior, scorn girl-type activities, and exclude girls from their play. Girls do many of the same teasing and chasing behaviors as boys, but do not see boys as being as polluted or inferior (Thorne & Luria, 1986).

As studies of parenting styles, childhood sexual abuse, and play patterns of boys and girls suggest, boys receive numerous messages that encourage them to use aggression to establish interpersonal control, and they have many opportunities to engage in aggressive interactions. Girls, on the other hand, receive messages to be submissive and apprehensive of men. Additionally, some girls learn that their bodies are not their own, and that the people who are supposed to care about them sometimes take sexual liberties. These experiences set the stage for patterns of behavior that emerge during adolescence when intimate, heterosexual interactions develop. Boys have learned, through observations in the home, from peer interactions, and from media depictions of male–female relationships, that they are dominant and entitled to female submission. Boys are more likely to develop a sense of "entitlement," a component of which is the right to dominate girls. Girls, too, learn that men are entitled, and they learn role prescriptions that push them to be submissive.

Gendered Violence in Adolescence

The gender-related patterns learned in childhood are played out in adolescent dating and committed relationships. It is not unusual for young dating couples in high school and college to act aggressively toward each other. Young people report that their most frequent conflicts with dating partners are over jealousy, sexual behavior, and alcohol use. A recent national survey of college students found that women and men reported directing various forms of verbal and physical aggression toward their dating partners with equal frequency (White & Koss, 1991), though many more students (80 to 88%) reported being verbally aggressive than physically aggressive (35 to 39%). Other studies have shown that the motives and consequences for such behavior are different for women and men (White, Koss, & Kissling, 1991). Women are more likely to be injured, and to feel surprised, scared, angry, and hurt by a partner's aggression than are men (Makepeace, 1986).

The best estimates of sexual assault among college students to date are that 14.4% of college women have experienced unwanted sexual contact; 11.9% have been verbally coerced into sexual intercourse; 12.1% have experienced attempted rape; and 15.4% have been raped (Koss, Gidycz, & Wisniewski, 1987). The estimate of rape found by Koss and her colleagues is 10 to 15 times higher than corresponding FBI estimates. To understand these results, you should realize that the word *rape* or the phrase *sexual assault* was not used to assess whether or not a woman was a rape victim. Instead, behavioral descriptions of the various forms of sexual assault were given, and the women were asked to indicate whether each had happened to them. When asked later in the survey, "Have you ever been raped?" 73% of the women who said they had experienced what meets the legal definition of rape answered "no." Furthermore, half of these women never told anyone about the assault. This survey revealed that most victims knew the perpetrator and the assaults frequently occurred in a dating context. A recent survey found similar rates of reported sexual assault among adolescents, indicating that sexual assault is not just a problem for college students. It is a frequent experience during the high school years as well (White & Humphrey, 1993).

Although research is limited, we know something about dating violence and sexual assault among adolescents who are not white, middle-class, heterosexual college students. Although it is difficult for any young person to admit being victimized by a dating partner, it is especially so for ethnic minorities. The legacy of slavery and distrust of white authority figures have made it difficult for African American teens to report abusive dating relationships (White, 1991). Women in Asian and Pacific Island communities, too, are reluctant to disclose abuse because of cultural traditions of male dominance and reticence to discuss private relationships in public (Yoshihamana, Parekh, & Boyington, 1991). For lesbian teens, the problem is complicated by the fact that, in reporting abuse, they may have to reveal their sexual orientation, something they may not be psychologically ready to do (Levy & Lobel, 1991).

It appears that dating violence and sexual assault among adolescents and college students is so prevalent, in part, because of the *overall structure and meaning of dating in our culture*, which give men greater power. Adolescent dating patterns follow a fairly well-defined script that has not changed much over several decades. A dating script is a set of rules to be followed by girls and boys that affords men greater power relative to women because they are expected to initiate and pay for dates, and because relationships generally are perceived as more important to women than to men (Breines & Gordon, 1983). A component of the dating script is a sexual script that prescribes the man to be the predator and the woman the prey (Weiss & Borges, 1973). Women are assumed to be responsible for how "far things go," and if things "get out of hand," it is their fault.

An in-depth study of college women's peer cultures discovered that young women believe that being attractive, attracting men, and having dates and boyfriends are very important (Holland & Eisenhart, 1990). Young women believe they will be judged as more attractive if they have a relationship with an attractive man. The more attractive the man, the more prestige and status a woman gains by dating him. Further, some college women believe that when a woman is more attractive than the man, he must treat her especially well as a means of equalizing power in the relationship, but if the woman is less attractive than the man, he can treat her poorly to compensate for her unattractiveness. The woman, if less attractive than the man, reduces her expectation for good treatment. Her expectations reflect her judgment of her relative attractiveness. Women also use a man's treatment as an index of their relative attractiveness. When mistreated, women blame themselves rather than the man for their victimization (Holland & Eisenhart, 1990).

Violence in Marriage and Other Committed Relationships

Abusive experiences in committed relationships include not only non-sexual physical violence, but also verbal harassment, insults, intimidation, threats, sexual coercion, sexual assault, rape, forced isolation, lack of control of money, and restrictions on medical visits (Yllo, 1993). Most researchers, however, focus on physical abuse, because it is seen as a more severe threat to safety and life and because it is easier to measure than emotional abuse. Although women report engaging in aggressive behaviors in committed relationships, most researchers acknowledge that these behaviors do not result in the same amount of physical and psychological damage as men's aggression (Straus, 1993).

The greatest threat of violence to women is from their intimate partners; for men, the greatest threat is from other men (Browne, 1993). Women are more likely to be physically or sexually assaulted by an intimate partner than by a stranger. It is estimated that 2 to 3 million women are assaulted by male partners in the United States each year and that at least half of these women are severely assaulted (that is, punched, kicked, choked, beaten, or threatened or injured with a knife or gun) (Straus & Gelles, 1990). As many as 21 to 34% of women will be assaulted by an intimate partner during adulthood (Browne, 1993). Further, it is estimated that 33 to 50% of all battered wives are also victims of partner rape (Randall, 1990). Most researchers agree that these numbers are underestimates and that the actual figures may be much higher. It is likely that many people do not admit to abusive behavior, even when guaranteed that their responses will be anonymous, because of shame, guilt, and the belief that wife abuse is normal (Dutton, 1988).

It isn't unusual for intimate violence to end in homicide. A woman's death can result from a severe beating or from the use of guns, knives, or other weapons. Approximately two-thirds of family violence deaths are women killed by their male partners and over one-half of all murders of women are committed by current or former partners (Browne & Williams, 1989). In contrast, only 6% of male murder victims are killed by wives or girlfriends (Uniform Crime Report, 1985). Murder–suicides are almost always cases where the man kills his partner or estranged partner and then kills himself (Stuart & Campbell, 1989). He also may kill the children or other family members before he kills himself. While men are homicide victims more often than women, if a woman is killed there is a 50% chance that she will be killed by her partner (Browne & Williams, 1989). Although there are instances in which a woman murders a partner who has been abusing her, this happens less frequently than men killing partners they have abused chronically (Browne, 1993).

When women do kill their partners, they often are reacting to abuse rather than initiating it. A recent study found several commonalities among women who kill their partners (Browne, 1987). The women were in situations where they were abused by their partners, and the abuse was increasing in frequency and severity. Along with the increased violence was a rise in the number and seriousness of the women's injuries. It was common for these men to have raped their spouses, to have forced them into other sexual acts, and to have made threats against their lives. The men typically used alcohol excessively each day as well as recreational drugs. Altogether, the desperation of battered women who kill has prompted attorneys to use "the battered woman syndrome" in court cases to describe the woman's psychological state (Walker, 1984).

The issue of gender differences in domestic violence is clouded by data on abuse in lesbian relationships. Until the 1980s, lesbian battery was rarely discussed. The idea of lesbian love as a utopia free of male violence permeated lesbian thought. Supposedly, if two women were together in a relationship, there should be no violence, only peace and harmony (Schilit, Lie, & Montagne, 1990). However, 31% of lesbian women report forced sexual activities in their intimate relationships (Waterman, Dawson, & Bologna, 1989). Even so, a study comparing heterosexual to lesbian women found that both groups of women had been victimized by men (72%) more often than women (28%). In dating relationships, heterosexual women were more likely to have been physically abused by their partner than were lesbian women. However, heterosexual and lesbian couples did not differ on physical abuse in committed relationships or sexual abuse in dating or committed relationships (Brand & Kidd, 1986). In sum, it appears that partner abuse is a problem that occurs with almost the same frequency in heterosexual and lesbian relationships, although there are differences in dating relationships. Gay male couples report slightly less sexual abuse than lesbian couples, but have more violence associated with abusive acts (Waterman et al., 1989).

UNDERSTANDING GENDERED VIOLENCE

To understand gendered violence, we must first recognize that culturally based socialization practices teach men to be aggressors and women to be victims. As this chapter has described, gendered violence is learned early in life and continues in our different relationships as we age. Although all men are not more powerful than all women, a social analysis focuses on overall patterns found in society. Statistics allow us to examine larger social influences. As this chapter has shown, the statistics reveal that women are the victims of intimate violence more often than men at every stage of development, with the exception of early childhood physical abuse.

Evidence of female abuse of children and spouses and the admission of lesbian violence create disagreement among researchers as to the relationship between gender and violence. Because mothers abuse their children and lesbians abuse their partners, some researchers argue that intimate violence is *not* related to gender and social roles. Other researchers disagree, arguing that patriarchy as a social system carries with it the message that the more powerful are entitled to dominate the less powerful. Because men more often hold higher status positions than women, it follows that men will abuse more than women, and because adults are more powerful than children, children will be victimized more than adults. But not all men are aggressors, and not all women are victims. Similarly, all men are not more powerful than all women.

Inequality in relationships, coupled with cultural values that embrace domination of the weaker by the stronger, creates the potential for violence. Theorists suggest that lesbian battery is motivated by factors common to all Western couples. Both lesbian and heterosexual couples are raised to see families as social units where hierarchical relationships exist. Parents have more power than children, and one partner has more power than the other. The more powerful partner can control money, resources, activities, and decisions. Partner abuse has been associated with issues of power and dependency in both lesbians (Renzetti, 1992) and heterosexual couples (Finkelhor, 1983). Both men and women learn that violence is a method people use to get their way. When individuals use violence and get their way, they are reinforced and thus more likely to use aggression in the future. Research indicates that women are as likely as men to aggress in situations that are congruent with their gender identities, and where they hold relatively more power (Towson & Zanna, 1982). White and Kowalski (1994) concluded that, "to the extent that power corrupts men, it may also corrupt women" (p. 485).

QUESTIONS FOR REFLECTION AND DISCUSSION

1. How might individuals and social systems encourage greater reporting of violence by minority and lesbian and gay individuals?

2. If violence is woven into the broad ideology of Western culture, how can we reduce it?

3. What are the merits of teaching young children about relationship violence? For various ages, what would be some of the ways to approach the topic?

4. Does it appear contradictory to conclude that women are the victims of many forms of intimate violence and yet frequently feel empowered in their day-to-day lives? How can you resolve this contradiction?

5. If a woman experiences several forms of victimization, for example childhood incest, adolescent dating violence, and marital rape, is she to blame? How can you account for her experiences?

6. Should physical abuse be considered "more serious" than verbal or emotional abuse? What kind of evidence would you consider necessary to answer this question?

REFERENCES

Brand, P. A., & Kidd, A. H. (1986). Frequency of physical aggression in heterosexual and female homosexual dyads. *Psychological Reports, 59,* 1307–1313.

Breines, W., & Gordon, L. (1983). The new scholarship on family violence. *Signs, 8,* 490–531.

Browne, A. (1987). *When battered women kill.* New York: Macmillan/Free Press.

Browne, A. (1993). Violence against women by male partners: Prevalence, outcomes, and policy implications. *American Psychologist, 48,* 1077–1087.

Browne, A., & Williams, K. R. (1989). Exploring the effect of resource availability and the likelihood of female-perpetrated homicides. *Law and Society Review, 23,* 75–94.

Campbell, A. (1993). *Men, women, and aggression.* New York: Basic Books.

Charlesworth, W. R., & Dzur, C. (1987). Gender comparisons of preschoolers' behavior and resource utilization in group problem-solving. *Child Development, 58,* 191–200.

Dutton, D. (1988). *The domestic assault of women: Psychological and criminal justice perspectives.* Boston: Allyn & Bacon.

Eron, L. D. (1992). Gender differences in violence: Biology and/or socialization? In K. Bjorkquist & P. Neimela (Eds.), *Of mice and women: Aspects of female aggression* (pp. 89–97). New York: Academic Press.

Finkelhor, D. (1983). Common features of family abuse. In D. Finkelhor, R. J. Gelles, G. T. Hotaling, & M. A. Straus (Eds.), *The dark side of families* (pp. 17–18). Beverly Hills, CA: Sage.

Finkelhor, D. (1984). *Child sexual abuse: New theory and research.* New York: Free Press.

Finkelhor, D., & Dziuba-Leatherman, J. (1994). Victimization of children. *American Psychologist, 49,* 173–183.

French, M. (1992). *The war against women.* New York: Summit.

Hicks, D. J. (1968). Imitation and retention of film-mediated aggressive peer and adult models. *Journal of Personality and Social Psychology, 2,* 97–100.

Holland, D. C., & Eisenhart, M. A. (1990). *Educated in romance: Women, achievement, and college culture.* Chicago: University of Chicago.

Huesmann, L. R., Eron, L. D., Lefkowitz, M. N., & Walder, L. O. (1984). The stability of aggression over time and generations. *Developmental Psychology, 20,* 1120–1134.

Hunt, M. (1974). *Sexual behavior in the 1970's.* Chicago: Playboy Press.

Koss, M. P., Gidycz, C. A., & Wisniewski, N. (1987). The scope of rape: Incidence and prevalence of sexual aggression and victimization in a national sample of higher education students. *Journal of Consulting and Clinical Psychology, 55,* 162–170.

Koss, M. P., Goodman, L., Fitzgerald, L., Russo, N., Keita, G., & Browne, A. (1994). *No safe haven.* Washington, DC: American Psychological Association.

Lagerspetz, K. M. J., Bjorkqvist, K., & Peltonen, T. (1988). Is indirect aggression typical of females? Gender differences in 11- to 12-year-old children. *Aggressive Behavior, 14,* 403–414.

Lerner, G. (1986). *The creation of patriarchy.* New York: Oxford University Press.

Levy, B., & Lobel, K. (1991). In B. Levy (Ed.), *Dating violence: Young women in danger* (pp. 203–208). Seattle, WA: Seal Press.

Lytton, H., & Romney, D. M. (1991). Parents' differential socialization of boys and girls: A meta-analysis. *Psychological Bulletin, 109,* 267–296.

Makepeace, J. (1986). Gender differences in courtship violence victimization. *Family Relations, 35,* 383–388.

Miller, J. B. (1986). *Toward a new psychology of women.* Boston: Beacon Press.

Perry, D. G., Perry, L. C., & Weiss, R. J. (1989). Sex differences in the consequences that children anticipate for aggression. *Developmental Psychology, 25,* 312–319.

Randall, T. (1990). Domestic violence intervention calls for more than treating injuries. *Journal of the American Medical Association, 264(8),* 939–944.

Reid, P. T. (1993). Poor women in psychological research: Shut up and shut out. *Psychology of Women Quarterly, 17,* 133–150.

Renzetti, C. (1992). *Violent betrayal: Partner abuse in lesbian relationships.* Newbury Park, CA: Sage.

Russell, D. E. H. (1982). The prevalence and incidence of forcible rape and attempted rape of females. *Victimology: An International Journal, 7,* 81–93.

Russell, D. E. H. (1984). The prevalence and seriousness of incestuous abuse: Stepfathers vs. biological fathers. *Child Abuse and Neglect, 8,* 15–22.

Schilit, R., Lie, G., & Montagne, M. (1990). Substance use as a correlate of violence in intimate lesbian relationships. *Journal of Homosexuality, 19,* 51–65.

Strassberg, Z., Dodge, K. A., Pettit, G. S., & Bates, J. E. (1994). Spanking in the home and children's subsequent aggression toward kindergarten peers. *Development and Psychopathology, 6,* 445–461.

Straus, M. A. (1993). Physical assaults by wives: A major social problem. In R. J. Gelles & D. R. Loseke (Eds.), *Current controversies on family violence.* Newbury Park, CA: Sage.

Straus, M. A., & Gelles, R. J. (1990). *Physical violence in American families: Risk factors and adaptations to violence in 8,145 families.* New Brunswick, NJ: Transaction.

Straus, M., Gelles, R., & Steinmetz, S. (Eds). (1980). *Behind closed doors: Violence in the American family.* Garden City, NY: Anchor/Doubleday.

Stuart, E. P., & Campbell, J. C. (1989). Assessment of patterns of dangerousness with battered women. *Issues in Mental Health Nursing, 10,* 245–260.

Thorne, B., & Luria, Z. (1986). Sexuality and gender in children's daily worlds. *Social Problems, 33,* 176–190.

Towson, S. M. J., & Zanna, M. P. (1982). Toward a situational analysis of gender differences in aggression. *Sex Roles, 8,* 903–914.

Uniform Crime Report. (1985). U.S. Federal Bureau of Investigations, U. S. Department of Justice. Washington, DC.

Walker, L. (1984). *The battered woman syndrome.* New York: Springer.

Warr, M. (1985). Fear of rape among urban women. *Social Problems, 32,* 238–250.

Waterman, C., Dawson, L., & Bologna, M. (1989). Sexual coercion in gay and lesbian relationships: Predictors and implications for support services. *Journal of Sex Research, 26,* 118–124.

Weiss, K., & Borges, S. (1973). Victimology and rape: The case of the legitimate victim. *Issues in Criminology, 8,* 71–115.

White, E. C. (1991). The abused black woman: Challenging a legacy of pain. In B. Levy (Ed.), *Dating violence: Young women in danger* (pp. 84–93). Seattle, WA: Seal Press.

White, J. W., & Humphrey, J. A. (1993, August 20). *Sexual revictimization: A longitudinal perspective.* Paper presented at the American Psychological Association, Toronto, Canada.

White, J. W., & Koss, M. P. (1991). Courtship violence: Incidence in a national sample of higher education students. *Violence and Victims, 6,* 247–257.

White, J. W., Koss, M. P., & Kissling, G. (1991, June 15). *An empirical test of a theoretical model of courtship violence.* Paper presented at the American Psychological Society, Washington, DC.

White, J. W., & Kowalski, R. M. (1994). Deconstructing the myth of the nonaggressive woman: A feminist analysis. *Psychology of Women Quarterly, 16,* 477–498.

Yllo, K. A. (1993). Through a feminist lens: Gender, power, and violence. In R. J. Gelles & D. R. Loseke (Eds.), *Current controversies on family violence.* Newbury Park, CA: Sage.

Yoshihamana, M., Parekh, A. L., & Boyington, D. (1991). Dating violence in Asian/Pacific communities. In B. Levy (Ed.), *Dating violence: Young women in danger* (pp. 184–195). Seattle, WA: Seal Press.

PART
FOUR

GENDERED
PROFESSIONAL
RELATIONSHIPS

CHAPTER

13

GENDERED INTERACTION IN PROFESSIONAL RELATIONSHIPS

BREN ORTEGA MURPHY
TED ZORN

You may be familiar with Murphy Brown, the television journalist portrayed by Candice Bergen; Grace Van Owen, the attorney played by Susan Dey in "LA Law"; and Joyce Davenport, the district attorney played by Veronica Hamel in "Hill Street Blues." Since the early 1980s, mass media in the United States have paid increasing attention to women working in professional settings. Although these depictions have often been distorted, exaggerating both the glamour and the problems of female professionals (Faludi, 1992; Vande Berg & Trujillo, 1989) contemporary popular culture seldom questions women's basic abilities and rights to pursue white-collar careers. Magazine articles, television talk shows, advertising campaigns, and movies may debate issues of good child rearing, "glass ceilings," overt discrimination and sexual harassment, and even proper attire. But a common thread is the assumption that women should be allowed to enter such fields as accounting, banking, corporate consulting, law, medicine, science, and higher education. This is not to say that gender-based prejudice, discrimination, and harassment don't exist. The 1992 U.S. Department of Labor statistics indicate that women "comprise only 2–3 percent of top management" and that "working women [overall] have median weekly earnings that are only 75 percent of similarly employed men" (Witt, 1994). Nor does our observation deny the charge that acceptance—especially within professional circles—is often limited to Caucasian, heterosexual, middle/upper-class women. Our point is that most of the conspicuous barriers for working women have been dismantled, especially in white-collar professions (Schwartz, 1992).

Ironically, it is this very "progress"—made, as Catalyst president Felice Schwartz observed, "from a zero point" (1992, p. 196)—that often prevents both women and men from recognizing that numerous subtle yet quite significant barriers persist. One such pivotal barrier is gendered conversational dynamics.

A widespread belief exists that neutral professional standards guide most professional behavior, including communication behavior. Thus, despite an equally widespread belief that men and women *in general* have trouble communicating with each other, many people persist in thinking that these difficulties evaporate at the office door. A good lawyer is expected to conduct himself or herself as a *lawyer,* regardless of gender. Moreover, many refuse to acknowledge the influence of gender on communication among professionals, preferring to explain differences in style and achievement as the result of circumstance, personality, or other individual attributes.

In our work as consultants, we encounter many men and some women who are reluctant to attribute any problems to gender differences. In private, however, gender often becomes the explicit topic of discussion and is viewed as the "cause" of many problems. This was apparent when a male friend recently confided that he would "never work for a woman again." We also hear from women who discuss in private, women-only groups their frustrations with male-only or male-dominated management teams who make decisions that affect them without understanding their points of view.

However, in part because our beliefs about gender are typically taken for granted and therefore difficult to notice (see Chapter 1 of this volume), and in part because other factors are more salient or less sensitive, it's easy to overlook gender's influence on interaction between professional men and women. Our research indicates that gender *does* affect the way professional men and women interact with each other. Moreover, it suggests that denying the influence of gender (often done in the name of promoting equality) can create a work environment imbued with suspicion, distrust, and frustration that is often polarized, ironically, along gender lines. We are not arguing that the differences we have seen are universal or innate. Our observations support those who contend that women and men are more alike than not. Nevertheless, we believe that there are significant gender-based issues in professional communication.

In this chapter, we draw on our work as scholars and corporate consultants to identify specific gender-based communication differences that can create problems in professional settings. Extensive field notes and written records of conversations from our consulting work provide examples of the differences we discuss. We also suggest strategies for addressing these problems and discuss factors that may impede the effectiveness of those strategies.

TWO DIFFERENT COMMUNICATION CULTURES

Many executives we have talked with, even some in their 40s, can recall when the first professional woman in their office was hired. And almost anyone who has worked for a few years can recall the first woman to be promoted to the executive ranks in his or her organization. This points to the fact that, with few exceptions, what we term "the professions" had very male beginnings. Thus, it is not surprising that scholars have been able to identify many aspects of a "normal professional environment" as essentially male in perspective (Haslett, Geis, & Carter, 1992). The largely unspoken rules for appropriate small talk, work hours, attire, on-the-job relationships, and displays of emotion were developed by men *for* men (albeit often unconsciously). As has been established throughout this book, men's and women's perspectives on many of these issues differ.

Thus, women entered a professional culture with meanings different from those they learned in the feminine speech communities discussed in Chapters 3, 5, and 9 of this book. When women entered professional environments, they first had to discover the rules, then decide to what extent they would conform to those rules or accept the consequences of breaking them. Even after the media announced that women had "made it," research indicated that a primary source of frustration for professional women came from their perception that they walked a narrow, sometimes impossible, line between demonstrating competence and maintaining a nonthreatening profile (Haslett et al., 1992; Morrison, White, & Van Velsor, 1987; Schwartz, 1992). Many of the women with whom we consult say that they constantly search for ways to convey just the right combination of masculine and feminine signals. To paraphrase former Texas governor Ann Richards, they—like Ginger Rogers—do everything Fred does, except backward and in high heels (Richards, 1988).

As professional demographics shifted, men also experienced frustration. Their "normal" patterns of interaction were challenged. Words, reactions, and norms that had worked for years became inadequate. Today, an increasing number of men complain of having to "walk on eggshells" in dealing with women at work. Some men so resent the discomfort that they resist making any change in their behavior. ("This chair*person* stuff is stupid.") Others are willing to adapt but feel caught in a tangle of mixed messages and vague directives ("Why can't you just give me a list of what to say and what not to say?")

It is in the context of these two cultures, then, the one that filters many men's experiences and the one that filters many women's experiences, that gendered communication patterns and their consequences arise and sometimes erupt. We turn now to specific gender dynamics that often plague professional interactions.

SHE SAYS/HE SAYS: GENDERED COMMUNICATION PRACTICES

The gendered perspectives professional women and men bring to the workplace manifest themselves in a number of specific ways. While there are many issues that we might discuss, we will limit ourselves to seven issues: double standards of expression, sports talk/family talk, sexist remarks, self-promotion, problem solving and understanding, inclusion in decision making, and humor. Each of these professional activities is saturated with gendered assumptions.

Double Standards for Expression

One major area of difficulty essentially involves double standards regarding displays of strength, power, and emotion. Women, especially Caucasian Americans, have traditionally conveyed their femininity by signaling submissiveness to men (Goffman, 1979; Henley, 1977). They smile more than men; in fact, they smile even when they're not happy. They keep their voices down and their language "clean." They cant their heads and express sympathy toward others. They may be terribly happy or sad but never angry or aggressive. Western men, on the other hand, convey dominance and control by speaking in a relatively loud voice, demonstrating little facial animation, invading others' space, and displaying outbursts of anger. Most of us are socialized to accept these norms about what's appropriate for women and men, and we implicitly (and sometimes explicitly) reward "appropriate" behavior and show disapproval of what we and society consider "inappropriate" (Morrison et al., 1987; Schwartz, 1989).

Much has been written about the price women pay when they display strength and power in private life (Haslett et al., 1992). In professional life, the consequence is often a glaring double bind (Morrison et al., 1987; Wood & Conrad, 1983). To display submissiveness is to be weak, and to be weak is not professional. To display strength and power is professional but not feminine, and therefore not approved. Hence the dilemma experienced by many women is manifested in comments such as "He's strong; he's got what it takes; she's a pushy bitch." Women in professional contexts often feel they must choose between being effective women or effective professionals, but they cannot be both simultaneously.

As a consequence of different behaviors and expectations, female professors report not being taken as seriously as their male counterparts because they are perceived by their students as more nurturing, hence less authoritative. Deborah Tannen (1990) told of a doctoral student who called her on a Sunday to ask questions she should have directed to her dissertation director, but didn't because she didn't want to disturb him. It was apparently okay to disturb a female professor. But when women professors try to convey more authority through stern (nonsmiling) facial expressions, for example, students often evaluate them less highly (Cooper, Stewart, & Gudykunst, 1982). The male manager who screams his displeasure may be regarded as a jerk, but "that's just how business is at times." The female who screams or cries is usually seen in a far worse light. He "just gets excited," but she's "too emotional."

One particularly insidious corollary of this double standard is the implication that certain jobs are still closed to "real women." An ad for a *Fortune* article on tough bosses bore the headline "You don't build a company like this with lace on your underwear" (*New York Times,* 1989). Put this next to all those lingerie ads featuring women with briefcases and what does this mean? It suggests women have to choose between being feminine and being tough, between being a "real" woman and being a leader in certain professional circles. And even if *you* don't accept that dichotomy, the majority of men and women with whom you work do, and will judge you accordingly.

This double standard can have negative consequences for men as well. If the standard for displaying strength and power includes a raised voice and aggressive nonverbals, soft-spoken and nonaggressive men may lose respect and influence, perhaps even more so than women with these characteristics. Crying in the office may undermine a woman's credibility as a tough professional, but it can destroy a man's reputation on both personal and professional levels.

For men, a far more common consequence of these double standards is extreme discomfort in having to deal with someone else who's crying. Many male executives tell us that the mere *anticipation* of some-one's crying leads them to soften criticism or withhold feedback. That "someone" is almost always female. As a result, women may not receive information they need, and the man involved, because of his dis-comfort, is not able to do his job well and persists in believing that he just can't "talk straight" to women.

Thus, men have traditionally displayed strength, power, and control more than women, and women have traditionally displayed more sub-missiveness, vulnerability, and sensitivity. These tendencies have led to expectations for what is and is not appropriate. Note that most of the emotions we've discussed are expressed by nonverbal communication, which we tend to be less aware of sending and receiving. Women seem to be in a "Catch-22," since communicating in these traditionally fem-inine ways lowers professional credibility, yet not being deferential and sensitive often results in negative labels such as *pushy* and *bitch*. Men, too, are constrained by these norms, and often feel compelled to live up to "macho" expectations of displaying power and not displaying vul-nerability. However, it is not only traditional nonverbal patterns and norms that create difficulties for men and women in interaction. The content of their talk also has differed traditionally, and this difference surfaces on the job.

Sports Talk/Family Talk

Sports talk is the unofficial small talk of American business. Not only are scores, plays, and statistics daily topics of conversation, but busi-ness talk itself is peppered with sports-oriented phrases. It is not uncommon to hear meetings, proposals, strategies, and the like described in terms such as *slam dunk, out of bounds, below the belt, score one for our side, struck out, defensive play, end run, dropped the ball, your turn at bat, the whole nine yards, easy lay up*, and *pass the ball*. During the 1970s, professional women were advised to take courses or read books to help them "learn the language" of competitive sports (Harragan, 1977; Hennig & Jardim, 1976). By the 1990s, direc-tives to women were less overt, but the prominence of sports talk con-tinued. An increasing number of women report avid interest in the topic and enjoy the camaraderie that grows out of talking about games, play-ers, and strategies. Yet even women who have interest and considerable expertise are often "shut out" by men who either can't imagine talking about sports with female colleagues or don't want to do so. Many women who have no interest in sports talk express disappointment at not finding other sources of informal connection with their coworkers.

What do non-sports-minded women want to talk about in casual interactions? The most common topics seem to be family and home. Although these topics (day-care issues, for example) may actually have more relevance to the workplace than sports, they are often regarded as unprofessional and, therefore, are frowned on except in all-female circles. Yet the criticism is seldom made that talk about the NFL and the NCAA Final Four is entirely unrelated to professions other than athletics! The point of small talk—whether about family, sports, or the weather—is to connect personally, not professionally.

A factor that exacerbates this conversational segregation is the tendency for informal as well as client/customer socializing to revolve around sports as well. We have heard numerous stories of conscious exclusion (country clubs that still exclude women or restrict the hours that women can play golf) and unconscious exclusion (the company baseball team that technically allows female players though none ever seems interested). Often, the decision to restrict participation *seems* logical: the male CEO with the one-room fishing lodge who doesn't think his lone female sales representative (or her spouse who would be left behind) will feel comfortable on the annual fishing and drinking trip; or the law firm senior partner who systematically invites all his male junior partners to pro-basketball games, reasoning that the one female manager wouldn't be interested, since she never participates in conversations about organized sports. No matter how reasonable these particular decisions may seem to the people making them, as a pattern they fuel the perception of a "boy's club" that facilitates informal mentoring for those inside and puts outsiders at a disadvantage.

Professional women often express apprehension about sex-segregated outings. What kinds of bonds develop in casual moments of give and take between men? When women express these concerns, some men dismiss them with denials, hostility, and/or accusations of paranoia. The following exchange took place in one of our workshops. Notice the emotional buildup the woman felt about being excluded and the men's defensiveness and dismissal of her concerns.

> *Woman:* I worked in a group of five, with four guys. They'd say once a week, "We're having a guys' night out." Finally, one week, I blew up.
> *Man A:* So, can't four guys go out together?
> *Man B:* You didn't miss anything.

The woman explained that she didn't say anything to the men in her work group for many weeks, but heard the invitations to "the guys" as well as discussions about their outings. Finally, her frustration at being excluded reached the boiling point. The two men's responses were, from their points of view at least, reasonable and logical. As Man A points out, surely four men can socialize together without having to have a woman along. And as Man B asserts, nothing work-related may have been discussed. But neither of these responses addresses the emotional anguish of being repeatedly excluded *because* of being female. (If it's difficult for you to see the woman's response as valid, imagine the same scenario played out along racial or class lines.) It's worth noting that many men have acknowledged that the comfort and bonding created through informal socializing can enhance valuable mentoring relationships and contribute to professional openness and trust. Yet despite these important effects on careers and advancement, many organizations and male professionals resist opening their social outings to women colleagues.

Is there any tangible impact to all this? Certainly the mere perception of being socially excluded has discouraged some talented women from staying in certain work environments (Schwartz, 1992). Why not go where building rapport isn't such an uphill struggle? Moreover, several public accounting partners have told us that knowing a partner candidate personally as well as professionally can be a tremendous asset to that person, since he or she usually needs an advocate who can go beyond the candidate's technical skills and speak to such subjective qualities as commitment or, as several partners called it, "fire in the belly" (itself, a masculine term that may not translate well to many women's approaches to commitment and success). These same partners admit that "not really knowing" a candidate as a person stands in the way of endorsement.

Sex-segregated socializing and interaction also limit individual and organizational effectiveness by undermining openness and trust between men and women. In our workshops, we repeatedly hear male executives express surprise at the difficulties and frustrations their women coworkers and subordinates describe. A typical comment was expressed by a senior male partner in a men-only group: "Marsha is one of our best up-and-coming managers. I can't believe I'm hearing about these problems for the first time [in this workshop]." What many men come to realize is that without a strong relationship, without concomitant trust and openness, people will not risk being perceived as complainers or as weak by sharing problems and concerns. And an all too frequent response by people who, correctly or incorrectly, do not believe their concerns will be listened to with empathy is simply to leave for what appear to be better opportunities.

To the extent that sex-segregated talk and socializing interfere with receiving effective mentoring, developing advocates, and creating trust, these "natural patterns" create problems, including gender inequity.

Sexist Remarks

In our experience, most professional men or women believe it's unacceptable to make blatant claims about a person's inferiority based on sex. Sexist remarks are, however, made in professional settings. For example, one accountant with whom we worked was told she was "thinking with her tits," while other professional women describe coworkers who respond to women's strong opinions by saying things like "Must be that time of the month." Men, on the other hand, have reported being offended when female coworkers comment, for instance, "You're a man. You wouldn't understand." Such sexist remarks are made in professional settings, but few people would defend them if publicly challenged to do so. Obviously sexist remarks are considered unprofessional (unless you work with Rush Limbaugh).

Numerous men complain that it's become "politically incorrect" to give compliments, make jokes, offer personal observations, and use "normal language." Why do women rebuke "innocent compliments" and take offense at what is obviously joking behavior? Why should women care if men make comments about other good-looking women, as long as it's not *them* they're discussing? Why should one person's opinion of "half-time" project managers have any bearing on those manager's self-confidence? And why *must* we say "women" instead of "ladies" and "girls"?

One rather maddening answer is that not all women respond the same way to remarks. We've met lots of professional women who will tell you that they welcome personal compliments and love being called ladies; other women can match any guy in the office for off-color jokes. As with *any* communication, relational context is the key. A compliment in and of itself is neither good nor bad. However, when appearance is repeatedly complimented but professional achievements are not, a woman may infer that only her looks and not her abilities are noticed and valued. Similarly, a compliment that suggests a professional woman's primary asset is her appearance may reasonably give offense to the woman who has worked hard to achieve her technical credentials. A female professor (Dr. Y) tells of being introduced around campus along with another new hire (Dr. X) who happened to be male. At one point, the chair (male) said jovially, "This is Dr. X from the University of Kansas, and this is Dr. Y from Northwestern....We're going to have to stop hiring these good-looking Ph.D.s, or the other women in the department will get jealous." Dr. Y commented later, "I felt like the chair was saying 'Here's the real doctor and here's the doctorette; isn't she cute?'"

Likewise, humor can signal judgment. A blond joke may seem like an innocent laugh to the speaker, but a blond woman standing nearby may wonder if her hair color presents one more obstacle to credibility that her male counterpart never encounters—even if he's blond.

Is it possible that some women overreact to particular remarks, or are too quick to allege sexism? Certainly. But the assertion that women generically are too sensitive ignores the historical context of sexism in the workplace and elsewhere. Men and masculine style are still the norm in most professional settings, especially at the higher levels of management and power. Thus, it is much easier for them to hear remarks as individual comments rather than categorical judgments. As a gay professor observes, "As a rule, straight, white men don't walk around the office wondering if things are being said or done to them *because* they're straight or white or male. And they're right—they've no reason to do so. Despite all the hyperbole about reverse discrimination, being white, straight and male has not worked against many people. Being black, being gay, being female has." So, for example, there's little reason for a man to wonder if his good looks undermine his credibility. No one has ever said to him "But you're too cute to be an accountant." The woman who's been told that even once, however, has reason to pause when others comment on her appearance. The historical context of sexism understandably influences how she interprets such a comment. Similarly, a Caucasian male intern may not like being called "boy" or "gentleman" by the male resident, but the intern is unlikely to wonder if the resident or anyone else in the hospital views male doctors as less qualified or less committed than their female counterparts. (The historical context of racism, however, might lead an African American intern to be offended by the label *boy*.)

Some sexist talk, such as unwelcome advances or talk of a sexual nature, can constitute sexual harassment. While Chapter 14 discusses this topic in detail, one aspect of sexual harassment is relevant to our discussion of gendered interaction between professionals. Men frequently joke that they don't understand all the fuss, since they would welcome sexual attention from female colleagues. These comments point to a misunderstanding of harassment, since, by definition, it consists of behavior deemed unacceptable by the target. In other words, victims don't have the opportunity to choose who makes advances or shows sexual attention. Furthermore, joking comments about welcoming sexual interest ignore the historical context in which women, more than men, have been treated primarily as sex objects. Even if it is true that some men would welcome sexual attention from women, their feeling is not universal.

Self-Promotion

Several researchers (Johnson, 1989; Tannen, 1990) have contended that men and women tend to see communication differently. Generally (and acknowledging a research population dominated by white, middle-class people), men place communication in the context of a fundamentally hierarchical and data-based world and, thus, see its primary functions as competing, gaining and holding status, and accomplishing tasks. The purpose of talk is to *do* something. As a rule, women place communication in a fundamentally communal and relationship-focused world, and see its functions as cooperating and building relationships. Talking is an end in itself because the process is both a sign and an ongoing basis for interpersonal connection. Our experience in consulting also provides evidence that "gender cultures" surface and sometimes clash in the workplace. One of the most obvious areas of impact relates to self-promotion.

If men tend to see communication as a competitive tool while women see it more as a way to build connections, then men are more likely than women to broadcast their professional abilities and accomplishments. Men also find it easier to take credit for ideas and jobs well done. Women, on the other hand, are less comfortable with what they see as boasting. They are more likely to let their work speak for itself or let their individual efforts be seen as part of a team achievement. The men and women with whom we work see this as a familiar pattern. One accountant told us that she was being counseled out of the firm, despite her acknowledged technical competence. She was told that she needed to be "more aggressive" in telling coworkers and clients what she did—simply doing it wasn't enough. A male professor at a major university has perfected a way of injecting the topic of his most recent accomplishments into almost any conversation and seems to feel no reluctance to pass along others' praise for his work. One of his female colleagues, on the other hand, asked permission of a friend to tell the news of a national research award she'd recently received: "Do you mind if I tell you some good news?" Another female professor, who had just had an extraordinary year of publishing and receiving awards for her work, used a tactic common to people who feel uncomfortable with self-promotion: deflecting compliments. When complimented for her achievements by a colleague, she downplayed the accomplishments and diverted attention to others: "The whole department had a good year, didn't we?" She even offered reasons why she hadn't been as productive as it seemed: "Really, much of this stuff had been completed for several years and just happened to come out at the same time."

Unlike the accountant described above, most women are not fired for lack of self-promotion. But they may be passed over for advancement, merit raises, special opportunities, awards, and other markers of success. Men seen by women as obnoxious in this respect may simply be doing what seems logical to them and what, in fact, results in career advancement. After all, there's no Promotion Fairy going from office to office asking worthy people if they want a promotion or raise. And many senior executives freely admit that being able to "market yourself" within an organization can help you get ahead.

Problem Solving and Understanding

Another area in which gender differences surface is that of problem solving. Research shows that men tend to discuss problems in order to solve them. The understanding fostered by such discussion is valuable only as a means to an end—problem resolution. Although women seek solutions as well, they tend to see understanding as worthwhile in and of itself. Thus, as a rule, women feel more comfortable than men talking about difficult situations that have no immediate or obvious solution (Johnson, 1989; Tannen, 1990). Chapter 9 in this book discusses this gendered dynamic as it occurs in personal relationships between women and men.

The contexts in which we see this difference involves problems that may be caused or exacerbated by the workplace but are not directly job dilemmas. The two most common of these "indirect" problems are family/work balance and networking. Professional women are much more likely than their male counterparts to have significant domestic responsibilities. They are also much more likely to experience difficulty with work-related socializing—especially when it comes to developing rapport with senior management, both internal and client, since both groups are predominantly male. Part of this latter problem stems from the male-oriented or male-only activities, such as sporting events, that we discussed earlier.

These problems are compounded for many women by the inadequate responses they receive whenever they try to discuss their situations with managers and mentors, who are predominantly male. In many cases, the men's perspective is something like this: "Look, neither I nor the firm caused these problems nor do I have any idea how to solve them. It's not my fault that the guy you married won't do laundry or that you feel guilty missing your kid's recital or that our clients like to play golf. So what's the point of talking about it? I can't change society." Many women point out that their workplaces aren't entirely blameless; yet, what really frustrates them is the seeming indifference of people who are supposed to be colleagues. "I'd much rather be truly understood than patronized and protected," said the lone female on a sales team. "I'm not asking for any extraordinary measures. I just want them to know that my life is different from theirs." As was often said after the Hill/Thomas hearings, women want men to "get it"—even those men who do not directly create the problems. If the men don't care enough to "get it," long-term solutions aren't possible.

Socialized to solve problems, men often express frustration at what they see as women's "pointless complaining" about problems. One male executive voiced what others have grumbled about when he said, "I don't mind if they come to me with a problem. But damn it, come in with a solution, too. Don't just lay the problem on me and expect me to fix it." From his solution-focused perspective, discussion of the problem is worthless if it doesn't lead to a solution. Therefore, someone who comes in with a problem and no solution is likely to be viewed as incompetent or a whiner. Such negative judgments unfortunately often result when a woman who uses communication to express feelings interacts with a man who uses communication to resolve problems.

A related complaint we hear from men is that women meet in women-only groups to discuss their concerns. Interestingly, from women's point of view, such discussions are helpful in getting the understanding and support they would like but often don't get from male colleagues. Since women value being listened to and understood, even when a solution doesn't result, these discussions are useful for them. Men sometimes view discussions among women as pointless ("They can't solve gender-related problems if they don't talk to us") and even harmful, since they act to separate men and women, may foster suspicion among men about what's being discussed, and may set up an us-versus-them atmosphere.

In sum, men and women may have different needs and values related to understanding and problem solution. However, if they don't recognize and respect the differences, they tend to judge the other group from their own norms. Thus, men often think women talk and complain too much on these issues, and women think men are insensitive. From each gender's own norms, such judgments make sense. However, when you realize the other is operating from a different sense of what is normal, the judgments seem less appropriate.

Inclusion in Decision Making

Because women tend to value inclusion and personal connections (Johnson, 1989, pp. 301–316), they often want to be involved in decisions that affect them, even when the men making the decisions can correctly forecast the women's answers (Tannen, 1990, pp. 26–42, 288–294). Numerous female accountants, for example, complain that they are never even considered for jobs that would require traveling to "bad neighborhoods" or handling sexist clients. Some say they would willingly take such risks if it meant getting high-profile work. Others admit they would turn down such work but say they still want to be asked. "What a total waste of time," says the man, focusing on information exchange as the point of communication. "Why should I ask you a question to which I know the answer?" "Because you might not always know the answer," she replies, "and besides, asking is the mark of a collegial relationship. The asking is as important as the answer."

We should note that both women and men have observed that question asking is not quite as benign as it sounds, since even women who *don't* want unpleasant or dangerous assignments might feel pressure to say yes. Few women, however, advocated not asking as the best solution.

Humor

A final area in which gendered communication surfaces is the use of humor in the office. Gender differences regarding humor are well documented. Men tell jokes; women laugh. Men trade insults and put-downs; women tell "cute" or "charming" stories and comment on situations. Seen from the perspective of gendered communication cultures, men are more likely than women to use humor in a competitive fashion. The outcome, in some cases, is undue discomfort on the part of women who have little idea how to respond in an atmosphere of seemingly relentless abuse. In response, men counter by arguing that women should "lighten up." Once again, the end result is a feeling that men and women live in two different worlds.

Additional Complications

In our experience, the difficulties raised by these gendered communication styles are generally complicated by two factors. One is a widespread norm against discussing such issues openly. The other is a belief among many men that the workplace has turned into the previously mentioned "eggshell environment"—a place in which men, especially white men, must constantly monitor what they say and do to avoid misinterpretation and negative judgments. Of course, not all men resist change; some admit feeling self-conscious but agree that changes have to be made. At the other end of the continuum are men who feel under attack. These men speak angrily of reverse discrimination and false accusations, although few have actually experienced either. Some even talk about becoming "an endangered species" although they work in places where top management is still 90% male. The title of a recent *Business Week* cover story—"White, Male, and Worried"—sums up this feeling (Galen, 1994), although the demographics of the professional world do not.

The depth of some men's feeling and its persistence in the face of contrary information fosters an atmosphere of distrust and fear in which open discussion is difficult and appreciation of different positions is next to impossible. Still, that is what is necessary if men and women are to learn how to work together effectively.

STRATEGIES FOR CREATING A COLLEGIAL ENVIRONMENT

Given the issues described above, we offer the following suggestions as ways men and women may interact more effectively in professional contexts.

- *Understand and appreciate differences in communication perspectives.* Many scholars encourage men and women to learn to speak each other's language. Rather than disparage a woman for engaging in "useless conversation," men should recognize that the conversation may *be* the point. Rather than dismiss a man as self-aggrandizing, women should realize that this may be what's required in the situation. Women and men both need to learn how to use talk to "get to the point" and how to use it to build and enhance collegial relationships. They also should learn to appreciate a variety of communication perspectives (for example, ethnically and otherwise culturally based) and to use talk to contribute to a rich and productive work environment.

- *Have open, honest discussions about these issues.* Do what it takes to keep conversation going. Give each other indications of understanding. Avoid responses such as automatic rebuttals ("That's not a gender issue!"), which function to stop conversation or turn it into point/counterpoint. Initiating and engaging in such discussions may be awkward and perhaps even painful at first. But focus on really trying to understand the other person's perspective and not reacting defensively. Your efforts at trying to understand will often encourage the other person to do the same.

- *Respect confidentiality.* When someone does open up, don't spread her or his remarks all over the office. If you hope to encourage candid discussions about any topic, you must support people when they take the risk of opening up. An important form of support is respecting confidentiality. When people know they can speak confidentially, they are more likely to be open and willing to work together to improve understanding.

- *Give timely feedback when you're confused or offended.* Make feedback specific, and focus it on behavior, as opposed to the other person's personality or character. By all means, avoid using labels or stereotypes to address these issues (for example, "This is just what I'd expect from a woman!"). Say, for example, "It really bothers me when you say I won't understand just because I'm a man. I'd like to try so why don't you give me a chance?" Remember that feedback need not be severe or overtly challenging in order to be effective. Wit and diplomacy can be more eloquent than rebuke.

- *Explain what you want out of a conversation, and ask when you're confused.* For example, say, "I'm not sure if there's a solution to this right now, but I'd like to let you know what's going on with me." Or, if you're on the receiving end of a complaint about a situation to which you don't have a solution, ask, "What would you like to get out of our conversation?"

- *Avoid remarks that imply less commitment on the part of one sex or the other.* For example, "Well, now that she's a mother, we'll have to pick up her slack." Or, "Don't worry about including him. Men aren't interested in relationships anyway." Even off-handed remarks made to one other person fuel negative stereotypes and solidify the barriers to individuals' success.

- *Object to offensive remarks even when you aren't the "target" and the "target" isn't there.* Sexist remarks are still sexist even when they're made outside the earshot of the person or group being maligned. When a man objects to calling the only female partner "the senior bitch," it carries weight that a woman's objection wouldn't have. Besides, a woman is unlikely to hear such overt comments. As with giving feedback, remember that humor and even silence can make your point. This is tricky, since these behaviors can also signal support or at least a willingness to "go along."

As with any communication, meaning depends on the context. Thus, it is possible that refusal to laugh (silence) at a sexist joke indicates dissent. Such indirect strategies are particularly useful when the person being rebuked is in a more powerful position than the one making objections.

- *Avoid certain double standards.* Not all double standards are bad. To the extent that a man and a woman differ in communication style, they may merit different responses. An effective communicator recognizes that *equitable* treatment doesn't always mean *equal* treatment. But certain double standards reinforce the devaluation of one sex and contribute to gender barriers in the workplace. For example, when a male manager sugarcoats his negative reaction to a female employee's work because he doesn't think she can handle "straight talk," he not only affirms his own misperception that women are categorically weak, but also withholds information that may be critical to her progress.

- *Consult with others about decisions that affect them.* Do so even if you think you can accurately anticipate their response. The purpose of asking people for input isn't merely to get information. It is also a sign of respect. We do this all the time in the name of common courtesy. We knock on doors, ask for permission to sit, and invite others to join us even when we are fairly sure they'll say no. The fact that most of us appreciate being asked is reason enough to do so.

- *Get to know each other as individuals, gender and all.* Here's the key. When we develop truly collegial relationships, when we know and trust each other as individuals, then we can hear and be heard effectively. As we stated earlier, meaning depends on context. What sounds like a compliment does not always convey positive regard. On the other hand, even the most outrageous comment can signal esteem. Throughout sessions of the 103rd Congress, Representative Charlie Wilson routinely called Representative Pat Schroeder "Babycakes" (unless she was with constituents, in which case he called her "Congressman Babycakes"). Schroeder knew Wilson well enough to realize that what seemed to be an overtly sexist reference was actually a put-down of such thinking. Further, Wilson knew that Schroeder would appreciate, rather than resent, the joke (Ivins, 1994). Similarly, we recently talked with a group of professional men and women together about this issue. One of the women said of Tom, a manager who was in the group, "Tom calls everyone 'Babe'—men and women. He's just having fun with us, and we know it. We all have a good time together and know he doesn't mean anything sexist by it." To know someone as an individual is not to ignore that person's gender but to understand how it, along with factors such as ethnicity, upbringing, sexual orientation, education, and personality, shapes her or his perceptions and behaviors. Knowing someone and letting that person know you can also lead to trust—trust that one understands another's intentions and can ask or even object when necessary. A workplace characterized by such true collegiality is just the opposite of an eggshell environment because it allows both women and men to contribute their best.

CONCLUSION

Although the gendered perspectives that women and men bring to the workplace create challenges for successful interaction, we are not pessimistic. We have seen many cases of men and women professionals working together respectfully and harmoniously, with good humor and competence. Although in almost every workshop we conduct we encounter examples of the problems described in this chapter, we also encounter some men or women who build supportive relationships with colleagues of the other sex. Additionally, we sometimes see communication improve before our eyes as people begin to open up and confront issues they have held inside, talking directly with each other in constructive ways. Simply talking more may not solve all the problems, but developing good relationships with coworkers and having an ongoing, open dialogue about issues of difference takes much of the poison out of difficulties that arise because of different perspectives. Implementing the strategies we've outlined above fosters strong, open relationships between men and women in professional life.

QUESTIONS FOR REFLECTION AND DISCUSSION

1. Talk to a successful professional woman in your community. Ask her about the challenges she has faced in her career and how she overcame them. Ask her to explain how she or other professional women balanced career and family goals, and if the challenges they faced were different from those of male colleagues.

2. Interview professional men who are in their 40s or 50s for their views on interacting with women. Ask them how the norms of interacting have changed with the influx of women into profes-

sional and executive ranks. How have they responded emotionally to these changes? In what ways have they altered their behavior?

3. Think of work contexts in which you've participated, such as university groups or summer jobs. What gendered communication practices can you recall? For example, did you notice differences in the ways men and women expressed opinions and emotions? Did you notice differences in others' reactions to their communication?

4. How are professional men and women's interactions portrayed in the media? Do you see the gendered communication practices described in this chapter reflected in these portrayals? How might such messages from the media influence or reflect what goes on in real-life professional interactions between men and women?

REFERENCES

Cooper, P. J., Stewart, L. P., & Gudykunst, W. B. (1982). Relationship with instructor and other variables influencing student evaluations of instructors. *Communication Quarterly, 30,* 308–315.

Faludi, S. (1992). *Backlash: The undeclared war against American women.* New York: Crown.

Galen, M. (1994, January 31). White, male and worried. *Business Week,* pp. 50+

Goffman, E. (1979). *Gender advertisements.* Cambridge: Harvard University Press.

Harragan, B. L. (1977). *Games mother never taught you.* New York: Warner Books.

Haslett, B., Geis, F. L., & Carter, M. R. (1992). *The organizational woman: Power and paradox.* Norwood, NJ: Ablex.

Henley, N. M. (1977). *Body politics: Power, sex and nonverbal communication.* Englewood Cliffs, NJ: Prentice-Hall.

Hennig, M., & Jardim, A. (1976). *The managerial woman.* New York: Pocket Books.

Ivans, M. (1994, September). Good time Charlie. *GQ,* pp. 132–137, 175.

Johnson, F. L. (1989). Women's culture and communication: An analytic perspective. In C. M. Lont, & S. A. Friedley (Eds.), *Beyond boundaries: Sex and gender diversity in communication.* Fairfax, VA: George Mason University Press.

Morrison, A. M., White, R. P., Van Velsor, E. (1987). The narrow band. *Issues and Observations. 7*(2), 1–15.

New York Times. (1989, February 17). Ad in *Fortune* magazine.

Richards, A. (1988, July). Keynote address, Democratic National Convention.

Schwartz, F. (1989, January/February). Management women and the new facts of life. *Harvard Business Review,* pp. 65–76.

Schwartz, F. (1992). *Breaking with tradition.* New York: Warner Books.

Tannen, D. (1990). *You just don't understand: Men and women in conversation.* New York: Ballantine Books.

Vande Berg, L., & Trujillo, N. (1989). *Organizational life on television.* Norwood, NJ: Ablex.

Witt, L. (1994, September/October). Woman warrior. *Mother Jones,* p. 15.

Wood, J. T., & Conrad, C. R. (1983). Paradox in the experience of professional women. *Western Journal of Speech Communication, 47,* 305–322.

SEXUAL HARASSMENT: ON THE JOB, ON THE CAMPUS

SHEREEN G. BINGHAM

My supervisor reached up my skirt at a business luncheon. My coworkers put a fake penis and an obscene note in my desk drawer. My boss grabbed my breasts and asked me to have sex with him. When I refused, he fired me. Nobody said anything to me about sexual harassment.

This story, told to me by a woman I met on an airplane last year, concerns events that happened more than 20 years ago. At the time, she didn't call what happened "sexual harassment," nor did thousands of other women who were similarly assaulted with unwanted and unwelcome sexual behaviors.

This woman's story isn't uncommon. Sexual harassment is prevalent, and victims often feel powerless to do anything to stop it or to punish harassers. In fact, sexual harassment in educational and professional settings is so pervasive that many of us who study it have come to believe it is systematically supported by practices and the gender ideology of Western culture. Like others who study sexual harassment, I've realized that cultural values and expectations about gender, power, and sexuality encourage us to see and experience sexual harassment as normal and unavoidable.

Let's return to my travel companion's story. Would you say she was sexually harassed? Do you think her sex, age, class, and sexual orientation had anything to do with what happened to her? Can you explain how the events she described could have happened without her realizing that she was being sexually harassed? Whether you believe this woman was sexually harassed depends on how you define sexual harassment. Whether you understand why she didn't know she was harassed at the time depends on your awareness of the ways in which communication shapes knowledge of experience.

This chapter focuses on those issues—what sexual harassment means and how its meanings are constructed and perpetuated through communication. As we will see, gender socialization in Western culture permits, and even encourages, sexual harassment by teaching women and men to communicate in ways that create the illusion that sexual harassment is inevitable, normal, and even desirable.

WHAT IS SEXUAL HARASSMENT?

The term *sexual harassment* wasn't coined until the mid-1970s (Wise & Stanley, 1987). Prior to that time, my travel companion and thousands of other individuals had no adequate language to describe what happened to them as wrong and unacceptable (Wood, 1993). Thus, when my travel companion was harassed and fired, she had no socially recognized term to speak out against what happened to her. All she could say was "My coworkers played pranks on me" or "My boss tried to make me go to bed with him." Language such as this fails to capture feelings of violation, humiliation, and outrage. The available language in the 1970s didn't allow victims of sexual harassment to name what happened as morally and professionally unconscionable.

Naming sexual harassment made us aware that particular kinds of conduct are wrong (Wood, 1993). At the same time, it propelled legal and public dialogue about how we should define and understand sexual harassment. Court rulings and social science research show that sexual harassment occurs in many different forms. Studies also suggest that a person's gender, race, class, affectional orientation, age, and marital status influence the frequency and nature of sexual harassment experiences.

Legal Definitions

Courts and policies recognize two general types of sexual harassment. *Quid pro quo* sexual harassment refers to the actual or threatened use of job-related or academic-related rewards or punishments to gain sexual compliance from a subordinate or student. For example, a professor might offer to give a student a higher grade in exchange for having sex, or an employer might subtly or overtly threaten to write a poor performance appraisal if an employee will not grant sexual favors. My travel companion was subjected to this form of sexual harassment when her boss fired her because she refused to have sex with him.

The second type of sexual harassment, *hostile environment*, refers to a wider and more ambiguous range of behaviors and conditions. According to the 1986 guidelines of the Equal Employment Opportunity Commission (EEOC), unwelcome sexual conduct creates a hostile environment that constitutes sexual harassment if it "has the purpose or effect of unreasonably interfering with an individual's work performance or creating an intimidating, hostile, or offensive working environment" (Paetzold & O'Leary-Kelly, 1993, p. 64). For example, an employee might create a hostile environment by groping a coworker or repeatedly make sexual gestures, comments, or propositions. One recent case in California involved a male lawyer who sexually harassed a secretary by touching and lunging at her breasts, pulling her arms back to "see which one (breast) is bigger," and making suggestive sexual comments ("Woman Awarded," 1994). However, individual perceptions aren't the legal standard for judging whether sexual harassment occurred. Most courts ask whether a "reasonable person" would experience an environment as hostile. More recently, some courts have adopted a "reasonable woman" standard to assess sexual harassment charges when the complainant is a woman (Forell, 1993). The behavior in question also must be judged "severe" or "pervasive" in addition to being "unwelcome" in order to be ruled unlawful (Shoop & Edwards, 1994). Legal standards based on broad social views prevent verdicts based solely on an individual's perceptions.

Legal definitions have not ended the debate about sexual harassment. Some people believe sexual harassment laws and policies are too restrictive and that fewer behaviors should be prohibited (Witteman, 1993). Some contend, for example, that making sexual comments, groping someone's body, or peeking down someone's clothing are natural and desirable in workplace and educational contexts (Roiphe, 1993), or that the U.S. Constitution guarantees free speech and nonverbal communication. In contrast, others argue that the courts tend to take an overly narrow view of sexual harassment, which sometimes discourages and disregards accusations that should be considered legitimate. For example, the "reasonable person" standard used to judge sexual harassment doesn't acknowledge that women and men have different social positions, experiences, and perspectives that affect their judgments of sexual harassment. Likewise, the "reasonable woman" standard presumes that people of the same gender all have common perceptions in spite of race, socioeconomic class, and affectional orientation. As we will see later in this chapter, these aspects of one's social position have implications for the frequency and nature of sexual harassment. The use of "reasonableness" standards therefore may fail to respect the experiences of marginalized groups and may distort and misjudge the legitimacy of many sexual harassment complaints.

Academic Definitions

Scholarly research supplements court rulings and legal definitions by identifying a variety of forms of sexual harassment (Bingham & Scherer, 1993; Fitzgerald & Hesson-McInnis, 1989; Gruber, 1992). Drawing from the literature as well as from experiences employees and students have shared with me, I can define and illustrate six forms of sexually harassing behavior that women and men experience in work and educational settings. Harassers often subject one person to several of these forms of harassment.

The first two forms, *quid pro quo* and coercive physical contact, are often considered the most severe types of sexual harassment. As noted in the previous section, *quid pro quo* sexual harassment involves the use of job- or school-related bribes or threats as pressure for sexual activity. The harasser may make explicit or subtle propositions that imply promises of rewards for complying or threats of punishment for refusing. Dziech and Weiner (1990) illustrate this form of sexual harassment with the narrative of a female student who had asked her male professor if she could write an extra-credit report to improve her grade. The professor refused the report but suggested an alternative: "There's one option I can give to you that I can't give to the males in the class. Sex?" (p. 94). The encounter left the student shocked, shaken, and wary of her professors.

The second form of sexual harassment, *coercive physical contact*, includes touching sexual or intimate areas of the body as well as physically coercing or assaulting someone. The harasser may use physical strength to trap, restrain, or push the victim while engaging in verbal forms of sexual harassment. A female employee, for example, told me of a man who held her arm for 15 minutes to prevent her escape while he made sexual propositions and comments. Another woman, a secretary, described a male superior who "shoved me against the copy machine, then rubbed up against me while telling me how nice I smelled." In a more unusual case, a male professor described a female student who he said "made a very determined pass at me, grabbing me and kissing me. I was surprised and shocked, and gave passive resistance." Victims describe these behaviors as unwanted, intimidating, degrading, and offensive.

The next two forms of sexual harassment, seduction and romantic imposition, involve conduct that is sometimes confused with romantic behaviors (see Witteman, 1993). These forms of sexual harassment differ from the behavior of consensual relationships, however, in that the harasser repeats or escalates the conduct even though the victim does not welcome or reciprocate it. These forms may be indistinguishable from *quid pro quo* harassment when the harasser is an organizational superior because the threat of punishment for refusing or objecting is implicit in relationships of unequal power (Tuana, 1985).

Seduction involves sexual propositions and other noncontact expressions of sexual interest that do not include or suggest threats or promises as pressure for compliance. For example, a coworker might repeatedly ask an employee to have sex with no implication that refusal would affect the employee's job. According to one female instructor, for instance: "This faculty member repeatedly harasses me with coy comments on my appearance, requests for sex, and complaints about his marriage and lack of sex life." Similarly, a male professor described a female employee who "approached me several times over the course of 6 weeks. She asked me explicitly to go to bed and dump my fiancée. She told me she was good in bed." More subtle forms of seduction also are common, as a female student described: "He constantly asks me if I have a boyfriend, and he says he knows that I make my boyfriend happy. He looks at my body instead of my eyes. He insists on knowing about my personal life and my likes and dislikes."

Romantic imposition differs from seduction in that nonsexual feelings and socializing are emphasized and sexual activity is not a focus. This form of harassment involves requests for dates and other repeated expressions of personal interest such as nonviolent and nonsexual touch, personal letters, gifts, telephone calls, and visits to the victim's home. For example, a female employee described a coworker who "began leaving presents on my desk, continually asked me out after I refused him several times, showed up at places where I was, kept calling me on the phone, and sent me love letters." Her coworker persisted even after she told him she was not interested and threatened to call his supervisor.

The last two forms of sexual harassment, antagonism and gender harassment, include sexist and sexual jokes, remarks, and other behaviors that highlight a person's sexuality or gender but do not convey expectations of sexual activity or socializing. These forms of conduct most clearly constitute sexual harassment when the harasser repeats them in spite of the victim's objections. *Antagonism* typically involves the use of sexual, obscene, or sexist jokes, comments, behaviors, and objects that degrade, insult, intimidate, or control the victim. For example, an employee might describe a coworker using obscene language or making insulting comments about the employee's sex life. Antagonism also includes expressed disapproval with the way the victim is fulfilling cultural expectations for femininity or masculinity. For example, a female secretary was subjected to "continuous remarks about my appearance—telling me how to dress, telling me I should wear perfume, telling me to be nicer to salespeople, and so on." Kramarae (1992) provides additional examples of how men convey disapproval of women's appearance, moral character, facial expressions, and sense of humor.

Gender harassment includes the use of sexist and sexual jokes, remarks, behaviors, and objects that harassers may intend to be nice, endearing, or funny, but that highlight the victim's gender or sexuality, usually in a condescending way. For example, an employer might use trivializing terms of address (*honey* or *sweetheart*) or express great surprise when a female employee aggressively negotiates a business deal. Gender harassment frequently takes the form of an apparent "compliment" (for example, a professor might tell a student he or she has a "great body"). A female employee described working conditions in which "I was called cute names, told I was good looking, and patted on the head." Another woman said that every time she wore a dress to work "there was continual dialogue about the color of my panty hose, the length of my skirt, and so on. Also, they never talked to my face, just to various body parts." As these examples suggest, gender harassment is intrusive and condescending; the harasser disrupts the target's concentration, makes the person's gender or sexuality more prominent than his or her role as a student or employee, and expresses superiority by presuming the right to evaluate the person's appearance or sexual attractiveness. When someone objects, harassers often manipulate the situation to suggest that the person's reaction is inappropriate, as a female university employee describes:

> A male faculty member continually makes flattering remarks or remarks of a "joking" nature but with sexual overtones. If I say I don't like it, he accuses me of being too sensitive or too serious. He also recalls how his female "adult" professional colleagues enjoyed such flirting in his previous job.

Although it is useful to identify sexual harassment in concrete, behavioral terms, focusing on behavior alone yields only partial understanding of sexual harassment. A behavioral focus doesn't help us understand the contexts in which sexual harassment is embedded. These contexts encourage harassment, influence interpretations of it, and suggest ways to respond. We turn to these issues in the remaining pages of this chapter.

Differences in Experiences with Sexual Harassment

Most research examining differences in sexual harassment experiences has focused on gender. Although limited by its neglect of cultural diversity, this research consistently indicates that sexual harassment differs for women and men. First, women report being sexually harassed by men far more often than men report being sexually harassed by women. In 1992, for example, men filed about one-tenth as many sexual harassment complaints with the EEOC as women did (Shoop & Edwards, 1994). Surveys show that about 30 to 50% of female students and as many as 75% of female employees have been sexually harassed by a man, compared to about 15 to 20% of males who report being sexually harassed in work and educational settings (Dziech & Weiner, 1990; LaFontaine & Tredeau, 1986; Leonard et al., 1993; McKinney & Maroules, 1991). Consistent with these findings, males report a greater likelihood than females of committing sexual harassment (Bingham, 1988). Sexual harassment of men may be increasing, however: The number of cases reported by men to the EEOC more than doubled between 1989 and 1992. While females are often the perpetrators in these cases, people of the same sex also sexually harass each other. In particular, gay men and heterosexual males who do not conform to masculine stereotypes are frequently the target of assault and sexual harassment from other men (Shoop & Edwards, 1994).

Second, women tend to find a broader range of behaviors to be sexually harassing and offensive than men (Hemphill & Pfeiffer, 1986). While both males and females generally see *quid pro quo* harassment and coercive physical contact as wrong, men tend to be less likely than women to see more subtle forms of intrusive conduct as sexual harassment (Gill, 1993). Research indicates that some men condone or approve of intrusive behaviors. In a study of male college students, for example, 29% reported being likely or highly likely to subject a female subordinate, who had already refused several date invitations, to behaviors such as persistent requests for a dinner date and comments on her appearance (Bingham & Burleson, 1993).

Third, although sexual harassment has serious effects on all victims, women report more distress and negative consequences than men

(Gutek, 1985). Sexual harassment may have enduring physical, psychological, social, academic, and career-related consequences (Loy & Stewart, 1984; "Our Stories," 1992). One reason for gender differences in the effects of sexual harassment may be that women typically have lower or similar levels of formal authority compared to their harassers, while many men identify their harassers as subordinates (Bingham & Scherer, 1993). Dzeich and Weiner (1990) suggest the term *sexual hassle* instead of *sexual harassment* when men receive sexual attention from subordinates, because these men have more power to control the situation.

Some research also has investigated the ways race, socioeconomic status, sexual orientation, age, and marital status affect experiences with sexual harassment. Minority women experience sexual harassment more frequently than white women (Fain & Anderton, 1987) and are subjected to different kinds of sexual harassment. For example, a white male may sexually harass a women of color in ways that draw on racial stereotypes. Also, working-class women experience sexual harassment differently than upper-middle-class women (Foss & Rogers, 1994). Among women working in predominantly male occupations, for example, blue-collar workers report more sexual harassment and respond to it less assertively than white-collar workers (Ragins & Scandura, 1992). Third, lesbian women may be subjected to more sexual harassment at work and perceive sexual harassment by men as even more offensive than heterosexual women (Schneider, 1982). Like gay males, lesbians are verbally and physically assaulted and harassed because of their sexual orientation (D'Augelli, 1988; Shoop & Edwards, 1994). Finally, younger women report more sexual harassment than older women (Schneider, 1982), and women who are not married report more sexual harassment than married women (Fain & Anderton, 1987).

Complex interactions of sex, race, class, sexual orientation, and age affect the nature of oppression and a harasser's conduct. Kramarae (1992), for example, reports the narrative of a black, working-class medical student who was an aspiring physician. The student was mistaken by an elderly, white, male patient to be a maid, and subsequently was forced to endure "jokes" from the attending physicians who wanted to see her "fluff up some pillows."

Pressure to define *quid pro quo* and especially *hostile environment* sexual harassment for legal purposes continues to fuel heated debate. Complicating these discussions is the diversity of sexual harassment in terms of both its form and how it is experienced. In the next section, we examine how cultural prescriptions for gender encourage various forms of sexual harassment.

CULTURAL PERPETUATION OF SEXUAL HARASSMENT

As we've seen in previous chapters, gender is a socially constructed system of meanings, values, and expectations that divides males and females into two nonoverlapping categories. This dualistic construction of gender disregards variation among individuals of the same sex, ignores facets of identity other than gender, and fails to acknowledge the qualities, activities, and interests that males and females have in common. Because our culture encourages us to embody idealized forms of masculinity and femininity, gender profoundly influences how we understand ourselves and how we behave and interact with others.

Western culture's views of gender encourage sexual harassment in four ways: The culture defines masculinity and femininity as oppositional and antagonistic; it produces disparities in the power, privilege, and value accorded to males and females; it links physical beauty, sexuality, and sexual interaction with power and self-worth; and it prescribes caring for females and career success for males.

Masculine and Feminine as Opposites

One way Western culture encourages sexual harassment is by instilling a "male versus female" mentality in us. Starting at a very early age, children often separate themselves based on biological sex to play, form friendships, and engage in social activities. Children's belief in the appropriateness of sex separation is reinforced when adults assign them to sex-based learning groups or place boys and girls on opposite sides in playground games and classroom competitions (Thorne, 1993). Oppositional views of women and men are further reinforced through portrayals of women and men as possessing opposite characteristics (Jewell, 1983); cultural phrases and jokes that pit males and females against each other ("the war between the sexes"); the policies of schools, clubs, and professional associations that exclude or discourage potential members based on sex; and legal practices that systematically favor one gender over the other (child custody decisions that favor mothers).

Barrie Thorne (1993) describes interactions that strengthen opposition and antagonism between males and females. In her study of gender relations among children, Thorne describes, for example, how a small number of boys regularly "invade" and disrupt the playground activities of girls, prompting the girls to protest verbally, chase the boys away, and complain to playground aides. While the male invaders insist that they were "just playing," the females "may define the situation as a serious violation" (Thorne, 1993, p. 80). Similarly, Lyman (1987) describes a college fraternity ritual in which a group of men perform a "joke" that promotes male bonding. They break into the dining room of a sorority during dinner and force the women to listen to a speech on Freud's theory of penis envy while a man demonstrates masturbation techniques with a rubber penis. In contrast to the men's view of this ritual as humorous, the sorority women respond with fear and anger. Thorne (1993) argues that antagonistic actions parallel the structure of sexual harassment episodes:

> The harasser, nearly always male, often claims that verbal and physical intrusions into the target's personal space are "all in fun," while the target, usually female, sees it as unwanted and even coercive attention. (p. 81)

Antagonistic interactions are encouraged by the cultural opposition of genders. For example, one current source of gender opposition is the feeling of some men that affirmative action policies give females an unfair advantage in gaining employment or entrance into college programs. Sexual harassment can be used by members of one gender, in this case men, to communicate that members of the other gender are not welcome or are not qualified. Opposition between genders is further reinforced when harassers succeed in making the work or learning environment so unbearable that victims decide to quit.

Gender Disparities

Beginning in childhood, most females and males learn that power and privilege are not equally distributed. The cultural construction of gender affords males a dominant and more socially esteemed position while providing females a subordinate and inferior social position. Gendered disparities in power affect sexual harassment, since power is often identified as the most important element of sexual harassment (Fain & Anderton, 1987; Kramarae, 1992). Specifically, unequal social and economic power and privilege both enable and are reinforced by sexual harassment. First, power disparities within society and organizations promote sexual harassment by giving men control of rewards, which enables male harassers to impose their behavior on others. If a man internalizes the cultural message of male superiority over women, he may even feel entitled to engage in sexual harassment, and be proud of himself for his masculinity (Wood, 1994). Women who sexually harass male subordinates may derive similar feelings of entitlement from positions of organizational authority. In turn, sexual harassment reinforces the prerogative of harassers to continue exploiting and intruding on others because it is itself a form of intimidation and control (Farley, 1978; Meissner, 1986).

Power disparities between women and men also give male harassers an advantage in gaining acceptance for their own interpretations of sexual harassment by absolving themselves of responsibility and placing blame on their targets (contending that a woman provoked or misunderstood the harassment). Women may also internalize an androcentric perspective that excuses the harasser's conduct or accepts it as natural or inevitable. Responses that excuse or trivialize sexual harassment reproduce power inequities, perpetuate the view that sexual harassment is normal, and promote the continuation of harassing behavior (Clair, 1994).

Power inequalities also encourage sexual harassment by making some people especially vulnerable. People who are less socially and institutionally powerful experience more difficulty dealing with harassing situations and are more susceptible to negative consequences if they object. Women who have less control over the circumstances of their lives, personal relationships, and working conditions have fewer resources to defend themselves against sexual harassment, and they may begin to view themselves as powerless and behave in powerless ways (Kaland & Geist, 1994). As a result, some women tolerate sexual harassment, quit their jobs, or leave school instead of standing up to a harasser or filing a complaint, even if particular circumstances suggest these latter strategies might be effective. Unfortunately, individuals who give up their jobs or educational goals to escape being harassed participate in a spiral of decreasing social and economic power and greater susceptibility to sexual harassment in the future.

Women as Sex Objects and Men as Sex Machines

Although most scholars argue that sexual harassment is a power issue and not really about sex, the meanings of sexuality and sexual harassment are unquestionably entangled. For example, legal guidelines describe sexual harassment as unwelcome conduct "of a sexual nature" (Shoop & Edwards, 1994), and the "sexual drive" of humans is often cited as a reason why sexual harassment occurs (Witteman, 1993, p. 37). It appears that prevailing cultural prescriptions for masculine and feminine sexuality encourage sexual harassment and make it seem natural.

In a number of ways, cultural prescriptions for sexuality encourage men to sexually harass women. Central in this process are sexual scripts that hold men responsible for initiating, engineering, and conducting sexual experiences with women, while women are assigned a gatekeeping responsibility, which requires setting limits on sexual activity (Alperstein, 1986; Struckman-Johnson & Struckman-Johnson, 1991). Prescriptions for masculine sexuality also link manliness to the quantity of sexual encounters a man achieves, and instruct men and women to view the masculine sex drive as naturally powerful and difficult to control. The initiator–gatekeeper script thus encourages males to view women as sex objects, and to see sexual interactions as a game or conquest in which it's fair to persuade or even coerce in order to "score" as much sex as possible. Consistent with this portrayal of masculine sexuality, males place less value than females on sexual consent (Margolin, Miller, & Moran, 1989) and perceive sexual rejection as less constraining and uncomfortable than females (Metts, Cupach, & Imahori, 1992). The initiator–gatekeeper script encourages men to persist in sexual activity even when it is unwanted by women, and to disregard or distort a woman's resistance and objections. This script creates a context in which sexual harassment seems to be a natural and acceptable form of male–female interaction.

Sexual harassment is further encouraged by cultural expectations for women to be sexually alluring and responsive. First, females learn that the ability to attract men physically and sexually is in large part what makes women valuable. Sexual objectification may be framed as a compliment because it validates a woman as desirable to men. Thus, sexual scripts dictate that women should feel flattered by sexual attention from men, even if the attention is not really wanted, because it confirms their feminine identity and self-worth. At the same time, the culture disparages women who respond negatively to sexual advances from men. For example, although both males and females generally endorse a woman's right to say "no" to unwanted kissing on a date, they only moderately approve of the woman who refuses (Margolin et al., 1989). Women who are viewed as sexually unresponsive may be labeled frigid, prudish, or man-haters. Cultural expectations that women should desire and enjoy men's sexual advances encourage women to tolerate coercive sexual behavior. In turn, victims' toleration helps to sustain sexual harassment by allowing the harasser to continue harassing.

The contradiction between cultural prescriptions for women to be both gatekeepers of sexual activity and sex objects also encourages sexual harassment. Sanford and Donovan (1984) explain the inconsistent expectations for feminine sexuality as the madonna/whore complex—the image of women as either madonnas untainted by sexual activity or promiscuous and immoral whores. The common belief that women pretend to be virtuous madonnas by giving token resistance to sex (Muehlenhard & Hollabaugh, 1988) gives men an incentive to doubt the seriousness of women's objections to sexual advances. This belief and incentive are strengthened if women object to sexual harassment ambiguously.

Certain cultural prescriptions for feminine sexuality also encourage women to sexually harass men. First, traditional femininity requires women to use their sexual attractiveness to incite a man to initiate sexual activity. As noted earlier, the culture defines the masculine sex drive as potentially too powerful for men to control. This gives women an incentive to persist in trying to excite a man until he can no longer control his response. Second, more recent portrayals of feminine sexuality propose that women's sexuality has been repressed by outmoded cultural scripts, and that progressive-thinking females should be sexually adventuresome (Sanford & Donovan, 1984). In this context, women may sexually harass men in order to obtain sexual pleasures that they believe men have denied women in the past. Further, women in powerful positions may use sexual harassment as a way to compensate for historical oppression of women by men. As Gochros and Ricketts (1986) indicate, treating men as sex objects may be a way for women to retaliate against men by showing them how it feels to be objectified.

Finally, sexual scripts for masculinity encourage men to respond with confusion to sexual harassment, especially if the harasser is a physically attractive woman. Many authors claim that middle- and working-class, heterosexual, American culture expects men to be ready and eager to engage in sexual activity with women at all times (Alperstein, 1986; Tiefer, 1987). Highlighting a man's sexuality may actually enhance his image of competence and potency on the job. Studies have found that individuals, and males in particular, are more accepting of unwanted sexual activity when it is initiated by a female toward a male than vice versa (Margolin, et al., 1989; Struckman-Johnson & Struckman-Johnson, 1991). Thus, in order to reject sexual harassment, a man must violate cultural expectations for masculinity. This sustains sexual harassment of men by making it difficult for males to admit or respond negatively when they are harassed.

In sum, sexual expectations and scripts for masculine and feminine sexuality are perpetuated within the culture and internalized by individuals. These expectations and scripts normalize sexual harassment and provide individuals with incentive to behave in ways that sustain it in work and educational contexts.

Feminine Sensitivity and Masculine Success

Part of the feminine role as defined by culture is the expectation that women should be sensitive and caring. Women are expected to care for and about others and to be emotionally sensitive, supportive, deferential, and nice. When this expectation for femininity interacts with the cultural prescription that men should be successful in their careers, women may be reluctant to challenge men who sexually harass them. A woman who objects to sexual harassment violates cultural expectations for feminine sensitivity by potentially harming the harasser's feelings or bruising his ego. Further, a woman who brings sexual harassment to the attention of legal or organizational authorities is likely to damage the harasser's reputation and career. This potential to harm a man's career sets the woman up as the villain responsible for his failure to fulfill the requirements of his masculine role. Not surprisingly, studies indicate that the most frequent ways women respond to sexual harassment include trying to avoid or ignore it (Gruber, 1989). In turn, failure to object to or report sexual harassment sustains the problem by allowing it to continue unimpeded.

In sum, cultural prescriptions for gender encourage sexual harassment even while laws and policies seek to prevent it. The prevailing cultural view of masculine and feminine as opposite identities encourages separation and antagonism between the sexes. In addition, Western culture confers greater power, privilege, and value on males than females, creating disparities that enable sexual harassment of women by men. Cultural scripts for masculine and feminine sexuality also promote sexual harassment by tying it to self-worth and by making it appear to fall within the realm of natural heterosexual interaction. Finally, cultural expectations for women to be sensitive and caring and for men to be successful in their careers enable sexual harassment by discouraging women from challenging or reporting male harassers.

RESPONDING TO SEXUAL HARASSMENT

Cultural prescriptions for masculinity and femininity exert a powerful influence on us, but they don't absolutely determine how we behave. It is possible to respond to sexual harassment in ways that resist and challenge the cultural prescriptions. The most promising solutions are those that challenge the structures, practices, meanings, and expectations that sustain sexual harassment. Formal complaints, mediation, educational programs, letters to harassers, and face-to-face communication are responses we will discuss.

Formal remedies such as filing a legal complaint with the EEOC or using the policy and grievance procedures of one's organization or school forcefully assert that sexual harassment is not acceptable. Students and employees can substantiate a formal complaint by collecting evidence such as harassing letters or pictures, and by keeping a detailed journal in which they record what happened, who was involved, when and where it happened, and with what effects (Shoop & Edwards, 1994). Formal responses are least preferred by victims of sexual harassment because they can be costly in terms of time, money, psychological well-being, personal relationships, and educational or career path. Formal complaints are especially valuable, however, because they force institutions to address sexual harassment in ways that may reduce future problems.

Efforts to encourage victims to file sexual harassment complaints sometimes stir concerns about false accusations (Carroll & Ellis, 1989). If a false accusation is made public and believed, even if it is not substantiated, the accused person's reputation and career may never be fully restored. Like fabricated rape charges, false sexual harassment accusations waste time and resources of the judicial system, can punish innocent people, undermine the credibility of individuals who actually have been sexually harassed, and provide ammunition for skeptics who doubt the legitimacy of all sexual harassment complaints. Because of this, it is absolutely essential that false accusations be discouraged and stopped whenever they occur.

Research indicates, however, that false accusations are extremely rare (Sandler, 1990). A survey of more than 300 institutions revealed that formal complaints of sexual harassment are intentionally fabricated less than 1% of the time (Robertson, Dyer, & D'Ann, 1988). Research also indicates that only a small minority of people who actually experience sexual harassment ever make their cases known to authorities (Fitzgerald et al., 1988). In light of these statistics, we should be less concerned with the potential for false accusations than with encouraging and enabling more victims to come forward.

Some universities and organizations offer mediation as an informal alternative to filing a formal charge of sexual harassment (Gadlin, 1991). A mediator is someone who facilitates communication between the grievant and the accused in sexual harassment cases to help them work out a successful resolution. Mediation can be a particulary useful way of handling sexual harassment disputes because it encourages empathic listening and nondefensive communication. To the extent that mediation creates a context in which each party comes to understand the other's perspective, it can be a means of educating harassers about the effects of their behavior (Gadlin, 1991).

Educational programs also may successfully challenge cultural meanings, values, and expectations that sustain sexual harassment. Students and employees can push for such programs where they don't exist and encourage full participation where they do. These programs should raise awareness of conventional meanings of gender and sexual scripts that foster sexual harassment and teach alternative meanings and expectations that promote other kinds of interaction (Wood, 1994).

A letter to the harasser is also a useful response. Rowe (1981) recommends a letter that has three parts. It should provide a factual account of what happened, describe the writer's feelings about the event and the damage he or she thinks has been done, and explain what the writer wants to happen next. The writer should keep a copy of the letter as evidence that objections to the harassment were clearly conveyed and deliver the original personally or by registered mail (Shoop & Edwards, 1994). Rowe (1981, p. 19) reports that the harasser usually "accepts the letter, says nothing, and reforms his or her behavior."

Finally, talking with a harasser can be a useful response to sexual harassment in some situations. Employees who talk to their harasser about the incident may improve their chances of resolving the situation in a satisfactory way (Bingham & Scherer, 1993). However, interpersonal responses are not recommended in all sexual harassment situations. Individuals may be hesitant to confront a harasser directly, for example, when they recognize the potential for bad feelings or retaliation. For example, a student nearing graduation may choose not to talk to a harassing professor until semester grades have been turned in. Interpersonal responses may have most potential for success when the harasser does not realize his or her conduct is being experienced as coercive, intimidating, and offensive.

SUMMARY

Behaviors that now are defined as illegal once were tolerated by employees and students who had no accepted term for naming them and no legal basis for objecting. The meaning of sexual harassment remains in process today as it is debated in the courts, the media, academic literature, organizational life, and everyday interactions. Our discussion suggests that our culture perpetuates sexual harassment in a number of ways in spite of laws and policies designed to prevent it. Sexual harassment is encouraged by prevailing beliefs and expectations regarding gender and sexuality, and by the inequitable positions of harassers and targets in a power-stratified society. Yet, it is possible to challenge the cultural meanings and conditions that foster sexual harassment. The most effective responses are those that reflect and support a view of sexual harassment as unacceptable, unnatural, and unjust in the workplace and on campus.

QUESTIONS FOR REFLECTION AND DISCUSSION

1. Familiarize yourself with the sexual harassment policy of your school or workplace. How is sexual harassment defined? What kinds of behaviors are likely to qualify as sexual harassment under this policy? What options are suggested for reporting and stopping sexual harassment?

2. Interview a person on your campus or in your workplace who deals with sexual harassment complaints. Ask him or her to explain how sexual harassment cases are reported, investigated, and resolved at your institution. How many cases of sexual harassment have been reported in the past 5 years? How were these cases handled? What was the outcome for the victims and the accused?

3. Conduct a sexual harassment survey on your campus or in your workplace. How pervasive is sexual harassment among students and employees? What forms of sexual harassment have students and employees experienced? What are the effects of sexual harassment on victims? How do victims usually respond?

4. Consider the ways sexual harassment is portrayed in the media. Watch evening television programs or movies and notice how characters of each sex commit and react to unwanted sexual attention in academic or professional contexts. What are the consequences for the characters? Is sexual harassment portrayed as a serious problem? Is it portrayed as a trivial or humorous issue?

REFERENCES

Alperstein, L. P. (1986). Men. In H. L. Gochros, J. S. Bochros, & J. Fisher (Eds.), *Helping the sexually oppressed* (pp. 66–81). Englewood Cliffs, NJ: Prentice-Hall.

Bingham, S. G. (1988). *Interpersonal responses to sexual harassment*. Unpublished doctoral dissertation, Purdue University, West Lafayette, IN.

Bingham, S. G., & Burleson, B. R. (1993, November). *The development of the sexual harassment proclivity scale: Construct validation and relationship to communication competence*. Paper presented at the conference of the Speech Communication Association, Miami, FL.

Bingham, S. G., & Scherer, L. L. (1993). Factors associated with responses to sexual harassment and satisfaction with outcome. *Sex Roles, 29*, 239–269.

Carroll, L., & Ellis, K. L. (1989). Faculty attitudes toward sexual harassment: Survey results, survey process. *Initiatives, 52*, 35–41.

Clair, R. P. (1994). Hegemony and harassment: A discursive practice. In S. G. Bingham (Ed.), *Conceptualizing sexual harassment as discursive practice* (pp. 59–70). Westport, CT: Praeger.

D'Augelli, A. R. (1988). Sexual harassment and affectional status: The hidden discrimination. *The Community Psychologist, 21*, 11–12.

Dziech, B. W., & Weiner, L. (1990). *The lecherous professor* (2nd ed.). Urbana: University of Illinois Press.

Fain, T. C., & Anderton, D. L. (1987). Sexual harassment: Organizational context and diffuse status. *Sex Roles, 5/6*, 291–311.

Farley, L. (1978). *Sexual shakedown: The sexual harassment of women on the job*. New York: McGraw-Hill.

Fitzgerald, L. F., Shullman, S. L., Bailey, N., Richards, M., Swecker, J., Gold, A., Ormerod, A. J., & Weitzman, L. (1988). The incidence and dimensions of sexual harassment in academia and the workplace. *Journal of Vocational Behavior, 32*, 152–175.

Fitzgerald, L. F., & Hesson-McInnis, M. (1989). The dimensions of sexual harassment: A structural analysis. *Journal of Vocational Behavior, 35*, 309–326.

Forell, C. (1993, March). Sexual and racial harassment: Whose perspective should control? *Trial*, pp. 70–76.

Foss, K. A., & Rogers, R. A. (1994). Particularities and possibilities: Reconceptualizing knowledge and power in sexual harassment research. In S. G. Bingham (Ed.), *Conceptualizing sexual harassment as discursive practice* (pp. 159–172). Westport, CT: Praeger.

Gadlin, H. (1991). Careful maneuvers: Mediating sexual harassment. *Negotiation Journal, 7*, 139–153.

Gill, M. J. (1993). Academic sexual harassment: Perceptions of behaviors. In G. L. Kreps (Ed.), *Sexual harassment: Communication implications* (pp. 149–169). Creskill, NJ: Hampton Press.

Gochros, J. S., & Ricketts, W. (1986). Women. In H. L. Gochros, J. S. Gochros, & J. Fisher (Eds.), *Helping the sexually oppressed* (pp. 51–65). Englewood Cliffs, NJ: Prentice-Hall.

Gruber, J. E. (1989). How women handle sexual harassment: A literature review. *Sociology and Social Research, 74*, 3–7.

Gruber, J. E. (1992). A typology of personal and environmental sexual harassment: Research and policy implications for the 1990's. *Sex Roles, 26*, 447–464.

Gutek, B. A. (1985). *Sex and the workplace*. San Francisco: Jossey-Bass.

Hemphill, M. R., & Pfeiffer, A. L. (1986). Sexual spillover in the workplace: Testing the appropriateness of male–female interaction. *Women's Studies in Communication, 9,* 52–66.

Jewell, K. S. (1983). Black male/female conflict: Internalization of negative definitions transmitted through imagery. *Western Journal of Black Studies, 7,* 43–48.

Kaland, D. M., & Geist, P. (1994). Secrets of the corporation: A model of ideological positioning of sexual harassment victims. In S. G. Bingham (Ed.), *Conceptualizing sexual harassment as discursive practice* (pp. 139–155). Westport, CT: Praeger.

Kramarae, C. (1992). Harassment and everyday life. In L. F. Rakow (Ed.), *Women making meaning: New feminist directions in communication* (pp. 100–120). New York: Routledge & Kegan Paul.

LaFontaine, E., & Tredeau, L. (1986). The frequency, sources, and correlates of sexual harassment among women in traditional male occupations. *Sex Roles, 15,* 433–442.

Leonard, R., Ling, L. C., Hankins, G. A., Maidon, C. H., Potorti, P. F., & Rogers, J. M. (1993). Sexual harassment at North Carolina State University. In G. L. Kreps (Ed.), *Sexual harassment: Communication implications* (pp. 170–194). Creskill, NJ: Hampton Press.

Loy, P. H., & Stewart, L. P. (1984). The extent and effects of sexual harassment of working women. *Sociological Focus, 17,* 31–43.

Lyman, P. (1987). The fraternal bond as a joking relationship: A case of the role of sexist jokes in male group bonding. In M. S. Kimmel (Ed.), *Changing men: New directions in research on men and masculinity.* Newbury Park, CA: Sage.

Margolin, L., Miller, M., & Moran, P. B. (1989). When a kiss is not just a kiss: Relating violations of consent in kissing to rape myth acceptance. *Sex Roles, 20,* 231–243.

McKinney, K., & Maroules, N. (1991). Sexual harassment. In E. Grauerholz & M. Koralewski (Eds.), *Sexual coercion: A sourcebook on its nature, causes and prevention* (pp. 29–44). Lexington, MA: Lexington Books.

Meissner, M. (1986). The reproduction of women's domination in organizational communication. In L. Thayer (Ed.), *Organization—communication: Emerging perspectives I* (pp. 51–70). Norwood, NJ: Ablex.

Metts, S., Cupach, W. R., & Imahori, T. T. (1992). Perceptions of sexual compliance-resisting messages in three types of cross-sex relationships. *Western Journal of Communication, 56,* 1–17.

Muehlenhard, C. L., & Hollabaugh, L. C. (1988). Do women sometimes say no when they mean yes? The prevalence and correlates of women's token resistance to sex. *Journal of Personality and Social Psychology, 54,* 872–879.

"Our stories": Communication professionals' narratives of sexual harassment. (1992). *Journal of Applied Communication Research, 20,* 363–391.

Paetzold, R., & O'Leary-Kelly, A. (1993). The legal context of sexual harassment. In G. L. Kreps (Ed.), *Sexual harassment: Communication implications* (pp. 63–77). Creskill, NJ: Hampton Press.

Ragins, B. R., & Scandura, T. A. (1992). *Antecedents and work-related correlates of sexual harassment: An empirical investigation of competing hypotheses.* Unpublished manuscript.

Riophe, K. (1993). Reckless eyeballing: Sexual harassment on campus. In K. Roiphe (Ed.), *The morning after: Sex, fear, and feminism on campus* (pp. 85–112). Boston: Little, Brown.

Robertson, C., Dyer, C. E., & D'Ann, C. (1988). Campus harassment: Sexual harassment policies and procedures at institutions of higher learning. *Signs: Journal of Women in Culture and Society, 46,* 792–812.

Rowe, M. P. (1981). Dealing with sexual harassment. *Harvard Business Review, 59,* 42–44/46.

Sandler, B. R. (1990). Sexual harassment: A new issue for institutions. *Initiatives, 52,* 5–10.

Sanford, L. T., & Donovan, M. E. (1984). *Women and self-esteem.* New York: Penguin.

Schneider, B. E. (1982). Consciousness about sexual harassment among heterosexual and lesbian women workers. *Journal of Social Issues, 4,* 75–98.

Shoop, R. J., & Edwards, D. L. (1994). *How to stop sexual harassment in our schools.* Boston: Allyn & Bacon.

Struckman-Johnson, D., & Struckman-Johnson, C. (1991). Men and women's acceptance of coercive sexual strategies varied by initiator gender and couple intimacy. *Sex Roles, 25,* 661–675.

Thorne, B. (1993). *Gender play: Girls and boys in school.* New Brunswick, NJ: Rutgers University Press.

Tiefer, L. (1987). In pursuit of the perfect penis. The medicalization of male sexuality. In Michael S. Kimmel (Ed.), *Changing men: New directions in research on men and masculinity* (pp. 165–184). Newbury Park: Sage.

Tuana, N. (1985). Sexual harassment in academe. Issues of power and coercion. *College Teaching, 33,* 53–64.

Wise, S., & Stanley, L. (1987). *Georgie Porgie: Sexual harassment in everyday life.* New York: Pandora.

Witteman, H. (1993). The interface between sexual harassment and organizational romance. In G. L. Kreps (Ed.), *Sexual harassment: Communication implications* (pp. 27–62). Creskill, NJ: Hampton Press.

Woman awarded $7.1 million in harassment case. (1994, September 2). *Omaha World-Herald,* p. 26.

Wood, J. T. (1993). Naming and interpreting sexual harassment: A conceptual framework for scholarship. In G. L. Kreps (Ed.), *Sexual harassment: Communication implications* (pp. 9–26). Creskill, NJ: Hampton Press.

Wood, J. T. (1994). Saying it makes it so: The discursive construction of sexual harassment. In S. G. Bingham (Ed.), *Conceptualizing sexual harassment as discursive practice* (pp. 17–30). Westport, CT: Praeger.

GENDERED ISSUES IN THE WORKPLACE

ELIZABETH J. NATALLE

In many ways, this chapter is a good endnote to a book on gendered relationships because it is about your future and the expectations many of you may have about your career. Although you, like many college students, may have work experience, your job has probably not been your priority in the past. You are about to enter a long period in your life in which your career and work environment will be prominent. What you expect and what you find in the real world may not match. The goal of this chapter is to help you to meet the demands of the workplace by demonstrating how gendered issues in the workplace are an integral part of daily professional life. With some advance knowledge of what to expect, perhaps you'll be able to anticipate situations and issues that will require mature and informed communication choices. For those of you who have already spent substantial time in a job or profession, this chapter may explain some of the gendered dynamics that you have encountered.

Communication in the workplace, like any type of communication, takes place within a context. But unlike other relationships in context, such as marriage, romance, or friendship, workplace relationships are embedded in complex situational constraints that often leave communicators with less control over relationships than they desire. For example, your job description, location in the organizational hierarchy, longevity, political influence, and likelihood for promotion (Daniels & Spiker, 1991) all influence the interpersonal choices that you make in communicating on the job. In addition to influences rooted in the workplace is an individual's *standpoint.* Wood (1995) describes standpoint as the way in which "the social, material, and symbolic circumstances of a social group shape how members think and perceive" (p. 74). Thus, people bring different perceptions and values to the workplace based on their standpoints. It is easy to see that workplace relationships are framed by unique, and often difficult, constraints that affect the kind of relationships we can form. Further, most of the time, we don't choose the people we work with as we choose our friends and romantic partners, yet all employees must learn to relate in a modern workplace that demands excellence in an increasingly competitive environment.

A central theme in this chapter is the difference between expectations and reality. The first part of the chapter discusses college students' *expectations* for the workplace from a gendered perspective. What do young men and women expect in a career and employment opportunities? The remainder of the chapter focuses on the *realities* of the workplace with particular attention to leadership styles, the structure of organizations, communication climate, and gendered views of organizational cultures.

EXPECTATIONS FOR CAREER AND THE WORKPLACE

Unless you are an exceptional undergraduate, your biggest concern right now is probably finding a job in your field after graduation. The majority of students I teach are also concerned about whether the first job will pay enough to cover living expenses without relying on family. While many students expect a lower wage than they would like, the reality is that first jobs often pay much less than even the lowest expectations. Despite discouraging employment trends of the past 2 years for new college graduates (Fowler, 1991; Meikle, 1993), students may expect to fare better than others if they develop excellent writing, listening, and oral communication skills ("Workers Need," 1992).

Affirmative action programs have set up interesting, and generally false, expectations among college students. Distorted news coverage of affirmative action as a "quota system" has left heretofore hopeful white males expecting to be victims of reverse discrimination in hiring and promotion (Gomez, 1994). Contrary to media myths, however, white men experienced a greater increase in professional employment between 1960 and 1980 than white women, black men, or black women (Sokoloff, 1992). Further, this same time period set the stage for white men to begin desegregating female-dominated professions such as nursing, social work, and elementary school teaching. Sokoloff (1992) concludes that even "during this period [1960 to 1980] of economic growth and expanding opportunities for disadvantaged groups, white men continued to be the overwhelming majority in the most desirable and visible of the professions" (p. 62). The professions referred to by Sokoloff include medicine, law, and engineering. What this means is that in spite of the predictions of documents such as *Workforce 2000* (Johnston & Packer, 1988), which reports that the American workplace will have more women and people of color than white males by the year 2000, statistically white men still have a better chance than women or minorities of gaining and maintaining high employment rates in the highest paid professional occupations.

A study by Fine, Johnson, and Foss (1991) examined students' career aspirations as part of a larger investigation of perceptions of gender in managerial communication. The authors were interested in the increasing complacency of younger women and men regarding sexual equality in the workplace. Responses to a survey from predominantly Caucasian preprofessional students revealed significant differences between women's and men's expectations for job positions and salary. Women expected to be in technical positions in their chosen field, while men saw themselves in management within the first 5 years of employment. Men expected to earn over $30,000 after 10 years, with 25% of the men expecting salaries of $60,000, and they expected to be self-employed. Compare that to female expectations after 10 years of employment: Women saw themselves in management positions, but expected salaries to be around $30,000 with only 10% of the women expecting to earn $60,000. Fine et al. (1991) concluded that women's lower expectations may be the result of reality, lack of role models, acculturation, and internalized negative sex-role stereotypes about themselves. To the extent that expectations affect motivation and negotiation for raises and advancement, the study raises the possibility that women's comparatively low expectations could be self-fulfilling prophecies.

Powell (1993) furthers the argument about acculturation and stereotyping with his claim that occupational *aspirations* (dreaming what to be when one grows up) are influenced by sex-role stereotypes that may be formed in the first 6 years of life. Even in the 1990s, children see work as sex-typed, and little girls aspire more to female jobs than boys aspire to male jobs. Even worse, occupational *expectations* (beliefs about the work one will do) show more sex-typed differences than aspirations. High school girls, more than boys, *expect* to work in female-dominated professions, such as teaching and nursing (Marini & Brinton, 1984). Aspirations and expectations are more consistent for boys growing up than for girls.

The reality of securing employment is threefold: First, professional occupations still tend to be sex-segregated, with men earning higher salaries than women and men having easier access to traditionally female jobs (such as nursing, teaching, librarianship, and social work) than women have to traditionally male jobs (such as medicine, computer science, law, architecture, and the ministry) (England & McCreary, 1987; "Female Workers," 1994; Sokoloff, 1992). Second, in spite of the dramatic increase in the presence of women in the workplace, few women have infiltrated top management and high-salaried positions (Natalle, Papa, & Graham, 1994; Stewart & Clarke-Kudless, 1993). Third, people of color, particularly African American women and men, have gained only modestly in professional employment opportunities (Bell, Denton, & Nkomo, 1993; Sokoloff, 1992).

It might be useful to pause for a moment and reflect on your own expectations. Have you considered how gender may influence your aspirations-turned-expectations for employment and career development? Think back to Chapter 1, where the argument was made that gender is a social construction. What has our culture helped you to construct in regard to expectations for a professional identity? What communication strategies will you use to gain employment and to advance, especially if socially accepted patterns of hiring do not favor your race or sex? How can you, as a man or woman, use communication to forge and develop an effective professional identity? As you think about answers to these important questions, let's now consider how the realities of the workplace compare to expectations. We will examine how gender influences leadership styles, organizational structure, communication climate, and organizational culture.

GENDERED LEADERSHIP STYLES

No other area in the research literature on gender and organizational communication has received as much attention as leadership. With the entrance of women into management, which began to be significant in numbers in the mid-1970s, leadership became a popular topic. Over the past 30 years, three basic questions about gendered leadership have emerged: (1) Can women perform effectively in leadership roles?

(2) Are there differences in how women and men lead? (3) Are men or women better leaders?

Can Women Lead?

When women first entered management, scholars realized that women might not communicate leadership in the same manner as their male counterparts. Schein's (1973, 1975) groundbreaking research found that middle-line managers, both male and female, paired management traits with masculine traits (for example, independent, assertive, acts like a leader) significantly more than with feminine traits (for example, understanding, cheerful, soft-spoken). The research results suggested that men were more likely to be selected for management positions because they held the desired characteristics of managers. This led to the question, Are women capable of exercising effective leadership? Deaux (1979) followed up Schein's research to see if the stereotyped differences discovered by Schein could be substantiated. Indeed, Deaux reported the different and inferior judgment of women's managerial ability by discovering that male managers rated themselves more positively than female managers in performance, ability, intelligence, and job difficulty. These findings, however, told us little about *actual* leadership ability, including how others (such as subordinates, peers, and superiors) rated women's and men's leadership behaviors. In actual fact, studies since the 1970s have documented positive results of women's leadership ability. For example, Baird and Bradley (1979) found that women foster high morale among subordinates, and Camden and Witt (1983) found a high correlation between female managers' communication and worker productivity. More recently, Wood (1994) reviewed a series of positive influences resulting from feminine leadership, including more concern for others, compassion, and a strong desire to help others.

Although Staley (1988) acknowledged mixed results in the research concerning differences in male and female managers' communication, she concluded that women managers sometimes do have doubts about having and exercising power because of cultural attitudes that keep society from accepting women in the role of leader. When differences in communication style were confirmed, Staley (1988) found that the *perception* of difference contributed to the frequent judgments that women managers were ineffective. Such findings remind us that perceptions and reality may not agree, but perceptions can easily dominate and distort our judgment and behavior. In the extreme, perceptions can lead to ingrained biases, such as the norm discovered by Larwood, Szwajkowski, and Rose (1988), which approved managers' discrimination against both women and African Americans when making decisions.

For many years, people have believed the stereotypes that masculine communication is the model for leadership and that men make better managers, but Wood (1994) and Powell (1993) show that such beliefs are mistaken, and there is no substantial evidence to support males' superiority as leaders. There is some evidence to show that men cling to the "masculine is superior" belief more than women. Brenner, Tomkiewicz, and Schein (1989) replicated Schein's (1973, 1975) research described above. The results indicated that male managers still rated masculine and management traits together, while female managers showed no significant differences in their pairings of masculine, feminine, and management traits. The researchers concluded that women managers do not practice sex-typing in their judgment and that "unlike her male counterpart, today's female manager would be expected to treat men and women equally in selection, promotion, and placement decisions" (Brenner et al., 1989, p. 668). Powell and Butterfield (1989) tested the notion that, with the presence of women in management, a good manager would be seen as *androgynous* (showing both masculine and feminine behaviors) rather than masculine. Their hypothesis was rejected, and Powell and Butterfield concluded that many people still cling to the old stereotypes, even though women are less likely than men to describe good managers as masculine.

Masculine and Feminine Leadership Models

Some popular writers (Helgesen, 1990; Loden, 1985) have distinguished male and female models of leadership and then argued that feminine models are better. Although it is tempting to make comparative value judgments, doing so limits our understanding of alternatives and their distinct advantages. It is more helpful to recognize that both masculine and feminine styles of leadership can be effective in particular organizational situations. Thus, the two styles are different, yet equally valid.

Loden's (1985) models of masculine and feminine leadership include five dimensions: operating style, organizational structure, basic objective, problem-solving style, and key characteristics. The masculine model is based on a competitive style and organizes people hierarchically. The basic objective is to win, and problems are solved rationally. Key characteristics of the masculine style include high control, strategic moves, low emotional involvement, and an analytical approach to business. In the feminine model, the bottom line is cooperation, and people are organized in teams. The basic objective is quality output, and problems are solved with a combination of intuitive and rational approaches. Key characteristics of the feminine style include shared control, empathy for employees, collaborative interaction, and an emphasis on high performance standards.

Using a case-study approach, Helgesen (1990) developed a model of female leadership to compare to Mintzberg's classic work, *The Nature of Managerial Work* (1973), which describes a male model of leadership. Of the eight characteristics that describe leadership, only one—maintains outside networks—is comparable in both models. The styles are dramatically different. In general, men prefer an unrelenting pace with no breaks, whereas women work at a steady pace with small, scheduled breaks. Men tend to view interruptions as a source of discontinuity and fragmentation, while women generally don't see unplanned conversations as interruptions. Men's outside activities often are work related and part of the male view of identifying self through the job. Women are more likely to see their identity as multifaceted and engage in activities away from work that may or may not be related to the job. Men typically prefer phone calls and face-to-face encounters, but avoid mail. Even though women also prefer face-to-face or telephone interaction, they schedule time to look at mail. Men typically do not take time to reflect and plan long term, but women focus on the ecology of leadership. Finally, men seem reluctant to share information with others because they believe that might diminish their personal power. Women, on the other hand, tend to schedule time to share information with employees and try to empower others.

Rather than pitting masculine and feminine models against each other, perhaps a better approach to gaining acceptance of male and female models of leadership is represented by Rosener's (1990) theorizing. Rosener describes male leadership as "transactional," where the job is viewed as a series of transactions with subordinates performing in a command-and-control style. Female leadership is "interactive" because the style involves more participation and information sharing. In contrast to Loden (1985) and Helgesen (1990), Rosener clearly delineates the advantages and disadvantages of each style and concludes that the best style depends on the context. In addition, Rosener cautions organizations to expand their ideas of what effective leadership means in order to give women more opportunity to develop careers in management.

Is One Gender Better at Leading?

Social scientists have not been able to verify that men or women are superior leaders or that one style is more advantageous in all situations. Eagly and Johnson (1990) conducted a meta-analysis of 162 studies in relation to four leadership styles and gender. They concluded that our views of how women and men lead need revision. In actual organizational settings, women were more democratic, but not more interpersonal, than men. Men were found to be more autocratic, but not more task oriented, than women.

Wilkins and Andersen (1991) conducted a meta-analysis of 25 studies in regard to sex differences and managers' communication behavior along with an investigation of several moderating variables such as type of participants, measurement tools, sex of the experimenter, and date of the research. The results consistently showed no real differences between men and women in their managerial communication. Wilkins and Andersen suggest that a more productive way to understand management behavior is to examine the interaction between traits of people and situational variables.

Overall, Powell (1993) reports no sex differences in leadership effectiveness or management traits; however, Powell cautions us about believing that male and female managers are interchangeable. Many situational variables may influence the success of any given manager, as Wilkins and Andersen (1991) suggested earlier. Powell argues that today's corporation has room for varied styles and traits in leadership. The burden is on the company to create a communication climate that allows a variety of leaders and leadership styles to thrive. Such findings as those by Powell (1993), Eagly and Johnson (1990), and Wilkins and Andersen (1991) challenge both the stereotypes and the assumptions many people hold about leaders and leadership.

ORGANIZATIONAL STRUCTURE AND COMMUNICATION CLIMATE

Organizations must have a structure if people, products, and services are to be coordinated in order to reach goals. Without *organizational structure,* patients could not recover from surgery, clients could not be represented in court, and motorists could not drive safely on the highways. No matter what the organization is—a hospital, a law firm, a social service agency, a state department of transportation—there is a need to structure the way employees interact with one another to perform their jobs and to create meaningful relationships. Furthermore, structure influences the communication climate in an organization. Just like temperature, the communication climate ranges from hot to cold and is produced partly by the flow of communication within the accepted structure of the organization. For example, if you are interviewing with a law firm where the prospective employer states that all attorneys are created equal, then you would expect a climate conducive to open communication for men and women alike. Yet, in actuality, structure and climate become gendered issues in the workplace. In this section of the chapter, we discuss how organizations create structures and climates parallel to the broad culture's socially constructed ideas of gender and race.

Organizational Structure

There are many ways to structure or organize people. Kreps (1995) outlines six perspectives on organizational structure: (1) classical theory, where organizations are viewed as highly structured and controlled mechanisms for creating efficient service and effective products; (2) human relations theory, which is just the opposite of classical theory because here the emphasis is on motivating employees to reach their highest potential; (3) social-systems theory, which views organizations as highly complex entities whose interdependent parts systematically influence growth and change; (4) Weick's (1979) model of organizing, which views communication as the core activity because organizations are social systems that need to reduce ambiguity and uncertainty; (5) organizational-culture theory, where organizations are viewed as symbolic cultures in which employees use communication to make sense of their roles and behavior; and (6) critical theory, which examines the relationship of political ideology to the organization's distribution of resources and opportunities for employee empowerment.

How does gender relate to organizational structure? Some communication scholars claim that "organizations are masculine creations" (Conrad, 1990, p. 327) that reflect masculine styles of behaving and communicating. Consider the classical approach defined above. The classically structured organization is the typical top-down American company. The organizational chart shows a highly centralized, vertical chain of command in which communication flows downward and is checked at several levels of management before moving outward to subordinates. The military, federal and state government agencies, and many private industries are structured on a classical model. Think back to the masculine models described by Loden (1985) and Rosener

(1990). Hierarchy and command-and-control characterize both mascu-line leadership style and classical organizational structure.

Although the human relations model is over 60 years old, we know it today as Theory Z (Ouchi, 1981) or as Japanese-style structure (Ju, 1994) where communication flows upward as well as downward and control is decentralized. Teamwork and participative decision making are hallmarks of a human relations approach to organizing. Inter-estingly, feminine models of leadership (Helgesen, 1990; Loden, 1985; Rosener, 1990) parallel almost· exactly the human relations model. Shared control, teamwork, collaborative interaction, and information sharing are commonalities of the two models.

Even though studies support the value of the human relations (fem-inine) model, the reality is that the majority of work environments in the United States are bureaucracies organized according to the classical (masculine) model. This has set up interesting dilemmas as more women enter management and as Japanese techniques are demon-strated to be effective. Conrad (1990) poses the problem faced by mod-ern corporations:

> It is not accidental, I think, that the history of organizational communica-tion theory and organizational theory has largely been a search for systems and procedures for incorporating values such as respect, fairness, equity, supportiveness, and cooperation into the operation of complex organiza-tions. It also is not accidental that members of organizations historically have accepted the techniques of these alternative ways of organizing but rejected the underlying values. (p. 327)

Conrad's point is very important. If the dominant organizational structure is masculine, but companies are interested in alternative struc-tures (that is, feminine or Japanese), they must accept the value system that underlies the alternative. If they do not, organizations cannot expect to adapt to meet a rapidly changing work force.

Kanter (1976, 1977) reports that opportunities for career advance-ment and the cultivation of meaningful interpersonal relationships are directly related to organizational structure. Position in the hierarchy carries with it power and opportunities to receive rewards in the form of promotions or the chance to meet people to whom one would oth-erwise not have access. While Kanter has focused her argument on sex differences, it is appropriate in the 1990s to extend her ideas to the standpoint (Wood, 1994) of any employee. The social location of an individual, coupled with organizational position, is an important deter-minant of how an employee will fare within the structure of any orga-nization. Kanter (1976) argues that women, and by extension people of color, are generally regarded and treated by organizations as people without power who perform routine service, while men in viable leadership positions constitute the real power to reward themselves and shape the system as a whole. These separate classes are marked by sex, race, and power, but within each class there may be "internal hierarchy, political grouping and allegiances, interactional rules, culture, and style, including demeanor and dress" (Kanter, 1976, p. 50).

Consider the example of a hospital social work department. The employees in social work are primarily female, but they work with physicians, who tend to be male. I have conducted numerous workshops with hospital social workers, and their common communication problems relate to the power structure of the hospital and the sex of the employees who populate different strata of the organization. Acker and Van Houten (1992) would explain the problem in the hospital as a *sex power differential* that is created when there are sex-segregated jobs that are ordered so that males are higher in the hierarchy than females, and males are not expected to take orders from females. In our workshops, we work on ways to bridge communication differences so that the social workers can gain power and effectiveness as communicators. These are difficult problems that involve the structure of the organization and the social construction of work and gender roles that intertwine to produce problems that are not readily eliminated with easy solutions.

An even larger problem with organizational structure emerges when one realizes that companies reflect the economic systems in which they are embedded. Natalle et al. (1994) argue that capitalism sustains a system of race, class, and gender oppression that directly contradicts the principles of democracy. The masculine corporation, unfortunately, can sustain practices of sex discrimination, racial prejudice, segregation of jobs by race and gender, harassing language, and promale bias in the structure of organizations. Unless people in power are willing to make radical changes, equality and opportunity are not likely to be offered to all employees in the near future. Of course, temporary solutions to structural defects include women and people of color creating their own organizations and fostering leadership within women's communities and the African American community in particular (Moore, Buttner, & Rosen, 1992; West, 1993). As we engage in a discussion over the solutions to these complex problems, let us remember that usurping power is probably not the answer in a democracy such as ours. A difficult but fair practice would be to redistribute resources and power so that all workers can enjoy a high quality of life, opportunities for advancement, and impact on the life of the organization.

Communication Climate

Earlier it was mentioned that *communication climate* is viewed like the temperature and weather conditions: A warm climate invites open communication, while a cool climate promotes defensive or closed communication. As Pace and Faules (1994) describe communication climate, it is indeed metaphorically linked to physical climate. Both are extremely important to our daily lives. Just like we check a weather report every day before leaving home, we are constantly monitoring the environment at work to make decisions about our communication with others. According to Pace and Faules, we judge the organizational communication climate based on how we perceive events and behavior as well as relatively enduring characteristics of the organization. It is clear that organizational structure has a relatively large influence on the climate, but Pace and Faules also note that other elements, such as management practices, the job itself, and company guidelines, help to create a communication climate.

Why is a communication climate so important, and how is this a gendered issue in the workplace? As Pace and Faules (1994) state, "A particular communication climate provides guidelines for individual decisions and behavior" (p. 105). Who you talk to, how you talk to others, the level of performance you achieve, how supportive you are of company policies, and how you interact with others are influenced by your perception of the communication climate. On a more personal level, your self-esteem and identity as a professional person will hinge on the communication that happens in relation to the organization. In the ideal communication climate, we would all feel positive and free to communicate honestly. In the real world, an organization's communication climate will change with certain economic and political conditions, and may change individually for certain employees, even though climate is generally seen as a shared attitude. Pace and Peterson (cited in Pace & Faules, 1994) indicate that the ideal communication climate consists of six factors: trust, participative decision making, supportiveness, openness in downward communication, listening in upward communication, and concern for high performance goals. We have already established in our discussion about organizational structure that gender and race factors enter into the picture to create bias. The same can be expected when individuals interpret an organization's communication climate.

Let's look at two examples from participants in focus groups I conducted to find out how the gender of the employees can create either a positive or a negative climate. The first example comes from a person who worked as a nurse recruiter in a health care employment agency. This person was one of 28 employees that included 25 women, 2 men, and a female manager. The office experienced almost 100% employee turnover a year, and the communication climate was generally perceived as extremely negative. The communication among the women was characterized as "competitive, catty, sniping, and back-biting." The manager was viewed as an instigator who pitted employees against each other and who spoke about the performance of individual employees to their peers. Male–female communication was viewed as nonproblematic and, in fact, the two male employees were generally not part of the mainstream communication in the office.

Interestingly, about 15 of the women created a support group where help was given to peers who were having trouble with the manager. The support group went for lunch or drinks and engaged in highly positive communication. While most of the employees eventually quit their high-paying jobs, several long-term friendships resulted from the support group.

What dynamics were at work in this real-life example? While the manager may have been incompetent as an individual, regardless of gender, she seemed to create a climate by playing off of some extremely negative cultural stereotypes about women competing against women. However, the employees appeared to play two different kinds of roles: one that reinforced a negative office climate and one that created a positive climate outside of the formal structure. This example reminds us that individuals, including ones without formal power, exercise choice about how they relate to one another.

A second example demonstrates how social construction of roles can generate a positive climate and thus create a highly desirable workplace. I once gave a workshop for a social work department in a rehabilitation hospital. There was one male social worker, but the other two dozen employees, including the department head, were women. In this workgroup, all of the positive feminine characteristics were displayed— respect, turn taking, positive facial expressions, politeness, collaboration in problem solving—even the details of refreshments were attended to throughout the workshop.

To my surprise, in addition to my consulting fee, the department head gave me a beautiful gift bag with items bearing the hospital's logo. After the workshop, I was invited to lunch where I had the opportunity to observe further the lively conversation and positive cohesion of this group. What a wonderful communication climate these employees had! There were few gender-related communication problems within the social work department. We spent most of our time talking about problems with the (male) physicians.

Note that in both examples, socially constructed gender roles contributed to the communication of workers' behavior, but the six factors of an ideal climate discussed earlier also influenced the overall climate. Trust, openness, and listening seemed to be missing in the employment agency, but those same factors all operated to a high degree in the social work department. One of the lessons to learn about effective communication is that individual behavior interacts with other factors, including but not limited to gender, to create an overall climate.

We have been discussing climate through the use of specific examples, but there is some evidence that the communication climate for the average female employee in the United States is "chilly" at best (Natalle et al., 1994). Even though women have dramatically increased their presence in the workplace, that presence has been greeted by an increasing amount of reported *sexual harassment* at all levels of the organization (Sandroff, 1992). The shocking revelations of women (Fraser, 1991; Fugh-Berman, 1992) since the Clarence Thomas confirmation hearings indicate that women who work alongside men often don't experience the kind of supportiveness that is conducive to effective professional relationships. There is also evidence that as our workplace relies more on computerized forms of communication, women are systematically sexually harassed through E-mail and other networks (Kantrowitz, 1994). What does this say about a climate for productive communication in the workplace? You may wish to review Chapter 14 to think further about the relationship of climate to sexual harassment on the job. It is also worth thinking about how an organizational climate may be constructed to reflect social attitudes toward women or specific ethnic groups.

In regard to other characteristics of people, Gomez (1994) challenges American companies to create a communication climate that is more accepting of workers who come from different racial and ethnic backgrounds. In her research and training in intercultural communication, Gomez discovered that companies are not perceived by minorities as responding well to a diverse work force. Among the problems are lack of equal treatment for all employees, failure to listen, failure to recognize and respect cultural differences, and a "predominant white male mentality" (p. 53).

A student in one of my focus groups illuminated these problems with a simple example. In his job as a waiter, this black male chose to wear his hair in a fashion that his manager judged "unacceptable." The waiter was told to go in the restroom and change his hair. Unfortunately, the hairstyle was the result of several hours worth of work and could not be changed simply by running a wet comb through his hair. When the waiter informed the manager of the time it would take to change the style, he was dismissed for the evening and lost his income from that shift. The waiter was angry because the hair incident was an indicator of a larger misunderstanding between blacks and whites over many cultural issues. The waiter felt that a negative communication climate had been created and reinforced by hierarchical differences in the chain of command and compounded by racial stereotypes. The waiter eventually quit his job in large part because he felt defensive all the time and couldn't enjoy his work.

A study on African American male communication (Orbe, 1994) revealed that differences in style resulted in African American men "keeping a safe distance" from European American men. The participants in the study reported that their careers had suffered at times because safe distance meant they couldn't access information through the informal channels of communication controlled by Caucasian men. On the other hand, there are some companies that realize the importance of considering *cultural diversity* in creating a healthy communication climate. For example, Wal Mart is addressing cultural diversity in its national advertising. In its Mother's Day flyer that consisted of 26 pages (Wal Mart, 1994), the company stated its commitment to cultural diversity on the first page and then featured culturally diverse vendors and business partners throughout the flyer.

In fact, among the most important corporate buzzwords for the 1990s is the term *managing diversity*. *Fortune* magazine explained the essence of managing diversity: "To survive population shifts and to prosper amid them, companies are training workers to be more tolerant of language and cultural differences, to identify and reject any racial and sexual prejudices, and to be more accommodating to the handicapped" (Dreyfuss, 1990, p. 165). Companies like Xerox, Avon, Hewlett-Packard, and AT&T are models of successful plans. Included in their programs are hiring guidelines to attract a variety of qualified workers, training and development of employees, and retention benefits including child care and access to professional networks. If these companies maintain their commitment to managing diversity, then the transformation of language, the rejection of prejudice, and cultural tolerance will create and maintain a communication climate that enhances the probabilities of effective interpersonal relationships and high productivity.

ORGANIZATIONAL CULTURE

Studying organizations as culture not only is a method for looking at structure (Kreps, 1995), but also is a leading perspective on how to define organizations (Conrad, 1990). Daniels and Spiker (1991) describe culture as "the artifacts of organizational life such as stories, myths, legends, and rituals" (p. 120) and as "a common interpretive frame of reference; a network of shared meanings" (p. 120). This implies *organizational culture* is "a system of shared meanings that are expressed through a number of different symbolic forms—symbols, rituals, stories, and myths—and that function to hold a group of people together" (Conrad, 1990, p. 6). Organizational culture can easily be seen as a gendered issue because artifacts and frames of reference often differ along gender, race, and class lines. Gender-related meanings and values (Bate, 1992; Belenky, Clinchy, Goldberger, & Tarule, 1986; Gilligan, 1982; Maltz & Borker, 1982; Tannen, 1990, 1994) can have a particularly strong impact on the creation and maintenance of an organization's culture. For example, sports clichés and war terms (*the ball's in your court* or *battle plans*) indicate masculine culture, while *cooking up an idea* or *putting a project on the back burner* reflect feminine culture. Gendered language can create mind-sets about how to conduct business. Different employees may have degrees of comfort with the dominant language and shared meanings created in a masculine or feminine culture.

Let's look at the Nike corporation as an example of what we mean by a gendered culture. Author Donald Katz (1994) clearly describes Nike as a male culture, even though gender is not an overt theme in his book called *Just Do It*. Nike is a company that targets the majority of its products to males and sponsors top professional athletes (for example, Michael Jordan, Charles Barkley, Pete Sampras) as a major part of the company's mission to make sports and sport performance an integral part of American culture. The stories and rituals of the company include famous food fights and beer parties along with a select group of employees known as "Ekins" (Nike spelled backward), who are hard-core sports fanatics and even have a Nike Swoosh tattoo. Although there are female employees in the company, the network of shared meanings and the frame of reference are decidedly masculine.

Compare Nike to the The Body Shop. Anita Roddick, founder of The Body Shop, runs the company on feminine principles such as caring and intuitive decision making (Helgesen, 1990). The stores and products reflect what Bullis and Glaser (1992) would call an *ecofemi-*

nist culture: No animals are used in product testing; the ingredients in the products include such items as grains, oils from fruit, seaweed, honey, and eucalyptus; and a percentage of company profits is donated to environmental causes. While Niketowns play rock music and sports videos to urban males waiting for the latest shoe style, The Body Shop staff sells cosmetics and soaps in a customer-friendly environment where rows of neatly stacked pastel-colored products rest against forest green shelves.

Organizational cultures are created by people; thus, a social reality emerges that reflects the dominant experience of the employees. Often, outsiders are unaware of the culture and experience a sort of culture shock (Conrad, 1990) when hired by the organization. In keeping with our theme of expectations versus reality, it is important to consider how you may "fit" with the culture of a particular profession or company. Is the profession one that welcomes and understands Hispanics or Latinos? Does the company hire and promote black women? Are males integrated into the rituals and shared meanings of the nursing field, for example, when they join the profession?

The concept of a cultural fit is very important to the success of a career and to the development of a healthy personal identity (Fitzgerald, 1993). The reality of the workplace, however, is that the culture of a company often does not value and support gay and lesbian workers, people of color, or women. In spite of the move toward trying to understand diversity, the media often fuel problems in the workplace. For example, network television and major newspapers continue to refer to the "battle of the sexes" or the "gender wars." Situation comedies spoof the men's movement, and the popular press makes fun of women and men attempting to get along in the workplace (Noble, 1994).

Serious attempts to help women and men communicate more effectively have received much attention from laypersons and professionals. Deborah Tannen's enormously popular book *You Just Don't Understand* (1990) tackled the stylistic differences in communication between women and men without placing blame on either sex. Her cultural framework helped many people to see how interpretive frames of reference begin in same-sex children's groups and are carried over into adult relationships only to cause miscommunication. Tannen's useful ideas tell us much about creating and sustaining a workplace culture; indeed, her new book, *Talking 9 to 5* (1994), is a response to the thousands of readers who want to learn how men and women can communicate effectively in professional life.

SUMMARY

While we have many choices to make in regard to working relationships, our expectations and the reality of the working world may not match. I have argued that numerous issues, such as leadership style, organizational structure, communication climate, and organizational culture, can be considered gendered because they are constructed by humans to reflect the larger society in which we live. Although there is nothing inherently wrong with a masculine leader or a feminine culture, for example, there is the danger that social constructions of any kind can restrict opportunities for certain groups of people.

Discovering the existence of prejudice and discrimination is never a satisfying experience, and some readers may now mistakenly expect that a career will not be rewarding because of gender or racial bias. Take heart! Your awareness can lead to changes in the organization you work for because you are aware of the potential problems created by bias. In one of my focus groups, a young assistant manager of a retail store described at length the communication problems he experienced with his manager, who was an older woman. After discussing the gender differences in style and his apparent frustration, I asked this man if he would just prefer not to work with women. "Oh no," he replied, "I think men and women should work together. It's enjoyable to have both sexes together!"

Perhaps the spirit of the assistant manager and the material in this chapter will inspire you to consider how you might approach career choices. By becoming sensitive to the biases and distortions that result from gendered organizational structures, for example, we are in a stronger position to initiate changes so that all individuals and social groups can be productive employees and enjoy supportive professional relationships. What is exciting about the workplace of the future is that it will allow each of us to grow personally by knowing and working with a range of people whose perspectives and styles differ from our own. You can take all that you have learned in this book and apply that knowledge toward making and sustaining happy and healthy relationships in your private and professional life.

QUESTIONS FOR REFLECTION AND DISCUSSION

1. Conduct informal observations to determine how gender influences the culture of your current workplace. Is the culture more masculine or feminine, or a combination of the two? What kind of struc-

ture is reflected in your workplace? How does the structure influence the culture?

2. Arrange to interview a man and a woman who hold a leadership or management position. Find out if gender influences their leadership style. Are race, age, or other factors influences as well? What reactions do these practicing managers have to the idea of gendered leadership style?

3. Design a content analysis of *Working Woman* magazine or *The Harvard Business Review* to discover how cultural diversity is covered in these periodicals. What conclusions can you draw about leadership, communication climate, or organizational culture based on your analysis?

4. Visit a local shopping mall and do a field study of how stores present themselves nonverbally. Based on the products, the store design, and the customer service, can you tell which stores embody feminine and masculine cultures? Is the communication climate friendly? Do the products seem appealing to you based on your standpoint? What factors encourage you to shop in particular stores?

5. Engage in a class discussion where students share some personal experiences about how their race, class, or gender may have affected their opportunity to get a job. What do these experiences tell you about how to strategize for successful job interviews?

REFERENCES

Acker, J., & Van Houten, D. R. (1992). Differential recruitment and control: The sex structuring of organizations. In A. J. Mills & P. Tancred (Eds.), *Gendering organizational analysis* (pp. 15–30). Newbury Park, CA: Sage.

Baird, J. E., & Bradley, P. H. (1979). Styles of management and communication: A comparative study of men and women. *Communication Monographs, 46,* 101–111.

Bate, B. (1992). *Communication and the sexes.* Prospect Heights, IL: Waveland.

Belenky, M. F., Clinchy, B. M., Goldberger, N. R., & Tarule, J. M. (1986). *Women's ways of knowing: The development of self, voice, and mind.* New York: Basic Books.

Bell, E. L., Denton, T. C., & Nkomo, S. (1993). Women of color in management: Toward an inclusive analysis. In E. A. Fagenson (Ed.), *Women in management: Trends, issues, and challenges in managerial diversity* (pp. 105–130). Newbury Park, CA: Sage.

Brenner, O. C., Tomkiewicz, J., & Schein, V. E. (1989). The relationship between sex role stereotypes and requisite management characteristics revisited. *Academy of Management Journal, 32,* 662–669.

Bullis, C., & Glaser, H. (1992). Bureaucratic discourse and the goddess: Towards an ecofeminist critique and rearticulation. *Journal of Organizational Change Management, 5(2),* 50–60.

Camden, C., & Witt, J. (1983). Manager communicative style and productivity: A study of female and male managers. *International Journal of Women's Studies, 6,* 258–269.

Conrad, C. (1990). *Strategic organizational communication: An integrated perspective* (2nd ed.). Ft. Worth, TX: Holt, Rinehart, & Winston.

Daniels, T. D., & Spiker, B. K. (1991). *Perspectives on organizational communication* (2nd ed.). Dubuque, IA: William C. Brown.

Deaux, K. (1979). Self-evaluations of male and female managers. *Sex Roles, 5,* 571–580.

Dreyfuss, J. (1990, April 23). Get ready for the new work force. *Fortune,* pp. 165, 181.

Eagly, A. H., & Johnson, B. T. (1990). Gender and leadership style: A meta analysis. *Psychological Bulletin, 108,* 233–256.

England, P., & McCreary, L. (1987). Gender inequality in paid employment. In B. B. Hess & M. M. Ferree (Eds.), *Analyzing gender: A handbook of social science research* (pp. 286–320). Newbury Park, CA: Sage.

Female workers say they're tired and underpaid. (1994, October 15). *Greensboro News & Record,* p. A4.

Fine, M. G., Johnson, F. L., & Foss, K. A. (1991). Student perceptions of gender in managerial communication. *Women's Studies in Communication, 14,* 24–48.

Fitzgerald, T. K. (1993). *Metaphors of identity: A culture-communication dialogue.* Albany, NY: SUNY Press.

Fowler, E. M. (1991, March 19). Students find job search much harder. *The New York Times,* p. D18.

Fraser, L. (1991, October). The doctor's dilemma. *Vogue,* pp. 306–311.

Fugh-Berman, A. (1992, January 20). Tales out of medical school. *The Nation,* pp. 1, 54–56.

Gilligan, C. (1982). *In a different voice: Psychological theory and women's development.* Cambridge, MA: Harvard University Press.

Gomez, A. M. (1994). Minorities in the work force: How satisfied? In P. Shockley-Zalabak (Ed.), *Understanding organizational communication: Cases, commentaries, and conversations* (pp. 51–54). New York: Longman.

Helgesen, S. (1990). *The female advantage: Women's ways of leadership.* New York: Doubleday.

Johnston, W., & Packer, A. (1988). *Workforce 2000: Work and workers for the 21st century.* Indianapolis: Hudson Institute.

Ju, Y. (1994). Supremacy of human relationships: A Japanese organizational model. In B. Kovacic (Ed.), *New approaches to organizational communication* (pp. 67–85). Albany, NY: SUNY Press.

Kanter, R. M. (1976). Women and the structure of organizations: Explorations in theory and behavior. In M. Millman & R. M. Kanter (Eds.), *Another voice: Feminist perspectives on social life and social science* (pp. 34–74). New York: Octagon.

Kanter, R. M. (1977). *Men and women of the corporation.* New York: Basic Books.

Kantrowitz, B. (1994, May 16). Men, women and computers. *Newsweek,* pp. 48–55.

Katz, D. (1994). *Just do it: The Nike spirit in the corporate world.* New York: Random House.

Kreps, G. L. (1995). *Organizational communication* (3rd ed.). New York: Longman.

Larwood, L., Szwajkowski, E., & Rose, S. (1988). Sex and race discrimination resulting from manager–client relationships: Applying the rational bias theory of managerial discrimination. *Sex Roles, 18,* 9–27.

Loden, M. (1985). *Feminine leadership, or how to succeed in business without being one of the boys.* New York: Times Books.

Maltz, D., & Borker, R. (1982). A cultural approach to male/female miscommunication. In J.J. Gumperz (Ed.), *Language and social identity: Studies in international sociolinguistics* (pp. 196–216). Cambridge: Cambridge University Press.

Marini, M. M., & Brinton, M. C. (1984). Sex typing in occupational socialization. In B. F. Reskin (Ed.), *Sex segregation in the workplace: Trends, explanations, remedies.* Washington, DC: National Academic Press.

Meikle, J. (1993, March 12). Recession hits graduate jobs. *The Guardian,* p. 3.

Mintzberg, H. (1973). *The nature of managerial work.* New York: Harper & Row.

Moore, D. P., Buttner, E. H., & Rosen, B. (1992). Stepping off the corporate track: The entrepreneurial alternative. In U. Sekaran & F. T. L. Leong (Eds.), *Womanpower: Managing in times of demographic turbulence* (pp. 85–109). Newbury Park, CA: Sage.

Natalle, E. J., Papa, M. J., & Graham, E. E. (1994). Feminist philosophy and the transformation of organizational communication. In B. Kovacic (Ed.), *New approaches to organizational communication* (pp. 245–270). Albany, NY: SUNY Press.

Noble, B. P. (1994, August 14). The gender wars: Talking peace. *The New York Times,* p. F21.

Orbe, M. P. (1994). "Remember, it's always whites' ball": Descriptions of African American male communication. *Communication Quarterly, 42,* 287–300.

Ouchi, W. G. (1981). *Theory Z: How American business can meet the Japanese challenge.* Reading, MA: Addison-Wesley.

Pace, R. W., & Faules, D. F. (1994). *Organizational communication* (3rd ed.). Englewood Cliffs, NJ: Prentice-Hall.

Powell, G. N. (1993). *Women and men in management.* Newbury Park, CA: Sage.

Powell, G. N., & Butterfield, D. A. (1989). The "good manager": Did androgyny fare better in the 1980s? *Group and Organization Studies, 14,* 216–233.

Rosener, J. B. (1990). Ways women lead. *Harvard Business Review, 68(6),* 119–125.

Sandroff, R. (1992, June). Sexual harassment: The inside story. *Working Woman,* pp. 47–51, 78.

Schein, V. E. (1973). The relationship between sex role stereotypes and requisite management characteristics. *Journal of Applied Psychology, 57,* 95–100.

Schein, V. E. (1975). Relationships between sex role stereotypes and requisite management characteristics among female managers. *Journal of Applied Psychology, 60,* 340–344.

Sokoloff, N. J. (1992). *Black women and white women in the professions: Occupational segregation by race and gender, 1960–1980.* London: Routledge & Kegan Paul.

Staley, C. C. (1988). The communicative power of women managers: Doubts, dilemmas, and management development programs. In C. A. Valentine & N. Hoar (Eds.), *Women and communicative power: Theory, research, and practice* (pp. 36–48). Annandale, VA: Speech Communication Association.

Stewart, L. P., & Clarke-Kudless, D. (1993). Communication in corporate settings. In L. P. Arliss & D. J. Borisoff (Eds.), *Women and men communicating: Challenges and changes* (pp. 142–152). Orlando, FL: Harcourt Brace Jovanovich.

Tannen, D. (1990). *You just don't understand: Women and men in conversation.* New York: William Morrow.

Tannen, D. (1994). *Talking 9 to 5.* New York: William Morrow.

Wal Mart. (1994, May 1). Mother's Day advertising supplement to *Greensboro News and Record.*

Weick, K. E.. (1979). *The social psychology of organizing* (2nd ed.). Reading, MA: Addison-Wesley.

West, C. (1993). *Race matters.* Boston: Beacon Press.

Wilkins, B. M. & Andersen, P. A. (1991). Gender differences and similarities in management communication. *Management Communication Quarterly, 5,* 6–35.

Wood, J. T. (1994). *Gendered lives: Communication, gender, and culture.* Belmont, CA: Wadsworth.

Wood, J.T. (1995). *Relational communication: Continuity and change in personal relationships.* Belmont, CA: Wadsworth.

Workers need help writing, talking. (1992, September 21). *Greensboro News and Record,* p. A1.